POWNALL, D

THE GARDENER

C & R Print 054 - 33460

THE GARDENER

David Pownall

F/359126

LONDON
VICTOR GOLLANCZ LTD
1990

First published in Great Britain 1990
by Victor Gollancz Ltd
14 Henrietta Street, London WC2E 8QJ

British Library Cataloguing in Publication Data
Pownall, David
  The gardener.
  I. Title
  823'.914[F]

  ISBN 0-575-04724-0

Typeset in Great Britain at The Spartan Press Ltd,
Lymington, Hants
and printed in Great Britain by
St Edmundsbury Press Ltd, Bury St Edmunds, Suffolk

For Michael Baldwin

Because of light airs
There's a tulip in the grass-rake
Because of God's arm
On my silly shoulder

I dare say I am blessed
I daresay I am blessed

Day of Light Airs
by the dedicatee

THE GARDENER

1

Mansergh faces east. When the sun rises from behind the mass of high ground which forms the border between old Westmorland and Yorkshire, a first flare of dawn leaps out of a nick in the dark line of the fells and shoots down to the bottom of the dale, vaulting the River Lune, piercing the eye of the observer; a mad lancer of original light.

The settlement of Mansergh sits upon one flank of a tipped valley: down it flows the Lune, wide between high banks and sweeping bends. The great glacier which rubbed this region down to its present femality of form created sheep and cattle country, smooth and forever green. Beneath the rounded surfaces of the fields lies boulder clay, hard to plough because it is full of stones. The dry-stone walls which mark out the land are as much a testimony to the patient harvesting of lumps of limestone and gritstone by generations of indefatigable farmers as they are to the boundaries of their holdings. When the dawn flash leaps up from the crack in the eastern fells and prances down into the dale it covers ground that has been sculpted in rough form by the ice-gods, then finely finished and given detail by human toil.

Mansergh is a silent place, protected from the winds of all directions by higher ground on every side. What sounds there are — the curlews and skylarks, the tractors and traffic on the valley roads — are merely the ornaments of this silence, a silence which is an extension of the land's contours, infinite as a circle is infinite with curves. As if struggling to escape from this powerful, universal hush, the sloping-shouldered church of Saint Peter commands the highest point practicable, a natural pulpit overlooking the valley, suggestive of words and sound with its glaring tower, but still cowed by the silence. After two hundred years the graveyard remains nearly empty and the cold in the nave has the bite of eternity. On the morning of the third Saturday in June, 1940, the chill had been lifted by the warmth of a summer morning flowing through the open door.

From the eastern wall of the graveyard where he stood smoking a cigarette, the Reverend Leo Midgely could see the party of people straggling up the lane behind a tall sober-suited man who was pushing a perambulator. The priest timed his own slow stroll in order to arrive at the west front as the christening-party got to the schoolhouse at the bottom of the path up to the lychgate. He spent the moments wondering why the people had chosen to walk all the way round on the road in preference to coming over the field on the footpath which was a third of the distance. He remembered the last baptism he had done at Mansergh and the image of the father striding over the field with the shawled baby held over his shoulder; the purposeful way he had handed the child to his wife while he climbed the broken gate, and the arrival of the family at the porch with mud clinging to their best shoes. With some pleasure he recalled how his own geniality had silenced their apologies.

He rested one arm on a tall tombstone and surveyed the contours of the farmlands which rolled north like the backs of a school of great whales. The family were now by the school, having halted there for a breather after the long climb up the lane. They were a little early, with enough time for a smoke and a chat before the final ascent to the church. Colours from their clothes moved bird-like in the swell of the scene. He could hear snatches of laughter on the breeze. Some of that could be for him: he was an outsider, a man apart whose life lacked openness, a priest who was never given the wholehearted trust of the people he served, even though he saw himself as their true spokesman.

As he watched the christening-party begin to toil up the slope in their bright and dark clothes he thought about the war. After a year of inertia the belligerents had finally got down to it. Hitler had swept through western Europe and now Mansergh was on his list, as was everywhere within a bomber's reach.

He finished his cigarette and stubbed it out on the green, crumbly gritstone he was leaning upon. With their winged hats and dresses in navy and white, the women were striding up the path to meet him. There was an expectancy and an optimism in their approach, unsteady though it was on high heels.

Inside the church was a memorial tablet for the men of Mansergh who had lost their lives in the last war. For such an empty, scattered parish it was a long list. The stonemason who had done the work had been an apprentice from Lancaster and he had overestimated the amount of space that the names, ranks and regiments would take up. When he had finished the job there was a large area of the tablet still unfilled which had displeased the Reverend Midgely as he considered it to be unartistic and unsightly. Often during the last fifteen years he had delivered his sermons with his eyes fixed on the left-over area, using it as a physical target for his ironical barbs against the crassness of contemporary attitudes and thought, and as a vacant tablet on which he could mentally carve out his individual moral code.

Today, he was glad that it was a christening morning. The service would take place at the west end, at the font, and the memorial tablet would be at his back so he would not have to look at it. The Reverend Midgely had been to Germany. He had been to Russia. He had been to America. For him, the dry-stone walls ran out of the parish and on into the greater world, penning in the peoples; they were diagrams of oppression and injustice engraved on the earth by an entrenched power.

The women were in front of him now. He noticed their lipstick, their strange hats and veils, and their ankles. Perfume was exhaled, breaking out with their shy, healthy smiles.

"Good morning," the mother said, trying to adjust her hat while holding on to the infant. "Aren't we lucky to get such weather?"

The Reverend Midgely looked at the baby in her arms which was wrapped in a silk, embroidered christening-robe of some quality. The woman's voice was soft and musical; Irish, he thought. She looked extraordinarily happy, transcending the lines of bad-temper around her slightly slanted green eyes.

She held the baby out to him.

"D'you want it now?" she asked. "Or shall I hold on to it until you're ready?"

"Haven't you determined the sex yet, Mrs Nash?" he replied with a crooked smile to temper his sarcasm. "I'd heard a rumour that you'd had a girl." And he held out his hands.

"Oh, I have, I have," the mother laughed, handing the baby over. "It's just that I can't believe she's here yet, if you know what I mean."

With the sweet-smelling baby held in his arms, the Reverend Leo Midgely led the family into the church. Glancing down into the baby's face he encountered a pair of steady, dark-blue eyes which seemed to be studying him closely, waiting for enlightenment, as were the dark-suited men who lagged behind, their eyes more uncertain, their hopes in confusion. From England's recent history they knew that war would call them all away. The promises which a father makes to care for his child's soul at baptism would have a hollow ring.

Within the hour the Reverend Midgely earned his fee and the name of the girl-child was entered in the parish register as Pauline Nash.

The previous entry had been made only seven weeks before: another baby from the same row of estate cottages. The Reverend Midgely glanced at the name and remembered the day. It had been the other face of Mansergh's weather, the green chambered gloom after rain, radiant with silence.

He remembered being a shade surprised at the Teutonic name *Eric* that the Sherwin family had chosen. It was not as bad as Hans or Wolfgang but he had remembered lots of Eriks in Berlin in the Twenties. Upon returning home to Kirkby Lonsdale he had looked it up in a book of reference and had been relieved to discover that it was essentially Old Norse, meaning (perhaps) *king for ever*, and was, therefore, as much English as German.

2

During the war the silence of Mansergh remained undisturbed; one incendiary bomb jettisoned by a German aircraft after an abortive raid on Barrow-in-Furness being the only violence perpetrated against it, and that landed in a midden.

To stand and watch the sun rise over Bull Pot and follow its flooding run over Long Hill, Calf Top and Raismoor to the Howgills was to be assured that nothing had changed. The war could not even aspire to the status of an earth-tremor where the fells were concerned. If the world was full of warring Titans they either flew far above or turned aside from this region's unbending strength.

Both of the children from Turner Row baptised at Saint Peter's in the early summer of 1940 looked out on to the same world from their windows: Eric, from number 3; Pauline, from number 7, only twenty feet apart. The same line of fells dominated the morning light and evening darkness, creating an electrocephalic pulse-line in the minds of all inhabitants of Mansergh. In later years *he* was conscious of it but *she* not so; but she could remember the names of every thwaite, garth, holme, pike and beck, because her father had tagged along after the hounds, looking for hunt subjects, with the pack crossing and recrossing the same ground, and he had taught her what each place was called. As a painter this was his approach: to study his scenes from many aspects in order to reveal their essences.

The painter, Pauline's father, Oswald, was a tall, fair man, kind but querulous. He had met Deidre, his wife, at the Royal College of Art in London and brought her to this part of the Lune Valley because it had been sketched and painted by J. M. W. Turner on his northern tours, and Turner was his inspiration. In his dry way Oswald Nash was enslaved by this fabulous colourist, going to the lengths of living in a cramped estate cottage in order to feel close to his hero. Deidre, herself a painter of sterner, more dramatic bent, used her husband's archaism to provoke her own aggressive creations, constantly resisting, resentful, but essentially tolerant of his dreamy obsession. From Belfast herself, she could never feel completely comfortable within the vast, green sweep of this landscape. She was bred in the city yet yearned to forget it, but it resolutely clung to her mind. She drew and painted figures reminiscent of the images of her childhood but set them in Oswald's vistas, thereby creating a fatal disunity of style.

The one point of coincidence in Oswald and Deidre Nash's vision of the beautiful was their child. They had little money, living off a small allowance made to Oswald by a disapproving father, and both sets of in-laws had thrown up their hands in horror when it was announced that Deidre was expecting a baby. However, this criticism had been quashed when they saw the child. That two people who had made their life's work the pursuit of beauty should engender such, and far beyond their own looks as if a greater force had intervened, was a source of some wonder.

And from birth she had been good in that sense that all parents understand. She was no trouble, passing through the routines of babyhood with no shrill alarms or colics. When Oswald and Deidre looked down on her, framed in her cot, her unflinching eyes gazing up with total calm, her quietness as enduring as the landscape's, they had to move closer together to support each other against disbelief. Before the birth of Pauline they had been worried about the decisions they had taken about their lives: leaving London, retreating to this out-of-the-way spot to paint rather than going into commercial art; not trying to find work in order to supplement Oswald's pittance. But once Pauline was there, in her inarticulate perfection, they accepted the gift and felt themselves to be blessed.

Eric's father, Andrew, was an under-foreman on the Rigmaden estate which, with Underley, dominated the west side of the dale. Most of his work was concerned with the maintenance of the huge mansion which had been built in 1822 but was now fast becoming ruinous through neglect. He was fighting a losing battle against dry rot, struggling with inadequate expenditure on the fabric and the feeling that the owners had already accepted defeat. Year by year he saw the rooms close down, the outbuildings go derelict, the roof fall in. The rest of the estate staff left to take up more essential war-work and he stayed on as caretaker of the collapsing house, a rôle he found humiliating. His trade was that of carpenter and he did what he could but he was only patching. By the time Eric was born his father knew that his days at Rigmaden were over.

Two months after the christening at Saint Peter's, Andrew Sherwin went down to Liverpool to visit some relatives. Upon his return he told Lily, his wife, that he had volunteered to join the Liverpool King's Regiment, the one his father had fought and died with on the Somme in the Great War.

Lily was a patriot and full of indignation against the Germans. She was a simple woman, full of energy, and she felt that she could manage while her man went off and did his bit. She could wash and clean for other people, do some sewing, and there was always her mother and father only a few miles up the road at Sedbergh if things got too tough. She cried when Andrew left but not because she was afraid for herself, or for him. There was no doubt in her mind that he would come back: that was part of his nature. Something in Andrew Sherwin was as durable as the wood stacked to weather by his shed at the back of the house. But she found herself crying for her son Eric who would only have the company of women, a sex that Lily Sherwin did not overly favour.

There were eight cottages in the terrace at Turner Row, all identical. What the inhabitants saw from the front and back windows was the same; the size of their gardens was the same; even their gates and coal-bunkers were of common design, as if a hillside terrace from a Lancashire mill town had been torn from its foundations and transplanted to another setting.

At the beginning of the war all the cottages were lived in by estate workers, bar two: one which was leased by the Nashes and the other rented weekly by the widow of the schoolmaster who had been forced to leave the schoolhouse upon the death of her husband. Margaret Brand had suffered greatly during her husband's final years of illness but nothing had dimmed her essential brightness of spirit. Now, as a widow, she was more alive than when she had been living with her husband. She flowered in a re-born way, a little guiltily, but with pleasure.

As the men went away to the war one by one and the women were left behind to manage as best they might with the children, Margaret Brand became the foster-mother of Turner Row. The wives found work in Kirkby Lonsdale or Sedbergh or on the farms and cycled off each morning, leaving the children under school-age at number 2, while the rest went off along the Chapel Road over the fields to the village school. When they returned in the afternoon they joined the younger children at Margaret's where they waited until their mothers came home.

Margaret Brand was a woman more able to communicate with children than with adults. This benign particularity had developed because no one had ever had the chance to listen to her while her cruelly loquacious husband had been alive and, once he was dead, no one would listen because everyone knew that Margaret had not the wit to sustain a conversation, her responses having been dulled by forty years of living with an arrogant, self-opinionated pedant.

Eric was the first child to go to Margaret Brand's house to be looked after while his mother went to work at a dairy across the river at Casterton. Others followed in quick succession once it was seen that Margaret was competent; but Pauline was not one of them. Because her father suffered from *petit mal* epilepsy, he was considered unfit for military service. So Pauline stayed in number 7 with both mother and father to look after her, and the rest of the Turner Row children packed into number 2.

If the Nash family had been off-comers before the war, now they were doubly so. Epilepsy not being a condition people advertise as it is popularly considered to be brother to madness, Oswald kept quiet about it, and proudly refused to accept that this quirk of his brain was not part of the super-sensitive equipment with which he responded to life and the universe. When folk asked him why he was sitting in a field painting instead of fighting in the war he always replied that it was because he chose to, which many found to be an inadequate and infuriating answer once the first casualties from the district were reported. His wife, Deidre, was no more diplomatic, her Ulster ire rising each time she was taken to task for keeping her man at home instead of placing him on the altar of national sacrifice.

Meanwhile, Pauline's beauty grew greater.

When the brood of Margaret Brand roared out on to the field to play in the sun, Pauline came out in her exquisitely colourful clothes, her black hair perfectly shaped and cut, and sat with her hand-made dolls on a huge scarlet and blue Moroccan blanket, her mother perched beside her on an artist's canvas stool, sketching or shelling peas.

Although envy was a component part of Margaret Brand's character, and she was fully aware of the hostility felt by the other residents of Turner Row to the Nash family, she could not resist admiring, then adoring the extraordinary loveliness of the one child who had escaped her. She approached Deidre Nash and suggested that Pauline might be better off joining in with all the other children at her house, otherwise the little girl would become lonely and isolated. The answer she received was cold and to the point: Pauline was perfectly happy as she was. No help was needed.

Into Margaret Brand's daily chatter to her charges floated the character Amaryllis, black-haired and dark-blue-eyed, a fiction recalled from her dead husband's erudition. Amaryllis had Pauline's beauty, a grace originating in myth and magic, and she became the principal heroine in the miscellany of gossip, fairy-tale and news with which she amused the children during the day. She wove Pauline into the royal family, into the films she saw at the cinema in Kirkby Lonsdale, into the news of great events she heard, even into her own past and childhood. As she babbled on, day after day, without any poison or malignancy, an obsession was revealed but there was no one to point it out because her audience was enchanted, first by the war and its distortions of the imagination, and secondly by their enjoyment of the reality behind the existence of Amaryllis, as they all knew from whence she arose: the girl at number 7, saviour of Europe, sprite of the river, spirit of the high moor, Cinderella and Snow White, all rolled into one.

Andrew Sherwin had been off in the army for four years when

Eric tried to run away from home; the cause being a beating given to him by his mother. Miserable, bored and lonely, Lily had allowed herself to fall in love with another man; a shameful betrayal of her husband's trust. The lover had left the dale and returned to the south, leaving Lily shaken, bitter and under siege as all the other spare males immediately assumed that she would continue with her amatory career. Turner Row was no place to be in such an exposed predicament and Lily received the brunt of righteous criticism for her infidelity. On the Sunday morning when Eric received his thrashing, a strap across the back of his legs, Lily was at the end of her tether, having been insulted by her own sister while taking a drink at the Durham Ox the previous night. The cause of this beating (his first) was his obstinate refusal to put his head in the basin so his mother could wash his hair.

Eric was a sturdy, well-knit boy, already strong in the leg and well used to wandering over the wide, close-cropped fields and clambering over the dry-stone walls. He often went down to the low road, crossing it to get down to play by the river, the main terror of the parents of Turner Row as it was deep enough to drown in. When he ran out of the back kitchen and on to the Chapel Road with his legs stinging and tears blinding him, he had to keep running because he knew that he must not turn on his mother, whom he worshipped. The best thing was just to keep going, breathing, keeping the house behind him. If his mother caught up with him he knew that he would attack her.

When he had passed the church and the school he was still sobbing and moving north, having not looked back. In fact his mother had not followed him out of the house but had collapsed into a chair, weeping herself at the cruelty of what she had done in taking her unhappiness out on her son.

He crossed Bank Hill to Fleshbeck, then went down by the Lune, following its great crook all the way along the edge. It was August and the water-level was well down, revealing the spits and banks of rounded stones. He walked along them, making his shoes crunch and clatter all he could, kicking and hacking to get rid of his temper.

Leaving the river at Blackbrow Wood he headed back towards the road. As he emerged from the trees he saw Rigmaden Park staring at him over the fields, its enormous windows gaping like the

eye-sockets in a skull. Affronted, drawn and impelled by stories of his
absent father, he allowed himself to drift along the narrow road
towards the mansion. He hated the sight of it with the same passion as
he temporarily hated his mother. With its family associations it
contrived to induce a vandalistic urge: he wanted to smash it up and
make it suffer, and, through that, his mother and father would suffer
as well. Mrs Brand had shown him pictures of the Blitz, houses
wrecked and writhing, which looked as gaunt, arrogant and hopeless
as Rigmaden Park. These ruined buildings were the faces of adults
who had failed their children, as his parents had by deserting, beating
and rejecting him. Adumbrated by this mood, his spirit hurt and
angry, he climbed the fence and walked towards the gaping entrance.

Everything salvageable had been removed. With the roof gone
from the front half and no glass in the windows, he found himself
standing in vast white chasms, silent except for the swish of swallows
and the flapping of doves. There were fireplaces where the tiles had
been hacked from the wall and empty doorways which carried only
rusting hinges. As he walked over the floorboards his shoes seemed to
thunder. This was the place which had failed his father and the
retribution it had suffered had been immense. No one loved it. Soon,
it would all fall down, destroyed. He laughed as he climbed the
wrecked stairs, stamping his shoes louder so the doves clattered off
the roof trusses. He was glad the house had been wrecked. It made
strong sense that the war should come so close and bellow its message
the full length of the valley, into all the uncomprehending houses and
the souls of women. The thought and feeling made him yell out and he
tore out a bannister.

Someone called from below.

He stood still, suddenly dwindling down from the giant storm of
his indignation. It was a woman's voice, not his mother's. The call
came again. He peered over the rail and saw Mrs Nash looking up at
him.

"What are you doing here, Eric?" she said.

He was unable to reply, dropping the bannister on the floor. After a
short wait for an answer, Deidre Nash cautiously climbed the stairs
and took him by the hand.

"I think you'd better come down, Eric," she said gently. "It's
dangerous up here."

He allowed her to lead him down the stairs and out of the house. Once they were outside he tried to wrest his hand from hers but she resisted and towed him round the side of the house to a courtyard by the stable-block where two easels stood with emergent oil-paintings on them. Oswald Nash sat on a canvas stool, a paint-spattered palette on his thumb. Beside him stood the Reverend Leo Midgely, leaning on a walking-stick.

"It's little Eric Sherwin," Deidre said. "He must be lost."

Oswald shrugged and smeared paint off his finger on to his overall, his eyes already back on what he had painted on his canvas.

"He can come back with us when we go home," he murmured. "Perhaps we should put him in the scene with Pauline? He's quite an interesting-looking fellow in a rough kind of way."

Pauline was enthroned, clad only in a pair of white cotton pants, on a blanket in a wheelbarrow, holding a bright-yellow flower to her chest. An old mounting-block with a rusty ring set into it stood beside the wheelbarrow, its cemented surfaces split by frost. Overhanging the wheelbarrow was a lilac tree in bloom, hundreds of tortoiseshell butterflies feeding off its nectar.

Deidre unbuttoned Eric's shirt and pulled it over his head then took down his shorts.

"Oh, dear, he's not wearing underpants," she said. "What now?"

"He's all right just like that," Oswald replied. "Hurry up."

"Take your socks off for us, there's a good boy," Deidre continued, her tone easy. "You don't mind doing this for us, do you? We're only making a pretty picture. There's a good boy."

Eric was at her mercy. He stood by the wheelbarrow, the butterflies in an orange cloud around his head, and slowly took off his shoes and socks. He felt his scalp tingle and his flesh turn into a singing cloud as Pauline stared at him.

When Deidre bent towards him he raised his arms to be lifted. He saw the dark figure of the clergyman react, waving his stick in the air and laughing.

"Stop!" Oswald said with alarm, hurrying over to take him out of Deidre's hands. "Will you look at that! At his age! God almighty, the boy's not five yet!"

He thrust Eric's clothes into his hands and pushed him to the rear of the easels.

"Cover it up," he muttered indignantly, "and stop being so silly!"

"He can't help it," Deidre protested humorously as she helped Eric to dress. "It's not his fault, is it? That's Nature for you! You're never too young. What a pity. I was looking forward to having him in the scene. He's got that very simple, basic look, don't you think? A true *helot*. Now, don't mention this to Mummy, will you? It was only for a picture. You sit down here and have a nice drink."

Deidre sat him down by her easel and gave him a glass of orange-juice and a sandwich. As Oswald and Deidre painted through the rest of the afternoon, Eric hardly moved, never taking his eyes off the girl in the wheelbarrow, except to look at the Reverend Leo Midgely in case he might make him laugh again.

When he was delivered back to his mother in the early evening, Deidre was surprised to note that Lily Sherwin did not appear to have missed him.

"We were painting up at Rigmaden Park and we found him in the ruined part of the house. It's quite dangerous," Deidre said with a cautious implication that Eric was not, perhaps, being properly supervised at home.

Lily reddened and sent Eric into the house with a flick of the drying-up towel in her hand.

"I hope he wasn't a nuisance," she said haltingly. "We had a bit of a row. I was trying to wash his hair."

Deidre smiled patronisingly, inwardly relieved that she was finding it so easy a matter to cover the blunder she had made by trying to use the boy in the scene. She lowered her voice so Eric would not be able to hear.

"I must say, he was in a state when we found him. We brushed him down and looked after him. Little boys are a handful, I'm sure, my dear."

"This one is," Lily replied grimly. "He misses his father, not that you'd get him to admit it."

The reference to the absent husband brought into play the subject of the war and the fact that Oswald was still at home instead of serving his country in some way. Deidre looked at Lily with a new, nervous respect, now finding her to be an equal contestant rather

than a walk-over. The encounter had been declared a draw, but Deidre was able to go back to Oswald and tell him that she anticipated no trouble from their *faux pas*.

That night Eric dreamed violently. He saw Pauline sat like a buddha by the river, her body coated with golden paint. Cattle drank close to her, framing her dark-blue eyes with their tangled horns. As he crawled towards her the round stones shifted under his hands and knees; then a huge wave reared up out of the river and swept him round the crook at Fleshbeck, round and round in a whirlpool.

His cries brought his mother stumbling from her bed and she nursed him for half-an-hour, until he was quiet, then crept back to her own room hoping that he would give her peace for the rest of the night.

Next morning found him flushed with a fever, his hands clutched between his thighs and his fair hair plastered to his head with sweat. His mother cycled into Kirkby Lonsdale to call the doctor. When he came it did not take him long to diagnose measles and by the end of that week every child at Turner Row who had not already had it, was afflicted: except one.

Oswald and Deidre Nash packed their bags and took Pauline on a visit to her grandfather in London until the epidemic was over, ignoring the neighbourly advice they received that it would be just as well to let Pauline have it now rather than later.

When he recovered, Eric was often found sitting on the front doorstep of the Nash house like a dog that awaits its owner's return.

3

When Pauline did return to Mansergh, Eric had gone. His father had been wounded and had ended up in a military hospital near Liverpool. His injuries were so bad that he was to be invalided out of the army and he had decided to leave Mansergh and work for an ironmonger whom he had met in his regiment. Eric's mother was overjoyed to be leaving Mansergh. Her husband's disability tempered her delight at the prospect of a new, guilt-free life, and she was very much a country girl who would have a lot of adjustments to make in order to live in Liverpool, now a shattered city; but she was willing and grateful for this chance to escape from what had happened to her. From the day of their first visit to see Andrew Sherwin at the military hospital to the time she moved into their rooms in Wharton Street, Walton, Lily only returned once to Mansergh, going up in a lorry with the ironmonger's brother to pack up and move out of number 3, Turner Row.

Eric did not accompany his mother on this journey. Since having measles he had been sickly and disturbed, difficult to deal with, taciturn, resentful; spending a lot of time hiding under the table. Lily could not get him to go out and play and he seemed to have no interest in amusing himself. The most upsetting feature of his behaviour was the way he reacted to his father: refusing to talk to him, or go to him. Andrew Sherwin had changed greatly while in the army: his face had thinned, he had developed a slight lisp, and his injury, a piece of shrapnel in his neck, made him walk in an exaggeratedly dignified manner as if struggling to hold his entire self together. But to Lily he was the same man, even an improvement on the one who had gone away to the war. He was good-natured, thoughtful and lively, wanting the best for his family, making light of his own pain.

To Eric his father was obsolete. What he had remembered of him had been incorporated into the ruinous dream of Rigmaden; he was no more than the broken stair or the clouds sailing across the roof timbers. Everything his father meant was disuse and decay: this whole city of Liverpool in its blackened ruin was his tomb, and the dark, damp rooms on the bottom floor of the old house full of the stink of a nearby meat-pie factory, were his coffin. In this gloomy, swirling madness of twisted houses and gaping craters there was no alleviating beauty. Without knowing the nature of his loss, Eric yearned to get back to Mansergh.

Andrew Sherwin was no longer a sad man. He had returned from Africa and Italy and four years of the comradeship of men with a good deal more understanding. Many of his friends had encountered problems with their children upon returning home and for a father to re-integrate himself into his family was not seen as an easy matter. As Eric resisted his attempts to win him over and drove himself deeper into silent fury, Andrew Sherwin bided his time and convinced his wife to conceive another child.

Eric remained in the thrall of his misery for six months. He was often ill with coughs and colds, kept wetting the bed, stayed away from the other children in the street, only taking pleasure in the ironmonger's shop where his father was employed. Although he would not talk to his father, he did allow himself to be taken along there while his mother went out to work. The smell was strong and exciting. Thousands of boxes and drawers contained shapes, lines and curves in countless variety. The tools had the blade-shine of rivers and the coils of hempen rope and wire were whirlpools.

Disguised, she was there: in graceful, secret parts, scattered (everything in this city was scattered); her whole fantastic nature lay hidden in those labelled drawers of nails and canisters of fuels and acids. When he walked into the shop behind his father, cruelly imitating his proud, tormented strut, Eric felt the freshness and headiness of his idol descend upon him.

Several times he asked to be taken back to Mansergh, though never admitting why. His mother told him that it would be best if they waited a year or so before returning, so he could get used to the change. This increased his frustration but he could not alter her attitude. When he broke his silence with his father to mutter a request on the same subject, his father feigned interest. Like his wife, he had his own reasons for avoiding the dale and its memories of disillusionment and degeneration. He did once promise to take Eric back for a visit; then the whole question was promptly forgotten.

The following September, after a hot summer amongst the blitzed ugliness and desolation of Liverpool, Eric was sent to school. It was only a hundred yards from the ironmonger's shop and it became his practice to go there as soon as school ended. His father, happy enough with his job and the prospect of the new baby, worked hard to bring Eric back into his fold. Ignoring the sulkiness and disdain, the ingratitude and peevishness, he slowly won back his son but was never aware that there was now a part of him that was forever lost.

For her part, Pauline had no memory of Eric whatsoever. When her parents returned to Turner Row at the beginning of October they found a new family at number 3 and the gossip about Lily over. Eric's absence from Margaret Brand's gang of children was not noticed and even when Oswald and Deidre returned to Rigmaden Park to make further sketches using the same scene and the same wheelbarrow to pose their cherished daughter, neither remembered the boy who had been there with them before. There were plenty of new things to think about with the war on its last legs. Oswald had been commissioned to go to Germany as a war artist — his father's influence being the cause of this choice appointment — and he wanted to finish off the Mansergh phase of his painting life before the full experience of war affected his style. So he threw himself into his work, his eye always on the date in the new year of 1945 when he would have to leave the dale and return, inevitably, a different man.

By the time he was due to leave, Deidre was pregnant. He offered to resign his commission but Deidre refused point blank. For her, after years of enduring the humiliation of having a husband unfit to serve, it was a matter of pride. She had stuck to him, defending his talent and her own as weapons against tyranny at all times, and now he had a chance to use it on the enemy but in the compassion that follows defeat. She saw this as a mission that any artist must be worthy of, and looked forward to his achievements.

Within two months of arriving in Germany Oswald was killed in a road accident near Frankfurt. Deidre bore this bravely enough but when the army sent her all his sketches and paintings from the war, she went to Manchester and procured herself an abortion.

At the end of the war Eric and Pauline were eighty miles apart, he in Liverpool, a blackened, broken city; she still in the dale. Deidre had tried to leave Mansergh, going back to her parents in Belfast for a while and even to London where she shared a house with Oswald's mother and father in Chiswick, but she eventually returned to the place where she had been happiest. The house at number 3 Turner Row was hers again and Oswald's father made her a generous allowance, eventually buying her the property she lived in when the terrace was put on the market. As the neighbours changed and changed again, often outpacing the seasons in their frequency, the girl at number 3 remained a constant wonder for her loveliness; a wonder felt most acutely by her mother, a woman struggling with grief and her own small talent for painting.

4

In 1950 Eric's family were living amid the bonfires and bulldozing of war-damage that was post-war Liverpool. Wharton Street, Walton, was a mean district of small factories and bad housing, riddled with squalid alleys and bomb-sites. The scars of cuts from corrugated-iron and glass were all over his knees and arms, signs of constant fighting. When he spoke in the street with his mates it was to swear or challenge, in his home he was quieter, gentler, unless thwarted. Then a passion of temper and hostility would be unleashed, something his father and mother could not master. They assumed that it was the place which antagonised him. As they could not afford to move they had to forgive the boy his anger, promising him better times ahead.

One August evening Eric was in the back alley behind his house. He had been playing with a gang of boys and girls and was on his way home for his tea when he saw a girl sitting against the alley wall playing with a few links of scrap chain which she held in the lap of her dress. On an immediate compulsion he went over, crouched down and kissed her on the cheek.

"What d'you want to do?" she asked.

"Nothing," he said abruptly.

She stood up, the chain dangling from her hands. He retreated a step as she raised her face to be kissed again. She followed him, coming out of the shadow. The illusion fled: all the colours and lights faded away, his heart slowed right down. He was staring at a girl he knew only too well and did not like.

As she shrugged and ran off to join the gang at the end of the alley to tell them what had happened, he opened the back door and went to stand by his mother at the stove.

She felt his trembling as he pressed himself against her and put a hand on his shoulder to steady him.

"Have you been fighting again, Eric?" she scolded him wearily. "When are you going to learn?"

At about this age Pauline became quite plump. Her beauty did not recede but expanded into a new dimension: she became, as Deidre put it, a Rubens rather than a black-haired Botticelli. The child did not concern herself with the loss of her earlier perfection but it came to trouble her mother who began to starve her, yearning for the return of the previous dignity of form and her pride in having the perfect child. Pauline did not protest but took to cooking for herself when her mother was out. Once this was discovered Deidre gave up the fight and accepted the advice of her doctor who promised her that Pauline would lose the puppy-fat later on. This proved to be a correct prognosis and by the age of thirteen Pauline had returned to her previous slenderness. One aspect of this period of adjustment became an incorporated feature in the household's domestic routine: from then on Pauline did all the cooking.

Deidre Nash's withdrawal from the normal world around her was primarily a conscious move. It was linked with her laziness which was as much self-indulgence as an expression of despair. Nothing mattered but her own inner life and the perception she had of her daughter as a vessel of some future vital greatness, the fulfilment of all her dead husband's promise. Pauline gave no indications of any intellectual or artistic talents but there was something in her temperament which encouraged her mother to carry on believing that the girl was unique: it was an eerie self-possession, an aloofness and passive calm which she had. Through-out the two years when she had been undeniably fat, a buddha-like serenity had been her retreat when the inevitable jeers and cruelties of other children assailed her. While her mother went frantic under the sneers of her neighbours — even Margaret Brand abandoned her Amaryllis, declaring that Pauline was destined to be a farmer's wife with a back broad enough to hump sacks — Pauline remained as tranquil and unruffled as ever, eating steadily as if she had learnt to trust natural forces more than any of the opinions of mankind.

This composure was not always deemed admirable by Deidre. When it was employed as a defence against her and Pauline retreated behind it rather than be involved in any dispute, Deidre found herself put in the wrong. It was always she who had to apologise because the heat and argument were all hers. Forgiveness became the child's monopoly. The skill with which Pauline administered this power became evident to Deidre and, although it was demeaning for her as an individual, she relished the quality in her daughter as proof of an original and extraordinary personality.

However, there was more to the child than this unusual maturity and inexcitability, this plateau of mind to which she could retire when under stress. At the opposite end of her being was a quirk which Deidre could not fathom. Pauline had displayed it only three times, all between the ages of eight and twelve. On her way towards the plateau, faced by the irascibilities and frustrations of her mother, her spirit in full retreat, anxious to put all the anger and foolishness behind her, she had suddenly and inexplicably turned, exploded into a screaming black rage and attacked her mother with all her strength. Deidre had cause to remember these transfigurations with awful clarity. Over the years she had struggled to incorporate them into her vision of Pauline's gifted nature as signs of psychic energy but she had failed. These incidents stood outside the girl's known nature and seemed to be visitations or possessions, or, far worse, warnings of possible epileptic tendencies inherited from her father. At no time did it occur to Deidre that they might be the result of her own behaviour: the response of a child made desperate by a mother's incessant demonstrations of inadequacy.

The last of these furies took place during a visit to a local beauty spot in the company of the Reverend Leo Midgely. After the death of her husband Deidre was uncommunicative and isolated by choice. She shunned all contact with her neighbours when she returned to Mansergh, even when Pauline began to attend the village school, which was situated a hundred yards from Saint Peter's church. The Reverend Leo Midgely became a frequent visitor there as he knew the teacher quite well and used the ground in front of the school building to park his car, there being no vehicular access to the church beyond that point. It became a habit of his to accompany the children of Turner Row home over the field to stretch his legs after church work. As a friend of the needy it was appropriate that he should single out the child who seemed to be the most lonely, and this was Pauline: though here was a misapprehension in itself as the little girl did not notice her lack of friends.

After he had delivered Pauline to the door of number 7 a few times, taking note of the strained, unhappy face of the mother who received her, he gained entry and set about relieving Deidre's gloom. He talked about his travels, his studies, his opinions, but most of all he talked about Pauline. She was, he said, the continuation of her father's spirit, the embodiment of the beauty he had worshipped in life. Whereas Oswald Nash had not been articulate, reserving all his creative energy for painting, he had frequently presented the Reverend Leo Midgely with enough evidence in discussion for him to deduce that Oswald Nash believed that his aesthetic sense, by which he lived and thrived, was not only God-given, but part of God. After a few months of confusion and suspicion during which she tried to avoid the clergyman, Deidre began to see what he was talking about and accepted his guidance. He had made life more whole, she assured him, and given her strength to go forward. Upon receiving this compliment, the Reverend Leo Midgely had reminded Deidre that it was he who had baptised Pauline — so powerful and pervasive was the widow's grief that she could scarcely recall any detail of her life before the tragedy — and he asked to be allowed to assume the mantle of godfather to the child, the ones appointed having neglected their duties and faded into history. Deidre gladly agreed and the Reverend Leo Midgely became the mediator between her and the world, and the arbitrator between mother's and daughter's interests whenever crises occurred.

It was in the latter rôle that he was most employed as the three of them toiled up the ferny slope of Farleton Knot, a limestone escarpment five miles to the west of Kirkby Lonsdale from which fine views could be had over four counties. Deidre was trailing far behind, a cigarette in her hand, while he and Pauline strode over the sheep-cropped grass of the path curling towards the summit. Eventually Deidre had fallen so far back that they had to stand and wait for her.

Pauline was still carrying puppy-fat but her future figure had begun to emerge. As she walked up ahead of him, he noticed how her legs had lengthened and the incipient development of a waist. To him this had more appeal than the fully-fledged woman he imagined: his mind relished the point between the exodus of childhood and the onset of experience as it conveyed motion, but motion impalpable. To his taste potential and promise were always superior to achievement, and success was a moribund condition. When he could he liked to influence and guess how a thing would grow.

"Here she comes!" Pauline said with a laugh as her mother toiled into view puffing on her cigarette. "She looks like a train. She shouldn't smoke while she's climbing, should she?"

He squatted on his haunches beside a gorse bush to keep out of the strong west wind that was blowing, beckoning Pauline to come beside him.

"We'll ambush her," he said conspiratorially. "Wait till she gets past then we'll jump out and frighten her."

"Oh, can we?" Pauline whispered, her eyes shining. "That would be marvellous."

When Deidre approached the point on the path by the gorse bush they could hear that she was talking to herself. At first it was inaudible, nothing but gasps and pants and expletives with no connecting sense, but as she drew nearer they could clearly hear what she was saying.

"I can't wear this, I can't wear that! Must have new clothes, Mummy. Where the hell is Mummy going to get the clothing coupons from, for Christ's sake? Why doesn't she do her own alterations? A lot of those clothes are nearly new, damn her, the fat little pig!"

Pauline sprang out of hiding and attacked her mother with terrible ferocity, her voice raised in a high scream. It took all the strength that the Reverend Leo Midgely had at his command to pull the girl off and pinion her. Once the fit had passed she sank into his arms muttering that she had always done her own sewing.

It was over in a few seconds. When Deidre picked herself up out of the ferns and walked around in a circle for a while to calm her nerves, they continued walking up the slope, but with Deidre energetically leading the way. This time it was Pauline who was left behind to dawdle, both females intuiting that it was better to keep some distance between them for a while.

The Reverend Leo Midgely had, for many years, been lulled by

31

the illusion that he had an acute and incisive insight into the human character, derived from his own disappointments. His chosen area of existence was no longer that of a parish priest operating within an orthodoxy laid down by a hamfisted, slumbering church. He had seen the great socialist experiment in the Soviet Union first-hand and found more of Christianity in that than in the Britain of the Thirties; he had seen India in its poverty, America in its wealth, Rome in its new brutality under Mussolini and Germany in its lunging, war-horse pride and madness. Greece he had found to be a picked bone, and Jerusalem a joke. His only choice had been to withdraw from a world in such chaos and concentrate on the inner world of the souls whose cure had been entrusted to his care. The dimensions here had been infinite but impossible to manage as his flock had remained obstinately fixed in their day-to-da preoccupations and soon they had begun to resent his sardonic gnosticisms. Step by step they had retreated until there was no one, then Deidre and Pauline had appeared on the scene; vulnerable, responsive, disturbed and proud: four conditions of soul which he had come to prize above all others after twenty years of lurching through the clayfields of the Anglican priesthood.

As he sat on the scalloped summit of Farleton Knot, the mother on one side of his cross, the daughter to the other, their silences trembling on the wind, he realised that his ministry had dwindled down to these two spirits; and the fells, crags, whalebacked mountains, plateaux, estuaries and coasts stretching out around him might just as well be the entire world for all the influence over human affairs he had attained.

Into the dreadfulness of this revelation came Deidre's voice. She shifted herself closer to him and was pulling at his sleeve.

"Oswald could never paint up here. He tried several times," she confided. "Too rocky, too bitty, no flow to it."

"Look out there!" he said, sweeping his hand through the panorama of Yorkshire, Lancashire, Cumberland and Westmorland.

"Oswald never looked out anywhere," Deidre said with a subdued snarl. "He could only paint things which were right under his nose."

"Then why do you choose to live in the scenes he painted if you disapprove? Get out of Mansergh, take your daughter somewhere new..."

"Ah, you don't understand, Leo. I only have the past. She only has the future. What I'd do without you I don't know, because you're the only guide we've got to the present."

The Reverend Midgely laughed wildly at the woman's compliment, but his mirth was a counterfeit. Deidre had appealed to what was left of his vanity and he was glad to hear what she had said. He suspected that the accuracy of her flattery had not been achieved by a random shot: Deidre knew of his yearning and, perhaps, had been able to sense the ache of his failures.

"Are you all right now?" he asked. "No hard feelings?"

"Oh, it was the heat of the moment. She's an angel, really. Come over here, my darling."

Pauline ran across, immediately willing to make up, and the Reverend Midgely left them to it, picking his way over the clints and grykes of the limestone pavement to look at a large erratic boulder which was balanced on one end, left behind by the retreat of the glacier in the Ice Age. Around the back of it he found footholds to get to the top and he scrambled up half-hoping that the thing would rock under his weight. Once there he stamped and pushed to disturb its equilibrium but it was unshakeable.

Twenty yards away the two females were sitting arm in arm on the summit watching him. They were not laughing at his antics but frowning as if they felt compelled to take whatever he did seriously.

Upon the death of his father, a communist doctor who had built up a prosperous practice in Manchester, Leo had inherited thirty thousand pounds. It had been the year of his graduation from Durham, a time when his mind was at its keenest and his ambitions untrammelled. What was urgent to him was that he should see and know the world, the context of sin, grace and the creation. Without this knowledge he reckoned that he would become only the most useless of priests, guessing, making assumptions, incapable of conducting experiments or giving advice. Salvation would remain a mystery, and God a robot powered by praise.

The essential weakness in his decision had been that he had overestimated the strength of the vessel into which this knowledge would be poured: himself. He had spent a fifth of his legacy on two

33

years of continuous travel, hoping to piece together the framework of a reality that would bear the weight of an ideology. His father had succeeded in accomplishing this, but his globe-trotting had been through the bodily systems of men and women. Out of these arduous, pain-filled journeys had come his communism; but the son could not find the same foundation in the sufferings which he had touched on as he travelled round the world. He had seen much that smacked of perdition, injustice and cruelty but he had had no means of feeling it through. What he had seen he had only witnessed: his nature and intellect were not the equipment of missionary, pastor or theologian. Upon his return to England he had spent a few months trying to piece together a future for himself. Politics had crossed his mind in the hearse of all his self-esteem but he had wisely let it go. Finally he had surrendered to the failure of his hungry rush on life and meaning and entered the Anglican ministry to give himself time to think the whole thing out again, placing the residual four-fifths of his patrimony in gilt-edged securities to provide a private income while he pondered.

5

Eric's father prospered in Liverpool. In spite of the post-war shortages, his friend's ironmongery business did well and he was able to borrow money from his family to buy in as a partner. When Eric was fifteen his father sold out and bought a business in Kendal, only thirteen miles from Mansergh.

Eric had gained entrance to grammar school and was given a place locally. It was not an easy move as he had always struggled to concentrate and hated to have his routine disturbed by outside pressures. The new life at Kendal Grammar was not as congenial as his old school in Liverpool and he spent more time on his own, riding the lanes on his bicycle, getting nearer to old haunts.

Living in Kendal brought both Lily and Andrew Sherwin back within the orbits of their families; something which she appreciated far less than he did. The long memories of country people were a threat and the prosperity of the family set them apart from their own sort. Before long, the gossip of the war years re-emerged to taint Lily and her husband got to hear of it. They argued over this barren ground, unsettling their marriage, which had been very sound until now. Andrew started to drink heavily and Lily avoided going out, becoming an anxious recluse. Both of them could see what was happening and the reason for it and they had enough combined sense to know the remedy. They must return to the anonymity of the city, heal the wound and start again.

Eric's education was the main stumbling-block. His brother John was only ten and due to move from primary to secondary school anyway, but to move Eric again after so short a time was decided to be inadvisable. While his mother and father returned to Liverpool with his brother, Eric was left behind to finish his schooling at Kendal over the next three years.

He lodged with a retired clergyman, the Reverend John Salmon who was the brother of the English master at the grammar school. The old house was a roomy, late Victorian parsonage, maintained as if the time of its construction had never slipped away. A housekeeper, Mrs Evans, presided, shepherding the male household (there were three other lodgers as well as Eric) through their daily routines. As it was his first time on his own, Eric was homesick, but he soon found friends and began to enjoy a sense of new independence. Not only that, his school work improved as he discovered that he was able to discipline himself more than he had reckoned. Ahead of him he saw university and a career as a veterinary surgeon; biology, chemistry and mathematics being his strong subjects. When he looked back upon this interlude in his life he enjoyed the sense of formality and manly order it provided, however brief.

Living at the Reverend Salmon's house in Stricklandgate was a boy in a similar position to himself. Daniel Fleck's father had been killed in the war and his mother, a local librarian, had married a Polish pilot who had escaped from Warsaw and flown with the Royal Air Force. After the war they had remained in Kendal and Daniel's step-father had started a second-hand car business. Tensions developed within the family and with business competitors so the Pole decided to go to the Yorkshire coal-fields where many of his countrymen had gone to work. They had left Daniel behind in Kendal to complete his secondary education for the same reason as Eric had been left: for the sake of continuity and to minimise the effects of domestic upheaval.

Daniel Fleck was five inches shorter than Eric who was already topping six foot. He was a studious but inspired friend, forever applying his intelligence to the minor details of daily life as well as to his omnivorous reading in history, geology, Freud, anthropology and the occult, drawing on all of them for his long discourses and stories. He was intrigued, provoked and tormented by the thought of girls but tongue-tied and abashed in their company, painfully conscious of his protruding ears which turned red when his blood was up, and his thick, bottle-end spectacles which gave him a befuddled, dangerous look.

If contact had ever been made, the girls would have encountered someone out of the ordinary: gentle, enquiring, thoughtful, and obsessed by history, science and sex.

Spending a lot of time in each other's rooms, the boys had many opportunities to work out each other's character but the art was lost to them. All that mattered was the crude rudiment of their understanding; their shared predicament, common enemies and the mystic union of finding each other agreeable.

They were both quite good athletes, although not sportsmen in spirit. Physical prowess only excited them during an actual contest and had far less to offer than the heroics of desire. To be able to run and throw were not the attributes of true conquistadors who were far too wily and subtle to be trapped into wasting energy on chaff. As outsiders they could never share the team ambition of the school, only scoff from inside at their own efforts, which were small aspirations when compared to what they hoped to win from the whole of life and the love of women.

Shortly after his sixteenth birthday, in June 1956, Eric found himself back in sight of the fells, a javelin in his hand. Kendal Grammar and the Queen Elizabeth School at Kirkby Lonsdale were holding an athletics meeting. Along the valley of the Lune came a cool wind, brushing the high white clouds towards him down the marked-out throwing-funnel. To one side sat a group of spent runners from the mile race; to the other a crowd of girls. A boy from the opposing team ran down the funnel, spikes tearing at the dry grass, and threw a javelin. It was a poor throw, too flat, and it meant that Eric had already won the competition from his last effort; but he had one throw in hand to better his distance which was close to a school record.

Daniel Fleck sat on the grass and hugged his knees as the wind cooled the sweat from the mile race on his skin. He had come third, which was creditable as he had done little training; but he had desperately wanted to win and impress these young women.

"No one notices who comes in third," he'd muttered to Eric as his eyes struggled to see through his steamed-up glasses after the race. "I might just as well have come bloody last!"

Eric raised the javelin over his head. Far down the funnel he could see the officials warily waiting with the measuring-tape. His eye went to the point of the aluminium spear as it gleamed against the dark, curving line of the fell; then he glanced at the girls to make sure they were watching.

The weapon shook in his grasp as he pelted down the approach; back went his arm, then he saw her. With a cry he hurled the javelin in a huge, spectacular arc.

The crowd watched the flight of the spear as it vibrated in the sun, then stuck quivering into the ground just past the record peg. Only two people had not followed the course of the weapon, their eyes fixed on each other.

Daniel ran over and hugged Eric in congratulation as the crowd applauded. He saw the tall, black-haired girl in school uniform who held a paint-splattered raffia bag to her breast, her dark eyes fastened on Eric. His body was as crouched and taut as a startled fox; cruel, fierce and direct. The girl began to blush, twisting her shoulders, but she could not look away.

"Steady on," Daniel said under his breath as he led Eric off towards the mass of spectators which had gathered for the next event. "Where're your manners?"

6

He followed her around all afternoon; from running to jumping to putting, his eyes feasting on her back because she now refused to look at him. Other girls kept him under surveillance and told her what he was doing, reporting on his dog-like insistence. When he had to perform again in the shot-put she walked away as he stepped into the circle with the iron ball. As he sank it into his shoulder and went into a low crouch, gearing himself up for the throw, he saw her wandering over the field towards the fence, the raffia bag swinging by her side. He impatiently shed the encumbrance of the shot by putting it badly, then set off after her, stepping out of the front half of the circle and thereby disqualifying his effort.

Behind him he heard laughter and jeering as the boys and girls in the crowd who were aware of what was going on mocked his undisguised pursuit. She stopped, lifted her head and looked round. For a moment he thought she was going to run but he was wrong. Standing back on one foot and folding her arms she waited for him, the raffia bag dangling from her fingers.

When he arrived he did not know what to say, but it hardly mattered: the pressure he had put her under had created a dialogue of its own. He had challenged her to recognise the attention he was paying.

"What is it you want?" she said. When he did not reply she repeated herself, her voice low, careful and troubled.

"What is it you want?"

Eric grinned and shrugged his shoulders, suddenly relaxed. Arrogance took over. The inner pursuit quietened. Beneath powder he could see a spot on the girl's chin.

"What's your name?" he asked.

"That's no business of yours!" she replied aloofly, beginning to walk away. Hoots and whistles from the distant onlookers followed this obvious rejection. His confidence wavered.

"Will you come out with me?" he pleaded.

"I will not!" she replied haughtily over her shoulder. "Go away. You're embarrassing me."

"Go on, come out with me," Eric persisted, now trotting along beside her. "Come to the pictures."

She stopped, her face a mask.

"Very well, but now you have to leave me alone," she said in a shaky voice. "My mother is waiting for me."

"I'll meet you on Saturday down by the Devil's Bridge at seven o'clock," Eric called as he turned to run back to the crowd. "Please, please come."

She hurried away, climbed over the dry-stone wall and fled down the slope of the field. Eric ran back to rejoin the crowd, ignoring the sardonic applause of his school-mates.

Eric had to receive a prize for his victory in the javelin. Before doing so, he was taken aside by the sports master and reprimanded for his behaviour.

"That kind of lewdness is not acceptable, Sherwin. If I thought it would do any good, apart from giving you a second opportunity to persecute her, I'd have you apologise to that young lady," he said, his ginger moustache twitching with amused irritation. "You thank your lucky stars that the Head isn't here today or he'd have been down on you like a ton of bricks."

Eric apologised, hinting that he had been put up to it by his mates as a test because he was shy.

"Well, you chose wrong there, Sherwin. That girl is no scrubber for the likes of you. She's got class, which you haven't, except when you're heaving javelins about the place. Go and get your prize, you animal," he said, chuckling indulgently.

When Eric received a copy of *Pilgrim's Progress* from the purple-clad Bishop of Carlisle as his prize, he noticed a tall, middle-aged clergyman of dark, serious looks in attendance who kept glancing at him with speculative interest and trying to attract his attention. As

Eric walked away the man came over and introduced himself as Leo Midgely, a curate and priest-in-charge of the Kirkby Lonsdale parish. He invited Eric over to the refreshment tent where they found a small table and ordered tea.

"Sit down, Eric," he said kindly. "You know, I was a javelin-thrower when I was a lad. I threw for my college and I made quite a study of the various techniques. You have a lot of promise. Your physique is right. I was always too tall but you're fairly thick-set as well as, what? Five eleven? Six foot? Perhaps you'd consider letting me train you? I've actually seen the great Finnish throwers, Jarvinen and Nikkanen. Danielsen's two hundred and eighty-one feet this year was a magnificent effort. I'd love to have seen him do it. . ."

Daniel Fleck came over to announce that the bus was leaving shortly to take the team back to Kendal.

"Don't worry," the Reverend Midgely said, his hand on Eric's shoulder, "I'll take you home. I know where you live."

"I should be getting back, sir," Eric replied, trying not to appear churlish. "I've got things to do."

"Leave them till tomorrow," the Reverend Midgely said grandly. "Oh, come on. Don't be a spoilsport. I'm the man who baptised you! My colleague, your landlord in Kendal, old John Salmon, told me all about you. There can't be all that many Sherwins about. Your father used to work at Rigmaden Park and you were born at Turner Row. Isn't that correct?"

"Yes, sir," Eric replied uneasily.

"How is your mother?"

"Very well, sir."

"Poor woman. She had a difficult time when your father went off to the war. I hope she's happy now."

"She's all right, sir."

The Reverend Midgely smiled affably, then sipped his tea. Some people came to the table and Eric was forced to sit and wait until they had finished chatting. He spent the time studying the clergy-man, paying him out for studying him so closely over the javelin. He was about forty, austerely impressive in a quizzical, gloomy way, but with laughter-lines crowded at the corners of his eyes and down-turning mouth. Eric particularly took note of his hands; long, brown and veined as a vine, nails as clean as a new book.

"Don't folk talk?" he said with a grin when the last batch of acquaintances had gone. "I've been working in this area for twenty-odd years now and, I suppose, I know everyone. Ah, the price of notoriety, eh, Eric? But I can't throw the javelin any more."

He got up and stubbed out his third Turkish cigarette since sitting down at the table.

"Come on, I'll drive you home. I'm having dinner with John Salmon tonight. Perhaps we can squeeze a place for you? Would you like that?"

Eric demurred. Too much had happened today and he had planned to get himself back down to the ground with some chemistry. He gave the excuse of too much homework.

"No matter. Another time. I tell you what, we'll drive to Kendal by the old road through Kearstwick and Old Hutton, and I'll make a diversion to take you past the place where you were born. How would you like that? Have you ever been back since you came to Kendal? It's not that far on a bike, is it?"

Continuing with his friendly, rambling discourse, the Reverend Midgely took Eric to his car and they set off north as the afternoon sun filled the western side of the valley.

That night Eric lay in bed awake until three in the morning, his mind racing backwards and forwards over the events of the day. He could not sleep because he did not wish to leave the colour and excitement of what had happened. At the fork of the Chapel Road, the Reverend Midgely had stopped his car and they had walked up the dirt track to Turner Row where he had pointed out number 3, Eric's birth-place. It looked small and anonymous, indistinguishable from the others and no one was in when the Reverend Midgely had knocked on the door. Walking further up the terrace he had stopped outside number 7.

"Quite a well-known artist used to live here. His pictures have started fetching good prices. I have a couple myself, some oils, water-colours he did of local scenes. Killed in the last months of the war, poor chap. His widow never married again. She still lives here, with her daughter, the young lady you encountered at the athletics meeting. Shall we pay them a visit?"

He had raised one hand and made a fist that looked as though it could batter the little door off its hinges. Eric had reacted sharply.

"No, I'd rather not . . . not now. . . ."

A face had appeared in the window, a pale blob between green, embroidered curtains, then had gone away. But the door had remained closed.

"Pauline is the light of her mother's life; too much so," the Reverend Midgely had said as they went back to the car. "She's a beautiful child but Deidre must learn to let her go."

Pauline walked the two miles back along the lanes to Mansergh, the shock of her confrontation with Eric still radiating through her mind. She had been flattered and humiliated both at once; also frightened by the force behind his approach. The boy had not seemed to be fully in control of himself. The vigour with which he had pursued her had had a barbaric feel to it; soldierly, mindless, unlike the sly and shy attentions of other boys who had attempted to attract her interest. She remembered the appraising vitality of his face as he had spoken to her, brushing aside all inhibitions, willing, urgent, wide open to any insulting brush-off she might have made. It was the behaviour of a masculine idolater. Her mother had warned her that, with her beauty, Pauline would provoke this response. Some men would react that strongly, pitching everything they had at her feet as sacrifices. They would not offer themselves as slaves, her mother had said. What they will feel for you will transcend that. They will simply say, I must have you, not as slave, or master, but as haver. That is how your father was with me. It was a collision not a union.

Over the years Pauline had learnt enough about her mother to doubt that her parents had had this kind of kinetic relationship. It did not fit in with her vague memories of her father, nor his photographs or his painting style. It was a fantasy, more to do with art than life, but this did not deprive it of strength in its effect on the girl. As an oft-repeated memory, a ritual performed in her mother's offices for the dead, it had great power. Knowing that it was primarily a fable did not preclude it from becoming part of her ambitions. She had been taught to expect this intense, single-minded passion from many men. Eric was the first of them to appear in her life and, as the herald, he quickly found grace in her mind.

By the time she reached the fork in the road where she had to turn off for Mansergh it had begun to rain. A squall had come in swiftly from the south-west and the sea, filling the sky with flying black clouds. There was plenty of shelter but she ignored it, walking along the lane with its rain-stirred, hissing hedges and fresh fragrances.

7

He knew that she wouldn't turn up.

After two days of heavy rain, the Lune was brown and swollen, pouring through the triple arch of the great medieval bridge, the air full of dampness and the rush of water.

Eric leant over the parapet, gloomily contemplating the rest of the evening. He had come on the bus with three other boys from Kendal Grammar, all of whom knew why he was going to Kirkby Lonsdale. If he saw any of them in the town or at the pictures and he was alone there would be too high a price to pay in terms of inane mockery. Whatever adverse comment his behaviour at the sports match had elicited, no one had been able to doubt his taste. The girl was agreed to be extraordinarily beautiful, but, as Daniel had said, not for the likes of Eric.

"We're talking about class," Daniel had said, sitting on the edge of Eric's bed the night after the athletics match. "You're a peasant, a prole, an erk. She's too good for you. Once she finds out what a barbarian you are it will all be over."

Eric rubbed his finger-tips on the stone, rationalising that she had made the date just to get rid of him. He stepped back from the parapet and walked down to a mobile café parked at the eastern side of the bridge. A fat man served him a cup of tea, small blue eyes twinkling in a huge, lumpen head.

"Been stood up?" he said with a knowing smirk.

Eric made no reply but moved away from the counter to avoid any further intrusions on his misery. Going to the southern edge of the bridge he sipped the hot tea and looked down into the broad pool which the waters poured into out of the limestone gorge. The air was alive with the relieved songs of birds after the rain and the muffled roar of upstream rapids.

She was standing in one of the central embrasures of the bridge, only the upper half of her body visible. He knew that she was completely aware of his presence and had been watching him as he drank. The cup in his hand made him feel stupid and exposed as if he had been caught performing some unmanly domestic chore. Without being concerned that the cup was china and the proprietor of the mobile café would like it back, he tossed the cup over the parapet and walked nonchalantly towards her, his mind whirling around the question of what would be the best opening remark he could possibly make.

"Quite a spate," he said finally as their manoeuvring eyes clashed.

She did not want to go to the cinema, nor for a walk. The only reason she had kept the appointment was because it was on the way to the Reverend Midgeley's house where she was headed for her private Latin lesson. Eric could come along if he liked but it would involve waiting.

"How long?" he asked, not succeeding in hiding his disappointment.

"My lesson is for an hour."

He suggested that he should go for a walk and then call back for her but this proposition was dismissed.

"If I finish early I won't wait for you and if you're not there exactly when it's over I won't remember you at all," she said without a tremor of amusement.

Eric shrugged and followed her meekly across the bridge. She would not allow him to walk fully alongside her all the way down the path back into town but kept striding ahead or falling back so that it would not appear as though they were walking out together. All this he accepted. From the moment he had got close to her again on the bridge he had been operating without self-respect.

When they arrived at the Reverend Midgely's house she let herself in with a key and took him into the sitting-room which was lined with book-shelves. There was a large elm table in the middle laid out with books and papers and two straight-backed chairs. She sat down in one of them and he, in his confusion, took the other.

"You can't sit there. That's Leo's place," she said after a pause in which her eyes roamed all over his head and shoulders as if searching for signs of dandruff.

"Where shall I sit then?" he asked, standing up obediently. "There're no more chairs."

She got up and went out of the room, returning a minute later with a stool which she put by the empty fireplace. It was a small piece of furniture and he lowered himself on to it with care.

"Won't . . . *Leo* mind me being here?" he said.

"No. It was his idea. Do you do Latin at your school?"

Eric nodded dumbly. He could not keep his gaze off her face and the way her mouth moved when she talked. Not daring to embarrass her he forced himself to look at her hands as they opened her exercise book. They were quite large for a girl, with very long, strong, well-formed fingers. When she took hold of her fountain-pen and shook it at a piece of blotting-paper he felt his legs tighten and had to grip the edges of the stool to steady himself.

The Reverend Midgely entered the room and immediately came over to Eric, a hand outstretched and a broad smile of welcome on his face. Eric got to his feet and shook hands, his other hand behind him against the fireplace.

"Eric! How delightful! You came. I'm so glad. Have you found a book to read? Perhaps you have one of your own with you or some private speculations you might dwell on? Do sit down, my dear boy. Don't mind us," he said rapidly, almost gabbling.

Without more ado the Latin lesson commenced and Eric was left on his stool. To get a book would have meant standing up and searching the shelves which would disturb Pauline so he sat tight and tried not to move. After ten minutes he was in agony. He knew that Pauline was looking directly at him every time she raised her head from the translation she was going through. To sit there like a hearth-ornament for an hour would be demeaning and ridiculous so he decided to stand up, take the nearest book to hand out of the book-case, then read it. Waiting for Pauline's attention to be drawn deep into a difficult passage of the Seneca she was struggling through, he suddenly got to his feet, grabbed a book that protruded from the others, pulled it out, opened it at random as he sat down, then attempted to read the page which was upside-down.

The Reverend Midgely had glanced in his direction as he carried out this manoeuvre, and Pauline had halted momentarily in her translation, but they immediately went back to their work once they had ascertained what he was about.

Listening to her light, northernly-flavoured voice as it wound itself round the Os and UMs and UNTs of the Latin; aware of the strangeness of the room and the authority of the dark, hunched figure of the clergyman always leaning closer and closer towards her, Eric found the problem of reading his book upside-down a welcome escape. His mind, at last, achieved some kind of independence from the girl: real distance appeared between his true self and the desire-driven tumults of his mind and body.

After five minutes of hard work he was able to ascertain that his wild choice from the book-shelves was a volume devoted to the agrarian policies of the Soviet Union from 1917 to 1941. In the time that it took for Pauline to complete her lesson he managed to read six pages upside-down, the thought of turning the book the right way up and thereby admitting his error being far too compromising to contemplate.

"What profession do you intend to pursue, Eric?"

The Reverend Midgely had left the table and was standing over Eric like a tree, his eyes directed down at the open book.

"I'd like to be a vet, sir," Eric replied, quickly shutting it.

"For that you'll need Latin, I should think," the Reverend Midgely said, taking the book out of Eric's hands, pointedly turning it round and re-opening it. "This is a very dull book, really, but the subject is of immense importance. Communism has many excellent ideas in it but it seems to take the edge off writers. Would you like extra Latin lessons? Perhaps you're good enough already? However, an aspirant veterinary surgeon should shine at the ancient languages. Are you studying Greek? You should. All the best early work on the doctoring of animals is in Greek."

Eric stood up. The nearest he had got to studying to be a vet was cutting pictures of prize cattle, sheep and pigs out of magazines. He was no good at Latin at all.

48

"I'm not sure my parents could afford to pay for extra Latin lessons," he said, knowing that he was lying.

The Reverend Midgely smiled and shut the book, returning it to the shelf.

"Oh, don't worry about that. The lessons will be free. Be here at the same time next week. Now, if you don't mind, I must get ready to go out."

Hardly giving Pauline time to collect her books and papers he ushered them out into the street. There was a measure of force and insistence in the man's movements which made Eric's hackles rise.

"Thank you, *sir*," he managed to mumble.

"I'm sure we'll get on, Eric," he said winningly.

"See you soon," Pauline said, kissing Leo on the cheek. "I learnt a lot today."

"Good. I will be along to see your mother on Tuesday. It's a lovely evening. Do something with it. Now," he said, turning to Eric, "two things: one, I insist that you call me Leo. I dislike being called sir, Reverend or Mr Midgely, all these being actual words I detest. Second, here is a pound-note for you to purchase the texts we require for your Latin studies. You can get them at the book-shop in Kendal."

With that he closed the door and left them standing on the step. Pauline put her head to one side and grinned encouragingly at Eric for the first time.

"Isn't he wonderful?" she said in a voice that brooked no disagreement; then she started to stride away down the pavement.

Eric ran after her, the pound-note fluttering in his hand. His mind was greatly confused and he felt ashamed at how he had allowed himself to be driven along by Leo, without protest. He was able to deal with other masters, even men who were more aggressive and skilful than Leo; but he could not handle this man with Pauline together. As he ran the few steps towards her retreating figure, these thoughts threaded through his inner heat and confusion, but then it happened again: his whole soul turned.

It was her back, the slope of her shoulders, the beginning of fullness in her hips, the flash of her bare legs and the sound of her shoes on the paving-stones which stunned him. He stopped running, stood with his hands against his ears, the bank-note fluttering against his cheek, and cursed, and cursed.

She had her bicycle with her, which she had left at another house. Once she had picked it up they walked through the old town's narrow alleys towards the church. She kept the bicycle between them, humming to herself. He was reduced to silence as anything he wanted to say dried on his tongue, condemned as idiocy before he could express it. He did not know what to communicate to her that would be sufficiently disguised for his love to avoid detection. To articulate the simplest thought or comment would mean confessing all, so charged with her presence was every action of his mind. He could not laugh. His sense of humour had fled in fear. To be light-hearted was an impossibility now his heart was as massive and overbearing as a planet running in orbit.

"I'm going to get on my bike and cycle now," she said, hitching up her skirt. "You're not very talkative are you?"

He stood and watched her ride off down the street. Over her head the evening sky was flushed with pink, pouring down between the high, old houses and flashing on the rims of her bicycle's wheels and the chromium of turning pedals. He was dragged into a further stage of his enchantment: there was the mechanism of the love, and he was deep within the machine.

Finally he managed to shout. What came out of his mouth had no words: it was as much a warning cry as anything. He repeated it as passers-by turned their heads to see what the danger was. This time he made it represent a possible good-bye.

Daniel sat on the window-ledge in Eric's room, his short legs dangling, consternation showing behind his spectacles.

"Are you telling me you just went for a walk?" he said.

"Yes," Eric replied, pretending to work at his table, his back turned on his interrogator. "That's all."

"You didn't go to the pictures after all? No snogging in the back row?"

Eric half-turned and gave his friend a scornful glance which implied as much mystery as contempt.

"Did you get a feel?" Daniel demanded, the black rubber heels of his shoes marking the wallpaper as he drummed them in frustration. "Come on! Tell me!"

"What's a feel?" Eric muttered, writing hard. "I don't understand your language."

"Yes, you do. Everyone knows what a feel is. You're just covering up because you got nowhere. Well, what a disappointment you are!"

Having delivered this condemnation with a cruel cackle, Daniel slid down from the window-ledge and took up a new position on the end of the bed from where he could get a better view of Eric's reactions.

"I was sure you'd come back with the full story. Incredible, not even getting a feel. That's criminal. If I was her I'd be insulted. What's the matter with you, anyway?" Daniel continued aggressively. "I thought you fancied her."

"I didn't say that I didn't kiss her," Eric said with forced patience.

"Ah! We're getting somewhere!" Daniel shouted, bouncing on the bed. "What did you kiss?"

"What do you think?"

"All over?"

Eric groaned and closed the exercise book he had been writing in.

"So what's *your* success-rate with women so far?" he asked meanly. "Let's hear about *your* triumphs."

Daniel sank his head into his shoulders and fingered his overhanging upper lip.

"If they knew what a tool I'd got they'd be queuing up," he mused. "As it is they just think I'm ugly. Did you really kiss her? Was it a French kiss?"

"Get out of my room, you tosser," Eric snapped, grabbing Daniel by the scruff. "You're too nosey."

"You didn't kiss her. She took a second look at you and decided you weren't worth knowing. Give me her address and I'll go and see her. . ."

Still gabbling excitedly, Daniel was thrust out of the room on to the landing. He encountered the eye of the Reverend John Salmon who was on his way to the bathroom.

"Keep it down, boys," he said sternly. "It's getting late for horseplay."

"Yes sir," Daniel replied meekly. "Sorry sir."

Eric still had the door of his room open. He caught Daniel's eye as he turned to go.

"Good night, you tosser!" Eric whispered. "Sweet dreams."

"Good night, you pathetic failure," Daniel hissed back.

Eric's dream that night was about a huge, concrete city. He was lost on the rooftops which were full of alleys and gardens with narrow bridges connecting them. He had to remember at all times that he was hundreds of feet above the ground. In one garden there was a river which flowed to the edge then plummeted down the side of a skyscraper on to the street below. He stood by the edge of the river and touched the water where it arced. In the balls of his feet he felt a sweet ache which told him to jump. He did so and the exquisite terror of his descent shocked him into consciousness, his heart thumping as he sat up in bed.

When he had recovered he lay back, his hands behind his head, and conjured up Pauline's face. He could not bring it clearly to mind. He had forgotten the way her nose went, what her mouth looked like, even how tall she was. It was not a true impression of her that lay in his mind, he decided, only a sensation. To have such an incomplete memory of her after such a day of shocks and confrontations made him suspect his mental powers. Maybe I'm not as sharp as I think? he mused. Maybe I'm not going to do so well?

Goaded by these reflective recriminations he slid back into a sleep that was dreamless. When he awoke in the morning with the housekeeper ringing her bell outside his door, the vivid image of Pauline was blazing in his mind and his cock crowed full-throated under his hand.

8

The week that had to elapse before he could meet Pauline again proved to be an epoch in the history of Eric's youth: so much happened that he faced her across the table in Leo's sitting-room for the next Latin lesson unsure of everything.

His father had died very suddenly of a brain haemorrhage. Eric had not seen him for several months; during his last visit to Liverpool his father had been away on business. When he was given the news over the telephone it was as if a total stranger had died. He could not even remember his father's face. When he went down to Liverpool, he found his mother racked by grief, hardly able to communicate with him. They spent most of the time together in silence, moving through the house and streets about the business of death. His younger brother was vague and embarrassingly cheerful, that being the only way he knew how to deal with such an event.

As the days went by and the funeral took place, Eric suffered a frightening distortion of self, aware that his thoughts and feelings had become too separate. He had loved and respected his father and grieved his loss, but he could not keep him in mind. Whenever he allowed his memory any freedom it persisted in bringing Pauline to him. It was this which caused Eric such incapacitating distress at the funeral: at the moment when the coffin was lowered into the ground at Walton Cemetery and the earth swallowed up his father for ever, he caught himself day-dreaming about Pauline and yearning to see her again. A powerful gust of shame shook him at the graveside and he had to walk away and be by himself while the hot tears flowed. All the family noted his grief and were satisfied: until then they had been questioning the apparent coolness with which both sons had taken the death of their father.

He had returned to Kendal on the Friday evening after going through the guilt-ridden business of lying to his mother about the reason why he had to be back. She had wanted him to stay with her in Liverpool over the weekend but Eric had told her that he had to sit an examination. His mother was not the kind of woman who knew much about her children's education and she took it on trust, saying that his father would never have wanted him to do anything that would jeopardise his future success in the world. After a protracted farewell, during which he promised to return to Liverpool in a couple of weeks' time, Eric had left his family in the depths of their bereavement and hurried back up north.

Upon arriving at the house in Kendal he was met at the door by old John Salmon who took him straight into his study, shut the door and demanded to know why he had told untruths to his mother at such a terrible time. She had made a telephone call from Liverpool to check if he had arrived back safely and, in talking to Salmon, had mentioned the examination. Salmon knew that there was no such need for Eric to return; however, he was good enough not to convey this to the distraught woman. Faced with the indignation of the old gentleman, and with one cruel lie already cradled in his conscience, Eric moved smoothly and inexorably on to the next. He told Salmon that he had been compelled to escape from the claws of his philistine family because discussions had been taking place which would take him away from Kendal Grammar School and pitchfork him into a leading rôle in the family business before his education was completed. Knowing Salmon's horror of all things bourgeois and commercial, and his worship of youth, Eric had designed his second lie with skill and eagle-eyed calculation. It had worked brilliantly, winning Salmon firmly on to his side from a previous position whereby the old clergyman had often looked at him askance, suspecting a fatal superficiality of mind.

As a result of these events, when Eric put his newly-purchased Latin texts into his school bag in order to set out for Kirkby Lonsdale and his lesson with Leo and Pauline he had to include his father and two great lies in what he would take with him. By the time he stood on the door-step of Leo's house and hammered with the large, black-iron ram knocker, he had consigned them all to the depths of his past. What he had been, and what he had become, were all one to him, but as Leo opened the door and ran an expert eye over Eric's face he could tell that his javelin-thrower had changed. Within all the freshness and vitality nodded a premature bud of age, wind-blackened and battered; and the knowledge that it was there strangely moved Leo's heart.

They worked on the second book of Virgil's *Aeneid* which was some distance from either Eric's ability, or interest. The lesson consisted of Leo and Pauline translating it line by line into English while Eric sat looking at her from under lowered brows. Leo never referred to him, or asked him a question: he seemed to have assumed that Eric would have no real involvement. After ten minutes of this stage-managed adoration, Eric could not endure it any longer: he excused himself and went in search of the lavatory. When he found it he combed his hair in the mirror and stared at himself closely. He was either being ignored or he was being patronised. What he should have done was to insist upon paying for the lessons. Sitting in that room in her presence, demonstrably stupid, obviously her inferior, was impossible to tolerate. He made up his mind to withdraw from the lesson and wait outside until she was finished. With a final flourish of the comb through his hair, then through his eyebrows, he left the lavatory and walked back down the stone-flagged passageway towards the sitting-room.

When he reached the room and opened the door he found Leo and Pauline in exactly the same positions. Neither of them looked up as he entered. Eric could not decide whether to say his piece standing or sitting. As he shut the door, his eyes on the perfect line of her parted jet-black hair as she bowed her head over the Virgil, the telephone rang. The instrument was on a writing-desk in the corner of the room. Leo got slowly to his feet, opened his dark length like a clasp-knife, and crossed the room in a couple of strides. As he answered the telephone he rummaged in his jacket pockets for his cigarettes and lit one up as he spoke. When he had finished he returned to the table and announced that he had been called to the bedside of a dying parishioner and had to go immediately. Leo then asked if they would wait for him as he did not expect to be more than an hour. Without asking for their agreement he left the room and a few moments later they heard the front door slam as he went out.

Pauline closed her book and crossed her big hands over it.

"What a hard job he has," she said. "I couldn't do it."

Eric felt the heat flood into his throat as he tried to answer her. He was still on his feet and she seemed to be looking up at him from a great distance, her eyes tearing into his face like cannon-fire. He flinched, attempted to smile but only succeeded in distorting his mouth.

"There's no point in trying to work without Leo," she declared with a small sigh, which might have been impatience as much as he understood it. "I'll show you the house."

They went from room to room of the three-storey, eighteenth-century town terrace. There were books in every room, not much furniture, many posters and pictures from the Thirties, many of them political in subject, a lot of well-worn fine carpets from the Middle East. It was very much a masculine house, almost devoid of prettiness, with lofty ceilings and broad, well-proportioned Georgian windows drawing in the summer light. As Eric followed Pauline in silence, desperately wondering what he should do with this gift of an hour alone with her, he did not notice the absence of any bed in the rooms which might ordinarily be expected to contain one.

She chattered on quietly. He heard her talk about Leo's travels, his knowledge of art and politics, his goodness and kindness, how he had been like a father to her. There were pictures in some rooms which she pointed out as being the work of her dead father, gifts that her mother had made to Leo in order to repay him for acts of generosity.

"My mother says that she doesn't know how she would have managed without him. He's been wonderful. In some ways I feel as though I am his child, though I know it would upset him to hear me talk so loosely. You know what people are like in a place like Kirkby Lonsdale. They'll get everything the wrong way round."

As she finished speaking, she opened a door to a narrow staircase leading to the attic level.

"Do you like surprises?" she added briefly, starting to climb up.

"Depends what kind they are," Eric replied with a covering laugh.

"Nothing to worry about. It's a nice surprise."

"Good."

Pauline opened another door at the head of the stairs and turned on several switches. Standing to one side, she ushered him in and closed the door behind them. Before he could look at what lay beyond she took his head in her hands and made him look hard into her eyes, then released him with a little shove into the room which was the complete attic width of the house, having pitched ceilings and six large dormer windows. The lack of beds in the house was compensated here: a huge double bed with a massive headboard of dark, carved wood capped with brass stood in the furthest corner from the door and an avenue of oriental carpets of various designs, some frayed and worn, led up to it. It was a traveller's room, full of items from Russia, Greece and the Near East set in some order; and a television set, its dull grey tank incongruous and out of place on a buhl table of inlaid brass. Beside it, black, unadorned, and equally inconsistent with its exotic surroundings, was a plain, black telephone.

There was not a single book to be seen.

"This is Leo's bedroom," Pauline said, awe and respect in her voice. "Isn't it smashing?"

"Is he married then?" Eric asked, dimly aware that it was an unnecessary and ridiculous question. "I never thought about it."

"Leo? Married? Ha!" Pauline laughed and strolled along the carpets. "He'd never marry anyone. What's the point?"

"So he lives here alone?" Eric persisted doggedly, unable to equate the man he knew as Leo with the room.

"Yes, quite alone. He has a housekeeper but she is very old and refuses to come this far because of the stairs, so Leo says. What do you think?" she added, suddenly mysterious. "Wouldn't it frighten an old lady?"

Eric walked along the avenue of carpets. To either side the stained and waxed floorboards had been polished until they were like glass, reflecting the light from the dormer windows. There was no dust.

"He keeps it this clean all by himself?" he asked, knowing the answer with a sudden deadness of heart.

"No, I help him. I insist upon it. How else can I pay him for my extra lessons? How else can I show my appreciation? My mother and I have nothing . . . oh, you wouldn't understand."

In a flurry of impatient gestures she turned and pulled at the counterpane of the bed. It was a vast embroidery in gold, amber, black and silver on a pink background.

"This comes from Armenia. Isn't it nice?" she said.

For the first time he detected what he thought might be acting. It was a suggestion of coquettishness, a sweet falseness created for his benefit. Instead of bridling, he responded to it greedily. She was trying to please him.

Letting the corner of the counterpane fall she sat down on the bed. The light of the cloudy summer afternoon poured down from the dormer windows upon her. Lying back on the bed she pointed upwards.

"You can see the fell from here," she said. "I never noticed that before."

Questions tumbled around in his mind as he lumbered towards her, his limbs as heavy and ancient as the memories which surfaced in jewelled confusion. He had no idea what she expected of him, or, indeed, whether she even liked him. His approach was, to him, as massive and ominous as a thunderstorm, but she did not even glance in his direction.

"He's not my lover, I promise you," she said in a matter-of-fact tone, her eyes still on the window. "I must admit, I often hoped that he'd marry my mother, until I realised she was mad. She is quite mad, my mother. But I love her. . ."

Bending over her, a precipice about to become a landfall, he allowed his weight to slowly carry him down. As he arrived in her vision, unstoppable, now mighty, she raised her head, insisting that he look straight into her eyes.

"I don't want to miss anything," she said.

She became unbearably conscious of fabrics. As his kiss lasted longer and longer and her skin shone, the touch of her skirt, her blouse, the counterpane, became rough and menacing. She felt that they were tangled up in great strangling lengths, struggling to get out. Clawing at her clothes she dragged them off while still crushed beneath his weight, then attacked his, ripping and tearing at his jacket and shirt, a prisoner dementedly seeking freedom from a cage. He was taken by surprise and fell from her, fear in his face.

"Take them off!" she commanded.

He obeyed, but he did not move fast enough for her.

"Stand up and do it, you'll be quicker," she murmured impatiently. "Oh, please hurry up."

Flustered and browbeaten he rolled off the bed and undid his belt, keeping his eyes away from her. She turned on her front and held her head wrapped in her arms.

"What's the matter?" he asked.

"I don't want to look any more," she replied, her voice muffled.

In a haze of indignation, bewilderment, paralysing excitement and desire, he stripped off his clothes, amazed to find himself folding them up and putting them carefully over the back of a chair. She kept her head covered, locking and unlocking her long, strong fingers. When he lay down beside her and she felt the nakedness of his body she turned to him as if he had scorched her. With no kiss, no prelude, no words, she guided him in. A few strenuous, shuddering lunges later it was over. As he cried out, the telephone rang.

She immediately broke their embrace and leapt from the bed, running over to answer it.

It was a brutal departure, hurting him. He hardly heard what was being said but lay still, nursing his loss until she returned.

She lay down beside him and took his frowning face to her breast, stroking his hair.

"That was Leo. He'll be back in half-an-hour," she whispered. "Look, I've been bleeding."

She moved to one side and forced him to look down at the small patch of bright-red blood lying with some of his pale sperm on the Armenian counterpane.

"That means I was a virgin. I want you to remember that," she said in a tone where pride and supplication were mixed. "Now we'd better get up and do some Latin."

When Leo returned they were both back in the sitting-room with their books open. They heard him walking down the stone-flagged passage and smelt his Turkish cigarette before he came through the door. He looked cross and distraught, sitting down abruptly without closing the door behind him, puffing agitatedly at his cigarette.

"That took a long time," Pauline ventured to say after a while. "You look upset, Leo."

"Yes," he snapped back at her, his eyes flashing with vexation. "I am upset. These things always upset me. That woman! People astonish me. After a lifetime of hypocrisy and viciousness, the most uncharitable person, I assure you, she has the cheek to believe herself to be saved."

"You don't think she is?" Pauline asked.

"If she is then all the good people aren't."

"Did you tell her that?"

Leo grunted savagely and lit another Turkish cigarette from the last, hurling the stub into the fireplace.

"I don't want to talk about it. You know her, Mrs Williams, an absolutely poisonous woman. I suppose she thinks heaven is administered by someone in the Conservative Party. They really are the limit, these old battle-axes."

Pauline smiled and winked across at Eric who was keeping quiet.

"Poor Leo," she said softly, "what lies he has to tell."

"Did you work hard?" Leo demanded suddenly, swivelling Eric's books around to look at them. "Nothing much here that I can see. Dare you taunt me about who goes to heaven and who doesn't, Eric?"

"No, sir," Eric replied quickly.

"Have you any idea of heaven? Did you ever take the time to think about it?"

"I'm not sure what you mean, sir."

Leo gave him a long, examinational look, peering straight into his eyes, then switched to Pauline. He grinned; a wide, happy grimace which instantly infused his whole presence.

"Good! Good! Let's get ahead and put all this behind us. We have so much to do!"

Stretching out across the table he took Pauline's hand, then did the same with Eric. For a moment he held on to them, leaning forward in his chair, his Turkish cigarette between his lips. He said nothing but the light in his eye was that of a fighter approving the contest of others.

"We will win," he said eventually.

Eric felt the hair rise on the back of his neck. He tried to withdraw his hand from Leo's grasp but it tightened and he was held.

"Be steadfast, Eric. There is nothing to worry about. I'm always here to help you. Understanding will come," he said with an expression of extreme kindness. "Why, you're trembling, boy."

Eric got to his feet, his hand still a prisoner.

"I have to go now, sir," he mumbled, attempting to shield his stricken features from Leo's gaze with his other hand.

"Make him stay, Pauline. Tell him he's among friends," Leo said, letting go. "I think it's all been a bit much for him."

But Eric was already out of the door and stumbling along the passageway. Pauline ran after him but she could not catch up before he reached the front door and got out into the street. As he ran away he looked once over his shoulder and saw her standing in the doorway, her hand raised.

9

Pauline returned to the sitting-room to find that Leo had gone. Standing in the passageway she heard his step on the stairs above. She followed him up, stopping at the bathroom to wash her face because she had been crying. In the mirror she discerned someone who was not the person she had known as herself: her mouth had lost its firmness, her eyes were more alert to danger, the way she carried her head was less erect. Looking at her hands as they squeezed out the flannel she could see tiny tremors.

When she got to the attic door, she heard the television on the other side. She entered the room and saw Leo lying on the bed, his arms behind his head, watching a news programme. The counterpane had been stripped off the bed. She looked round the room for it but could not find it anywhere.

Leo held out a hand.

"Come here, little one," he said sorrowfully, "come and rest."

She went over and sat on the bed beside him. He put his arm round her and she fell on to his chest, overcome by a fresh outbreak of tears. He patted her shoulder, his eyes still on the television screen which carried pictures from a flood disaster in the United States.

"He'll be back," Leo said with a sigh. "Try to understand."

Pauline violently shook her head and moaned.

"Now, now, enough of that. Eric's been through a great turmoil lately. The boy needs time to sort himself out. He'll re-compose himself, all in good time," Leo murmured soothingly. "And you must take a few days to get over what happened."

"I never want to see him again!" Pauline seethed.

Leo lit a Turkish cigarette and blew the smoke up into the air.

"He is your mate. You were made for each other," he said, giving her a reassuring squeeze.

"But you said I wasn't to fall in love with him," Pauline protested.

"Did I?" Leo responded quizzically. "I can't think why."

"Well, I have, so there!"

"That's because you couldn't help yourself. I knew that I must allow for a certain leeway, youthful defiance being what it is. It strikes me things have worked out rather well," he added with a twinkle in his eye. "You should have a lot of fun."

"I wish I knew what it is you and my mother want of me," she whispered.

"Only your happiness. Have a sleep now. Is the television disturbing you?"

Pauline shook her head and rammed her face deeper into his shoulder. The aroma of countless Turkish cigarettes had impregnated the cloth of his jacket and she lay there inhaling it, not daring to let Eric back into her mind.

There was no one else to tell, but, before he opened his mouth, Eric knew that it was a mistake to share his story with Daniel. He had to talk, however, or go mad. Knowing the capacity Daniel had for harvesting the most sumptuous sexuality from the scantiest hints, he feared that the massive ornateness of his experience would sink any chance of credibility. To be disbelieved was the last thing he wanted. To go along with his account of what had happened at Leo's house was the confession that he now loved Pauline and already needed her again. To put this proposition to someone with such a jejune experience of women was an act of craziness; but then, he was crazy, and lonely inside the tumult she had caused.

Daniel listened, open mouthed, his big head thrust forward. Often, he sniffed and frowned, then pursed his lips as if calculating the truth of what he was being expected to believe.

"You lucky bugger," he breathed when it was all over. "I'd pay to have made that up."

"I didn't make it up!" Eric protested. "That's what happened."

"I don't understand why you're not brilliant at English essays when you've got an imagination like that," Daniel persisted. "You could make a fortune writing pornography."

They were in the walled garden at the back of John Salmon's house sitting at a garden table, supposed to be revising for a history examination by testing each other for dates. Eric had the list in his hand. Instead of hitting Daniel — which was what he felt urged to do — he carried on where they had left off.

"The Treaty of Locarno?"

"Nineteen twenty-five."

"Who was the British delegate?"

"Austen Chamberlain."

"What was agreed?"

"Everybody agreed to betray everybody else when they felt like it," Daniel said with a diabolical grin. "If she heard you talking about her like that she'd sue you."

Eric turned the list over and got up from the table.

"Don't expect me to confide in you again," he said grimly. "It just isn't worth it."

"Come on, Eric, it's all a bit far-fetched, you must admit," Daniel complained, turning the list back over. "Let's drop it, eh? My turn. When did Germany enter the League of Nations?"

Eric walked away, his treachery like vomit in his mouth. He had not had the courage to tell Daniel the necessary prelude: how he adored this girl. Instead he had conformed to the ritual rôle of the irresistible conqueror and had been scoffed at for his pains.

"When did Germany enter the League of Nations? No? Nineteen twenty-six. The occupation of the Rhineland? Of Pauline?"

"How are we going to stop you being so envious?" Eric said wearily. "We'll have to get you a girlfriend somehow."

"Get stuffed. You're going to fail this exam. You know sweet F.A."

"Do you want me to ask her if she's got a friend?"

Daniel's eyes widened, then he pulled himself together.

"Okay," he said, feigning indifference. "But I doubt if she'll ever see you again. If you go around telling such bloody great lies about her she'll be sure to hear of it."

"Do you want me to mention it to her or not?" Eric snapped.

"All right, keep your hair on. Bad temper is a sign of someone who's still a virgin, so Freud says. Any idea about the occupation of the Rhineland?"

"No!"

Daniel sniggered and rolled up the list.

"Nineteen thirty-six. That's only four years before you were born. And if your kind of imaginary sex had been used by your mother and father you'd still be waiting to get started."

10

Eric had already decided to put in an appearance at the next Latin lesson before he received Pauline's letter. It was written on headed beige notepaper which not only carried her address but also her telephone number. The letter was clearly scribed in a round, looping hand, and full of commonplaces. Reading it made him feel as though she had become his sister. There was no apparent connection between the reality of what had happened between them and what she was able to write about. This dissociation troubled him but he reasoned that it was probably all she dared to express to someone who had run away from her in fear. Besides, the message he had hoped for was there: she asked Eric to meet her on the Saturday — the same day as the next scheduled Latin lesson with Leo — at a private bridge over the Lune about a mile north of Kirkby Lonsdale. To get there he would have to trespass on the Underley Hall estate, she wrote, but no one ever seemed to care about that. Enclosed in the envelope was a rough sketch-plan to help him get there. The time she requested him to arrive was six o'clock in the morning.

He decided to write back.

tel: Kendal 3 3 4 7

Beechcroft,
Slynegate,
Kendal.
18th June 1956.

Dear Pauline,

Thank you for your letter. I will do everything I can to meet you on Saturday. Will you be supplying breakfast or should I bring my own?

Do you know a girl at your school who'd be prepared to

meet a friend of mine? He's very intelligent and not bad-looking. I'm not suggesting that you bring her along this time but at some future date, perhaps?

I hope you don't mind me asking this.

See you Saturday.

Yours truly,

Eric.

The response was a telephone call from Pauline's mother which came through during dinner on Thursday evening. Eric had to take it in the corridor with the housekeeper walking backwards and forwards to serve the meal from the kitchen. Deidre Nash was in a rage, pouring obscenities and blasphemies down the telephone. She had found his letter in her daughter's satchel and wanted to know whether he thought they were running a brothel.

"I don't know what you mean. . ." Eric stammered in reply.

"You know well enough," she screamed. "I've read your letter!"

Eric stood with the receiver jammed hard against his ear so no one else could pick up what was being said. He was not given an opportunity to answer before Deidre Nash put the telephone down. Before he had time to leave the corridor it rang again. This time it was Pauline.

"I'm sorry," she said, her voice tense and shrill. "Mummy's not very well."

"I'm drunk!" shouted Deidre from close by. "And why not after what that sacrilegious animal has done to you?"

"Please come on Saturday," Pauline said, her voice well lowered. "I must talk to you."

"D'you mean in the morning?" Eric asked numbly.

"Yes, yes! Goodbye."

The line went dead. He replaced the receiver and wandered back down the corridor, his mind reeling. When he entered the dining-room, John Salmon gave him a suspicious look.

"Were both calls for you, Eric?" he asked.

"Yes, sir."

"Quite a coincidence. You don't get that many calls, usually," the old clergyman sniffed. "Try to keep the number down. This isn't a social club."

"Sorry, sir," Eric said, resuming his seat, "but it was the same person. There was a technical fault and they had to ring back."

Eric set his alarm for four o'clock when he went to bed on Friday night. In the first light of the June day he woke before it went off, dressed and crept out of the house. Getting on his bicycle he set out on the A65 to Kirkby Lonsdale. There was no other traffic. Even the farmers were still asleep.

He had calculated that it would take him between sixty and seventy-five minutes to cover the twelve miles, leaving half-an-hour to find the private bridge. Having never heard of it before, he assumed that it must be a small structure and not easy to locate. He arrived in Kirkby Lonsdale after a fast hour's ride, his body livened and loosened by his journey through the silvery landscape of smooth hills and beck valleys, rode through the town where only the milkman was up and about, passed the great church of Saint Mary and the end of the street where Leo lived, and pedalled north.

At the southern corner of the Underley estate he turned right for Mansergh, keeping his eye open for the gates. He had not gone further than half-a-mile when he came upon them. Stopping, he stood in the road with his bicycle between his legs and looked at her map. It was only twenty-five past five and he was nearly there. He pondered whether to find the bridge straight away or cycle on a little to Mansergh and wait for her by the Chapel Road junction as she came down from Turner Row. Then, behind him, he heard a vehicle approaching from the direction of Kirkby Lonsdale. Hurriedly he rode through the gates and between the trees until it passed, then followed the drive, searching for the left turn she had described as leading down to the bridge.

He was there very quickly, emerging from between tall firs and silver birch to see the bridge and a long track leading across the flood-plain of the Lune. His initial impression was that it was a short, almost ornamental edifice, part of the architectural style of the estate, built in stone of quality over a narrow part of the river. But as he got nearer the full size of the bridge emerged: it was a magnificent, broad, twin-arched road bridge with crenellated parapets and rounded piers, straddling the Lune at a wide bend where the water swung through an acute arc. He was so taken aback by the enormous dimensions and power of the bridge that he stopped, puzzled as to how such a huge piece of building could be tucked away and unheard of: but this enigma was soon overtaken by the beauty of the scene it introduced.

Near the churchyard of Saint Mary's was a point on the high left-hand bank, going north, from which the Victorian aesthete Ruskin had looked and been so amazed that he had immediately sanctified it as being *naturally divine*; in addition, Turner painted the scene from a different point of view, profoundly touched by the vista. It was impossible to arrive in Kirkby Lonsdale and escape without coming by this pearl; but here, hidden, obscured, guarded from the general gaze, was its superior.

The fells were dark blue to black in the morning flood of light from the east, their edges sharply defined, running, folding into one another, lifting, plunging. Below them the ground faded into the farmland and its careful grey walling, loaded with green, round-shouldered woods. Between the first white house and the bridge's broad, grey, military strength were perfect, smooth fields, sheep-cropped, dotted with massive, individual beech trees. Nothing was out of place; even the lambs seemed to move in time with the antiphonal choirs of birds.

"Hello," she said, almost in his ear. "You're early, aren't you?"

She was wearing a black raincoat and a pair of wellingtons, her hair tied up in a coloured scarf. Her eyes looked tired, delicately ringed with blue beneath the bottom lids. When she spoke again he noticed with peculiarly objective clarity how her mouth moved unevenly, as if her lips were hindered. Leaning over the bicycle cross-bar, he kissed her. Her lips were cold and unresponsive. He kissed her again, taking hold of her big, cool hands. This time she warmed to him.

"I'm sorry about the other night and my mother's 'phone call," she said stiffly, withdrawing her hands. "You must imagine that I live in a madhouse."

She guided him over the bridge as she spoke, linking his arm. Suddenly he felt more at ease; the ache of strangeness and acute excitement subsiding in his blood. He became aware of their

69

complete isolation in the scene, indeed, in the universe, so wide and high were his feelings.

"I've missed you," he said, expecting her to be touched by this. "But I did get a bit of a shock."

"If I hadn't written that letter I don't think I would ever have seen you again," she replied simply, taking his arm.

Eric was flustered. He bumped his front wheel against her by accident and muttered an apology.

Below them, there was a splash.

Pauline let go of his arm and looked over the parapet.

"That might have been a salmon," she said blandly.

Eric leant his bicycle against the parapet. He did this very carefully so it would not fall down and embarrass him in his weakness. Pauline came over and took his hand, leading him round the end of the bridge and down the river bank to a shingle beach beneath the arch. She sat down on a long, flat stone, tugging the hem of his jacket to make him sit down beside her.

"I'm not a harlot," she said calmly, once he was settled, "if that's what you're thinking."

Her use of the archaic word, plangent and reverberative with its biblical associations, took him aback.

She put her feet together and stared down the black cylinders of her wellingtons, then glanced at him.

"It's love I want to talk to you about," she said, in the tone she might have used to a slow child.

A shout came from the bridge above.

Pauline stiffened and stood up, putting a finger to her lips. She walked out from under the arch and looked up.

"Hello?" she called back. "Who's that?"

A stocky man peered down at her, his face shadowed by an old trilby. He lifted the bicycle up by the cross-bar.

"Oh, it's you, Pauline," he said with a laugh. "Why are you riding a man's bicycle?"

"Mine's got a puncture so I had to borrow one," Pauline replied. "I saw a salmon just now."

"Probably a sea-trout. I've had poachers out netting during the night, the devils. Are you doing some drawing?"

"Yes."

She looked up at the man, leaving a large silence between them so he would take the hint to go away. Bouncing the bicycle on its tyres he propped it back against the parapet.

"Nice bike," he grunted. "You look after it now."

Then he was gone, back across the bridge.

Pauline returned to Eric and sat down.

"It doesn't matter where you go, there's always someone spying on you," she said, bitterly. "That man follows me around. He watches me with binoculars."

Eric said nothing. He had encountered a new side of her: a cunning and paranoia which he recognised in others, it being common enough behaviour; but she should have been different. He did not believe that the man spied on Pauline.

"Is this whole thing just a joke to you?" he blurted out.

"Why should you think that?" she replied, with great concern.

"Getting me here at an unearthly hour of the morning when we could easily have met somewhere else later on. That would make a good story for your friends, wouldn't it?"

"What friends? I don't have any friends. It's impossible to have any friends," she said sharply. "You're the only friend I've got except Leo."

He lowered his head, trying to marshal his thoughts and emotions. How could someone so beautiful be friendless? It was unimaginable. Then he realised that he did not want to believe that she was friendless out of pride. This was the girl he had come to worship; everyone should seek after her and admire her, as he did.

"I'm sorry," he said lamely. "I shouldn't have thought that of you."

"Why get so upset over a lie?" she said in a sudden spurt of vexation, her eyes glittering with suppressed anger. "You didn't like it when I told that idiot an untruth about your bicycle being mine, did you?"

Eric attempted a smile.

"That's got nothing to do with it," he replied, hoping to sound reasonable, "but since we're talking about it, why did you lie? I'm doing no harm here, am I? Are you ashamed of me, or something? If you can trespass here, so can I."

She shook her head emphatically.

71

"No, no. I'm expected to trespass. I'm expected to be where people will automatically take notice of me."

There was a silence under the arch. Only the rush of water over the spit of pebbles could be heard. He felt his heart tighten with fear.

"I don't know what you mean," he said finally, anticipating that there was worse to come. "You'll have to explain, I'm afraid."

She turned to him, anger distorting her brows. Suddenly, all he saw of her were her teeth and eyes and the choleric flush running through her skin.

"If I tell lies it is because I've been strictly taught," she said harshly. "Didn't you know that there's nothing the matter with lying, provided you get what you want? Haven't you read Lenin, Trotsky, Mao Tse-Tung, *Mein Kampf*, Machiavelli, the pamphlets of the Free Spirits? Well, if you're telling the truth and everyone else is telling lies then you're putting yourself at a disadvantage all the time, aren't you? The truth belongs to God so perhaps he's the only one with use for it."

She finished her tirade and put her big hands to her cheeks, shaking her face as if she could not credit what had poured out of her mouth. To have mocked Leo and his teaching struck her with the force of sin, perhaps the only sin. Immediately, she recanted within, staring sadly at Eric. From his expression of wonderment she deduced that he was bewildered rather than shocked, but she was wrong. His wonder was at the power of her beauty's return after her disfigurement. Trailing far behind was his intellect, struggling with the implications of what she had so furiously expounded.

"Do you love me?" he asked humbly. "I have to know."

She nodded, aware of his journeys, and letting the point pass when she could have cut him loose to return to his world and leave her to endure her own.

11

She had to confess to herself that she was disappointed at his lack of interest in the knowledge Leo had taught her. All the boy seemed to care about was whether they were in love, and, if so, what they should do about it. He walked up and down the pebbles, crunching them underfoot, clearly moved by what he had learnt about her and the strangeness of her teaching, but far more involved with the learning she had conveyed to him by a simple nod of the head by affirming that she loved him.

"Are you sure about it?" he asked after several progresses from one side of the arch to the other. "I need to know."

"Yes, but. . ."

"No *buts*. I'll deal with the *buts* later. What I can't really believe is that you mean it as I mean it. I can't get inside your mind."

"Perhaps you wouldn't like it there," she said, sphinxlike in her desire to bring him out of his anxious trance. "Don't forget, you know very little about me. It's not all that simple."

"Of course it's simple!" he snarled suddenly, booting a large pebble into the water. "What's happened is simple."

"Wait till you find out. . ." she began to say, but he silenced her with a sharp movement of his hand.

"I don't care what you tell me. All I know is, I've had it. Even if you tell me you're a witch, I don't mind. Whatever I thought I was going to do about you has gone out the window . . . oh, hell . . ."

He squatted on his haunches in front of her and pressed the toes of her wellingtons.

"I don't know what I'm saying," he said regretfully. "Ignore me. I'll be all right in a while."

"What were you going to do about me?"

"Have a fling, then break it off," he declared with a short laugh. "You know, find 'em, fuck 'em and forget 'em."

She stared at him, obviously insulted.

"Then you didn't reckon on Leo and my mother, did you?" she said sharply. "But worse, you didn't reckon on me."

"It's just a thing people say at school."

"Then don't be a parrot!"

He retreated a few steps, more unsure of himself. There had to be a level where they could talk about what had happened to them. It was proving difficult to find.

"I didn't mean to upset you," he said apologetically.

"Yes you did. I know that word. Everyone knows it. It's for abusing people." She paused, measuring him up. "Am I a nut-case?" she said.

"I don't care if you are," he replied swiftly.

"You should if you've got any sense. I might make you as bad as I am."

"So be it," he declared with a cavalier's flourish. "We can be nut-cases together."

They climbed back up on to the bridge, picked up the bicycle and walked back into Kirkby Lonsdale.

While she talked, he listened.

"It's not that they practise it, they can't, they wouldn't be allowed to," she said as they sat at a corner table at the back of a workman's café in the main street, "but they believe it; not that they don't change what they believe when they feel like it. It just goes on and on. Leo says its the process of argument about life that is life, so there's never a conclusion. But the big thing for them is not to end up being conventional. They hate that. For the last two years it's been antinomianism. . ."

From within his self-imposed vow of silence until he had heard her out, Eric balked. She noticed his frown and paused, one eyebrow raised.

"Surely you've got to ask me what that is?" she asked impishly, "or are you brilliant at Scripture?"

"I'm not," he replied. "I think it's a waste of time."

She fiddled with the spoon in her saucer and shrugged as she spoke.

"Oh, I don't. I suppose that's not surprising. Do you want to know what antinomianism is, then?"

"Why not?"

"It means that if a Christian has grace then it's not necessary to keep the moral law."

"Oh, yes?"

"It's a contradiction, don't you think?"

Eric smiled uncertainly.

"If you say so," he answered, demurring. "But how does Leo manage to keep his job if he thinks like that?"

Pauline leant forward on her elbows, her finger-tips together.

"No one knows. He did have some problems with his bishop before the war, that was after he went to Russia and came back and wrote some articles about how wonderful communism was, but then they sent him down here into semi-retirement and told him to keep his opinions to himself," she said with a giggle. "No one ever asks any questions. He performs a few services, buries people, marries people — though he avoids that if he can get out of it."

She paused, aware that he was already thinking on to the next phase of her explanation.

"My mother's not his girlfriend, if that's what you're thinking," she said with assurance. "He sublimates all his sexual feelings."

He found himself incapable of suppressing a burning blush. He could not hide or disguise it and it was such a dramatic change in his complexion that Pauline leant over to touch his cheek.

"Are you going to explode?" she asked mockingly. "Shouldn't I mention sex in your presence?"

"Sorry," he muttered. "I don't know why I went red."

"Are you really that naive?"

"Perhaps I am, deep down; but you know enough for both of us."

"What d'you mean by that?"

"Leo's place, all that. He must have taught you a lot; opened your mind, told you a thing or two."

"Would you rather we were both ignorant?" she said acidly.

Eric paused, catching the flash of haughtiness in her eyes; but it died away and she took his hand.

75

"We can go there now, if you like," she whispered, "I've got my own key."

Eric bridled and snatched his hand away, jealousy flaring up in his face.

"Why do you have to have your own key?" he demanded hotly.

"It's my refuge. . ." she started to explain, tentatively groping for his hand; but he moved away, standing up and pushing his chair back.

"Where are you going?" she asked fearfully. "Please don't run off again."

Eric strode down the length of the room then halted and came back, his expression dark with self-ridicule.

"Refuge from what?" he asked bitterly. "How d'you think it makes me feel when you treat yourself like his nun?"

Pauline got up from the table. He watched her rise, avidly scrutinising every small action and the alterations as her body achieved its full dimension, her breasts and arms bearing up her head. The full power of his feelings for her struck hard, a force from outside, without mercy or thought. He stepped back, an involuntary exclamation on his lips as the strength of it shook him.

"Do you want to come or not?" she said in a voice which seemed to come from a third person. "Anyway, there's nowhere else for us to go."

Leo's housekeeper, Mrs Ackenthwaite, was mopping the stone flags in the hall when they arrived. She was an old, deaf woman with a resolutely private manner, economising on speech and contact and having that skill of always being in the parts of the house where no one would want to be at the same time as she was. She recognised Pauline with a nod of her long, grey-haired head and stood back to watch them walk over the newly-washed flags. Eric took giant strides to keep the marks he made down to a minimum.

"Don't bother tha'self wi' hoppin' about," she muttered. "I'll have to do it over again like as not."

"We're going upstairs, Mrs A," Pauline said with a touch of patronising authority. "We'll be out of your way."

Mrs Ackenthwaite made no reply but moved her galvanised-zinc bucket noisily across the stone floor.

As they went up the stairs, Eric asked Pauline whether the housekeeper would be suspicious of them going up to the bedroom together.

"She couldn't care less. It's not her territory," Pauline assured him, "and she thinks Leo is wonderful. He pays her twice as much as she'd get elsewhere."

"But mightn't she talk?"

"Mrs A? Never. Listen, she often finds me here first thing in the morning. I don't explain, she doesn't ask."

She stopped on the stairs, waiting until his head was as high as her hips.

"I think she knows this is partly my home. She was a farmer's wife, used to people coming and going, making do, making the best of things, like we have to." She resumed climbing the stairs, still talking. "I think Leo takes her to visit her sister in Barrow-in-Furness now and again. She's an invalid, some strange disease, nobody knows what it is."

She reached the top of the stairs and opened the door to the attic. A wave of tobaccoed air floated down to Eric as he followed Pauline into the room, but he found his way blocked when she halted one step from the door, her hand raised to warn him against entering any further.

He looked into the room over her shoulder.

A woman sat reading a pile of papers and talking to herself, her back pointedly turned to the door. Her hair was a rusty shade of red and piled up on top of her head, held in place by two tortoiseshell combs. From the lobes of her ears hung a pair of silver hoops which were so large that they touched her collar-bones. As she muttered over the papers the hoops swung about like scanners.

When she turned to look at Eric the first thing he noticed were her hands: every finger carried a ring, some flashy, some dainty and discreet. From there he progressed to her off-the-shoulder evening gown in rose madder satin with a low neck-line which could not contain her bosom. Eric stared, recoiling from the grossness of her overblown breasts which seemed to lunge towards him like white whales. She threw her papers on the floor, grunted an incoherent curse, picked up a glass from the table beside her and raised it in his direction.

"Cheers!" she said with a huge smile, revealing a set of large, white, even teeth. "I've been waiting for you."

Pauline turned and pushed Eric so hard out of the door that he fell down the stairs, slamming it shut behind him. When he had recovered he sat on the stairs and listened to the row coming from the room. After a while he realised that it was not a row at all as there was only one voice raised, and it was not Pauline's; it was the voice which had abused him over the telephone. Climbing back up the stairs he stood by the closed door and listened, suppressing an instinct within himself to re-enter and tackle the woman.

"You whore! You bitch! Isn't my body your body?" he heard her scream. "What is there to be ashamed of? You'll look like me one day!"

He strained to hear Pauline's reply which was low and unintelligible.

"I do want to meet him. I said I wanted to meet him, the young goat! I'm here, as arranged, aren't I? What have I done wrong? Don't you want me to dress up for him?" the woman said, in a lower voice.

The cackle which followed was big and indulgent rather than malicious. Once again he heard Pauline's murmur, then a screeching outburst from the mother that was so loud and crazed that he could not follow it except to pick up the repetition of *whore* and *bitch*. The urge to enter the room became very strong. He was surprised to find himself so unafraid. Turning the handle of the door he pushed it open. It crashed shut on him with tremendous force as if someone had hurled themselves against it. He heard panting from the other side, then the door being hammered.

"Keep out of here, you animal!" the woman shrieked, "I'll deal with you later. Don't you ever try to come between my daughter and me or I'll kill you fucking dead!"

Eric sat on the stairs and put his head in his hands. Somehow he knew that he had been finally drawn into this agonising world of theirs on their terms. A week ago he would have fled, as he did the first time he encountered it at the Latin lesson. But now he wanted more. A new courage had been created to deal with the strangeness. Standing up he seized the door handle, turned it and strode into the room.

Pauline was standing with her mother held sobbing in her arms, the pale, freckled shoulders and vast satined buttocks quivering. When Pauline saw him enter she smiled wanly and shrugged.

"It's all over now," she said, rocking her mother's body as if she were a child, "we'll be all right, won't we?"

Her mother nodded, blubbering.

"Give us five minutes, Eric, then come back," Pauline said in a voice that belonged to a nurse handling a difficult patient. "Then we can have a talk."

He obeyed her without question. As he ran down the stairs taking three at a time and swinging on the bannisters he felt glad that he had had the guts to go into that room and show his love how much he could take.

When he returned there was a different woman in the room. She sat quietly in a chair, her sturdy legs crossed, her chin supported by her hand, and surveyed him with a cool but amicable eye as he crossed the room. Her hair was now down and tied in a bunch at the back; the ear-rings, the rings and the make-up had disappeared; and she was dressed in a pair of brown slacks and a light blue sweater with white sandals on her feet.

"Hello," she said, firmly offering her hand, "I'm Pauline's mother. I've heard so much about you."

He shook her hand, noticing its warmth and the strong, lingering squeeze she gave him.

"Hello, Mrs Nash," he answered, keeping his voice as normal as he could make it.

"I'm quite well now," she said with a gracious little tip of her head and a coy smile. "I do get into these moods, as you saw. But they mean nothing. I don't know what it was that upset me so much."

"Mummy," Pauline remonstrated gently. "There's no need to explain. Just forget it."

"I'm damned if I will! This poor boy must have been absolutely appalled by what he walked into. Eric, you must understand my philosophy. God made us as we are. When I contemplate the mysteries, and there aren't many to a woman like myself, I like to go the whole hog."

Eric smiled to cover his confusion. Mrs Nash was behaving in the most artful, exquisite manner, fluttering her hands like a Balinese dancer to illustrate her points. There was accomplishment and experience in her demeanour now; gone was the wildness he had first encountered.

"Dante is your man. Life is hell but you have to laugh. Now, when Dante thought about Beatrice he eventually had to arrive at one point. It's the same with me when I think about my daughter's future. Frankly, I'd like to stop at the spot where she becomes truly happy, but the imagination travels on, always in motion because that's its essential quality, is it not? If an imagination doesn't move then it's not an imagination, is it?"

She paused, staring at him with renewed hostility. He decided to meet her gaze, encountering a green, feral smokiness under curiously folded eyelids. He noticed how short the lashes were, almost as if they had been trimmed.

"I do hope you're intelligent, Eric," she sighed after he had refused to look away and their staring-match had ceased to be subtle.

"He's very intelligent," Pauline chipped in protectively.

"Is he now?" Deidre countered archly. "And as brave as a lion, no doubt."

"Oh, don't start again, Mummy," Pauline whined again, the thin, wheedling grief-note in her voice painfully reminiscent to him of his own family and their recent lamentations. He found it disturbing to have Pauline reduced to echoing those dreary obsequies so he drove the parallels from his mind. But that did not stop the two women as they fitted themselves into the groove of oft-repeated disputes and carpings.

"I'm not starting anything, darling," Deidre said with theatrical self-control, her smile monumentally false. "Eric and I are just trying to get to know each other."

"Well, don't be sarcastic, then. . ."

"I wasn't being sarcastic," Deidre insisted with an air of injured innocence. "Was I being sarcastic, Eric?"

Eric refused to be drawn, adjusting his expression to disguise his disappointment as mother and daughter continued with their ritual. All his fear had gone. At any moment he expected the scene to fall into the ultimate classic pattern and the bickering to culminate in recourse to the tea-pot.

"What does your father do?" Deidre said suddenly.

He heard the question and felt a chilling gap open in his mind. With everything that had happened between them, he had forgotten to tell Pauline that his father had died. It had not emerged as something important, something to be shared. This mad woman had more power over his memory, with her rantings and eccentricities. He collapsed into shame, unable to frame a reply without incriminating himself.

"Didn't you say he was an ironmonger?" Pauline said helpfully.

He nodded, holding back a tide of tears as he remembered the other life. His father was an ironmonger. That is what he was. Nothing else.

"Nails and dustbins and things?" Deidre asked, her smile benevolently condescending. "How very, very nice."

"He had a chain of shops in Liverpool!" Eric stated with spontaneous aggression, his eyes fierce and defensive. "He built them up from nothing."

Pauline looked at him questioningly. He could not announce his father's death to her in words so he put the truth into his expression, hoping that she would be able to read it.

"When did he die, dear?" Deidre asked solicitously.

"Not very long ago."

It was Pauline quickly answering for him.

He was saved from further interrogation by the entrance of Leo into the room carrying a brand-new javelin, its point taped up in corrugated brown cardboard. He ripped this off and brandished the gleaming spear over his head as Deidre laughed with delight, all interest in Eric's past forgotten.

"See what's come, Eric?" Leo said with an actor's warrior-roar. "Now we can really start your training."

12

"This is the latest model, Eric," Leo said, balancing the javelin on the edge of his forefinger. "Look at that! Perfect! When I was a lad javelins had to be made of the outer, sunside layer of the finest Finnish birch . . ."

"Good morning," Deidre interjected sourly. "Please remember us girls."

Leo laughed and put the javelin into Eric's hand.

"I'll be with you in a minute, Deidre. I'm so thrilled with our new toy. Feel it, Eric!"

Eric awkwardly hefted the aluminium spear in his hand then dipped the point down to rest against the floorboards.

"The unofficial record is two hundred and eighty-three feet, would you believe?" Leo said enthusiastically, gathering up the corrugated brown paper. "A black man, Arep Kibiege of Kenya in nineteen fifty-two. But it doesn't stand. I believe the throw was incorrectly supervised. We mustn't be surprised at this. After all, Kenya is a British colony full of innumerate public-school ignoramuses."

Deidre stood up and went over to a hide suitcase which was tucked behind a wardrobe. As she picked it up Eric could see a corner of the rose madder satin dress sticking out of the lid.

"I didn't come here to be ignored, Leo" she said with offended dignity. "If you'll kindly carry this down to the hall for me and ring for a taxi, we'll be off."

"I didn't ask you to come, Deidre," Leo replied, "but as you're here why not stay for a cup of coffee?"

"I'll have my own coffee at home, thank you. I have never been so insulted in my life."

Deidre put the case down and rooted in her handbag for a handkerchief, checking Leo's response to her display of chagrin with sharp, tearful glances. He merely shrugged and opened the door, bowing.

"Leave if you must. May I ask how you knew Eric would be here?"

"I accidentally saw a letter which had been written to him," Deidre said with a sniff, stuffing her handkerchief away in the jumble of her handbag. "I knew she'd bring him here. She never brings anyone home."

"Can you blame her?" Leo asked flatly.

Deidre started to totter towards the door making heavy weather of the suitcase. Pauline and Leo watched her, refusing to react. Eric stepped forward and took it from her.

"There's at least one person with manners here then," she said haughtily.

Eric found that the case was very light. He stood by the door, ready to take it down the stairs, unable to meet Pauline's eye.

"Take it to the hall!" Deidre ordered him.

"The boy's not a porter, Deidre," Leo rejoined sharply. "You really must stop being so bossy. Eric will take it down when he's good and ready."

Deidre held her handbag under her bosom and gave Leo a hostile glare.

"And you're supposed to be a tactful man. Can't you work it out that I'm trying to get a few moments alone with you and my daughter to discuss something crucial to her career?" She paused, inflating herself like a toad. "I trust you more than any man on earth. I've put my future in your hands many times."

Leo turned to Eric with a resigned grimace.

"Perhaps you had better go. Deidre has something on her mind. Wait for me in the hall and we'll go and try out the javelin. A farmer friend has let me mark out a throwing area in one of his fields so we can be private. Don't run away!" he added.

Eric went down the stairs with the suitcase and sat on a chair in the hall. Mrs Ackenthwaite came through a couple of times while he was sitting there. On the last occasion she bent down, tugged the protruding piece of the rose madder satin dress and chuckled.

"Bet tha' cut a dash in that," she said with a meagre grin. "It would go with thy blushes should tha' have the sense to have any."

Pauline accompanied her mother in the taxi, sitting in silence on the back seat, keeping as far away from her as possible. In this mood Deidre Nash was a volcano, her eruption predictable. Her pride had been hurt. She felt no guilt for her actions, thinking only of her child, treasuring every atom of growth and change as if it were a second phase of her own earlier happiness. Pauline would never have accused her mother of despotism but she was aware that, as do those who live under self-righteous tyrannies, the way to survive was skilfully to resist only the worst excesses of injustice. This she did by the use of some light guile plus great affection and sacrifice, all her tactics governed by the regrettable knowledge that her mother was mad.

Choosing to live wholly in the past except for the existence of one other, her daughter, Deidre Nash had preserved her sense of purpose. When Pauline grew up and left her, so she often told the girl, she would simply kill herself. There would be nothing left to live for and everything to die for. Pauline would be liberated from her influence; the grandchildren would be spared the shame of having a mad grandmother (long ago she had diagnosed her own malaise of the mind); and she would join her husband in death, painting somewhere. But before all this could happen Deidre Nash wanted to be sure that her daughter was in touch with all the potential of her beauty and talents; alive, awakened, firmly placed in the best position from which true fulfilment could come. That men would fall in love with her was obvious, so Pauline must learn how to deal with this and to choose the right one — not out of innocence but out of knowledge. Hence the grilling at the end of each day when Pauline had been out of the house in the world alone. Things happened, she reminded Pauline constantly during these interrogatory sessions, things happened all the time when mothers weren't around.

"I liked Eric. I liked him very much," Deidre said kindly. "He has a nice way with him. Not too complicated. Not too much brain, perhaps. An artisan at heart."

Pauline had no wish to encourage further comments of this kind by her mother as the taxi-driver was a local man who knew them both. She looked out of the window and kept quiet.

"Leo says the boy dreams of becoming a vet. He hasn't got the brain for that. One has to study for something like seven years. Well, Eric's got plenty of time to realise his own limitations. God knows, it didn't take me long."

Pauline wriggled uncomfortably, longing to tell her mother to shut up. The driver stopped to let some sheep across the road, lowering his window to exchange a few words with the farmer who was following them on a bicycle.

"You must marry a great man," Deidre whispered, "not someone with limitations."

"Can't this wait until we get home?" Pauline said under her breath.

"All I'm saying is that your gift must not be wasted. Have this one for a lover if you like but, for God's sake, remember what I've told you. Be ready for a greater world than this. That's what you were intended for, my darling."

That evening Deidre returned to the subject of Eric. She was drawing very small sketches of her own left hand held between two mirrors at right angles. As she drew, her frayed Chinese silk dressing-gown kept falling open. Each time this happened she clutched the lapels together and shook herself as if she had stopped a decline into indecency.

"What are your feelings for that nice, stupid boy?" she drawled, lighting a cigarette with her drawing-hand.

"He's all right, I suppose," Pauline replied, tidying up the mess around her mother's chair.

"All right? All right?" Deidre puffed. "What kind of an analysis is that? He's all brawn. Don't get taken in. Worse still, don't get bowled over."

"I'm not going to," Pauline said humbly, her eyes averted from the varicose veins which disfigured her mother's strong, white legs like graffiti on a marble statue. "I promise."

Deidre completed her sketch. Once she had examined it, she shredded the paper and scattered the pieces on to the carpet where her daughter had just cleared up.

"Not a scrap of talent, my darling; unlike you," she said with a proud, serene smile as Pauline obediently bent down to pick them up.

That night Pauline went to bed early. Her room at the front of the house was the only private territory she had and it was respected as such by her mother. There was even a bolt on the door and a length of strong rope tied by Deidre herself to the leg of the bed by the window to enable Pauline to escape from the house when her mother's disordered and agonised mind went into its crucial nocturnal phases. Deidre only took sleep by cat-napping at any time she felt tired, which might be over breakfast or while she was having a conversation, but these sporadic slumbers never took place at night as this was the time when her energy-level rose and she prowled around the small house thinking aloud. This had been her practice since the death of her husband and it was a loving mother's instinct that had made her exclude herself from Pauline's bedroom. In her grief she had pestered the child to such a degree with picking her up and putting her down, weeping over her and talking to her, that Pauline had become ill. It was then that the bolt had been put on the door. The rope had made its appearance ten years later after a night when Deidre broke the door down in a paroxysm of possessive, maternal anguish; Pauline had had to beat off the smothering attack, hitting her with a heavy shoe. From that time on Deidre never entered her daughter's room, even when one of her whisky-drinking bouts pushed her into the most furious excesses of remorse and misery.

This did not stop her pushing notes under her daughter's door. Some mornings there were twenty or thirty of these missives for Pauline to wade through when she got up to go to the bathroom. These days, she never read them; nor did Deidre refer to anything written therein. They were thoughts from the night and belonged to the darkness.

Pauline lay in bed, a book in her hand. Someone further down Turner Row had the radio on with the window open and she could not help listening to the music. Turning off the light, she opened the curtains and the window wider, then climbed back into bed. She could imagine the family sitting around the radio in a way which she had never been able to remember happening in her own home. Deidre had no need of stimulation from outside.

Pauline heard the stairboards creak as her mother's weight depressed them. Tonight Deidre would wander the rooms of the house as if they were the infernal regions. She would stop at her daughter's door a hundred times before daybreak and listen for her breathing. The girl sighed and closed her eyes, opening them when she heard her mother move away, then she slept.

When Deidre and Pauline had gone, Leo changed into a black track-suit, put his old throwing-spikes into a shopping-bag and went downstairs with the javelin. He found Eric sitting in the hall.

"Ready?" he asked. "Let's get cracking!"

Eric got to his feet and moved unwillingly towards the door. He would have preferred to go back upstairs and talk to Leo about Pauline as she represented a challenge far greater than the javelin. On her way out, Deidre had berated him for misleading her daughter, calling him callow and arrogant. As the door shut in his face, Eric had been startled to realise that Pauline had not spoken a word in his defence.

As they walked along the Main Street, Eric recounted the incident to Leo who seemed not to take it very seriously, interspersing his advice with jovial brandishes of the javelin as he greeted passers-by. He had not changed his clerical collar and vest under the track-suit, which gave him a frequent cue for comedy.

"A soldier of the Lord!" he shouted to an erect, white-haired old man who was approaching them with two Irish Setters on the lead. "Your ally, Major! The Church militant!"

The old warrior frowned and pulled his dogs to cross the street, indicating his displeasure. Leo shook the javelin at him.

"An old War Office desk-man, one of the privileged scions of the upper classes, too gutless to fight," Leo breathed fierily. "That congenital moron sent thousands of our best young men to their deaths in 1917. No wonder he can't take a joke these days."

Eric would have dearly loved to disengage himself by now, his embarrassment increasing with each encounter they made. Leo

87

went into the butcher's and offered to do the slaughtering for him; into the wool shop to do some knitting with his giant needle; finally he pricked a melon from the greengrocer's on the point of the javelin and gave it to Eric.

"For lunch, comrade. After we've laid down the basic rules and I've shown you a thing or two."

Leo took him down to the Lune by the road bridge, then into the meadow crossed by the footpath to Whittington. He had marked out a throwing funnel on the south side, the white thick and new. Leo sat on the grass and took off his shoes, shaking his spikes out of the shopping-bag beside him.

"This morning I just want you to watch me, Eric. I won't be able to throw far, but my technique is good and my style was always something to behold," he said merrily. "Oh, I must say it feels good to be doing something like this again. I was quite a physical young man when I was at college."

Eric looked down the funnel as it reached out. He recalled seeing Pauline standing beside the same diagram at the athletics meeting. Why should I have noticed her? he wondered. I should have been concentrating on what I was doing.

If I had run past her then all this need never have happened, he reasoned to himself. But he had a direct apprehension that there had been no choice. The girl had been summoned out of the earth to confront him. Now, examining the ugly design which had been drawn over the empty field, seeing the position she had occupied void, he was able to be glad that it had all happened.

"We'll have to watch out for the sheep," Leo said with a grin. "If we impale one we'll have to pay for it."

"Why do you take such an interest in Pauline and me?" Eric asked abruptly.

Leo looked at him sideways, fingering his long-lobed ear while he thought out his answer. There was relief and pleasure in his voice when he eventually spoke.

"Because I believe in God, I'd say."

"Does that mean I should shut up and not ask any more questions?"

Leo laughed, stretching out his legs and touching his toes to loosen up his back.

"Ask all you like. I have nothing to hide. To save time I might explain a few things?"

Eric nodded. He had garnered up all his courage to quiz Leo about his bedroom but had so far failed to come up with a subtle way of doing it. He hoped that Leo might touch upon it of his own accord.

"In the first place," Leo began, "since the death of Deidre Nash's husband during the war, I have become . . . if you like . . . Pauline's surrogate father. Deidre has not recovered from her grief, nor will she. Her condition is border-line, certainly more eccentric than psychotic, and, between us, Pauline and I can manage most of her frequent crises."

He paused, giving Eric time to assimilate the information.

"You don't have any problem understanding that, surely?" he said, indicating that he would like to continue.

"No, I'd gathered that much, but . . ."

"Ah, you must wait," Leo warned him, smiling. "First we must talk about my function in all this, then how I perceive it, which is what troubles you, I should guess."

"Well, there're fathers and fathers. Mine was pretty straightforward," Eric said, immediately regretting it as he saw Leo's long face darken.

"Are you saying I'm not straightforward merely because you haven't heard my arguments?" he demanded stiffly. "What I believe in is as valid as anyone else's creed. I have my integrity, Eric, please don't imagine that I haven't." His expression eased as he saw Eric's discomfort. "All right, I have my own way of looking at things. And it's workable, I can promise. Do I hear you asking what I believe in? Do you care? There's no real reason why you should, but I'll tell you anyway." He paused, re-tying the laces of his spikes.

He looked at Eric, searching for a sign that the boy was anxious to hear what was going to be said.

"It is a divided world but in the beginning it was created as one. Everything in it is God and belongs to God; sin, evil, tragedy included. Political power is of God. What is not of God is disintegration. Are you following me?"

"Not in detail. . ." Eric muttered unhappily.

"It's the detail that is interesting, Eric. Always look for the detail. That way you learn. I'm unpopular. One or two in the Church like me, but that is because I am provocative and they like to be stirred out of their spiritual sloth now and again. But they will never take the risks I take. Oh, no, that might jeopardise their positions. Over the years I've had a long list of colleagues and friends who have enjoyed talking to me then, as they get older and smugger and more set in their ways, they abandon me as a communist, radical, trouble-maker etc."

Leo bent forward and attempted to touch his knees with his forehead but failed.

"Stiff in the lumbar region," he gasped, still pressing to get down. "Not good. One throws from the hips."

"Would some people say you were corrupting me?" Eric asked levelly.

Leo straightened up, his eyes full of admiration.

"Yes, they would. But my disproof of that accusation would be the very fact that you have got the intelligence and insight to ask that question. Thank you, Eric. Thank you very much indeed. It means that you will not be anyone's victim and I need to have that confidence in you. We have some strange places to visit, you and I. Having you creeping along behind me complaining about being corrupted would get on my nerves."

"Leo, I'm quite ordinary, really. I don't come from a family that's used to . . . well, much attacking the system and all that," Eric said apologetically. "My mother isn't like Mrs Nash."

"I wouldn't want her to be. I knew your parents, of course, when you lived at Mansergh. A couple of typical rural working-class Conservatives, church three times a year and baptisms, weddings and funerals. The usual intellectual framework, which is a cage, you realise? A cage."

Eric pulled back from continuing the conversation, aware that he was on the verge of betraying his family. The implied insult was curiously inflammatory, even though it was obvious that Leo had merely put his mother and father in with the general mass.

"Perhaps I'd be happier sticking to their view of things?" was the only challenge he could dredge up. "The system my mum and dad supported won the war, didn't it?"

Leo laughed and put his hands behind his head, bending from side to side.

"That's very staunch, Eric, very loyal. It's only right you should back up your parents, but you'll have to grow out of it sometime. Their generation simply got it all wrong: far too subservient, far too superficial. They never got below the surface."

Eric frowned, avoiding the gnomic gaze which Leo had fixed upon him. He had a notion of what was being said but it was not yet transparent to him. He began to retreat towards the one secure territory of his mind: Pauline. He had told her that he loved her, a confession that had swept him into the purview of this peculiar man. But, at least, Leo had some kind of perceptible logic underlying his actions and opinions: Pauline's mother struck him as being merely deranged; yet they were allies.

"I'm not sure how to deal with Mrs Nash," Eric said, hoping to divert Leo from any further onslaughts on his background.

"You must be very strong, my lad," Leo said encouragingly. "I know what you're going through. Don't worry about Deidre Nash. Leave her to me. I've known her for years. She's difficult, yes, but at least she's alive, unlike most of them round here."

"Does she ever hit Pauline? I couldn't have that."

Leo laughed out loud, standing up and digging his spikes into the turf.

"Deidre hit Pauline? Never!" he exclaimed. "They're very close, those two women, almost one person."

"I don't like to think of her that way. . ."

"No, you wouldn't. To you she's Amaryllis in the shade, your country girl, hair full of flowers, kisses of honey — and quite right too! *Amor vincit omnia et nos cedamus amori!*"

Eric's face fell and Leo clapped him on the shoulder with a hearty laugh. "Eric, everyone knows the first half of that bit of Virgil, but not the second. Love conquers all *and let us yield to it*. I wonder why it is so zealously neglected? Comrade, do you want it all to be easier? Things that are worthwhile aren't easy, Eric. You have to suffer for them." He paused, slowly rotating the javelin in his hand like a bandmaster's mace. "Are you with me?"

"Am I free to decide?"

Leo chuckled, his fingers flexing with machine-like rapidity.

"Another excellent question. I don't think you are free. She is your new reality," he said from behind the silver blur of the whirling spear, his voice raised over its thrumming.

"I don't know what you mean," Eric complained, trying to read Leo's expression through the propeller effect.

Leo turned sideways, edging closer to Eric, the javelin now moving at a very high speed.

"First-class exercise for the fingers. Used it for the piano. Got up to standard eight but then I lost interest," he said nonchalantly, then his features hardened and he twirled the javelin faster, his wrist like a crankshaft. "Pauline is the glass through which you will see everything from now on. Be glad. Love is a great gift. It is the one sure way of knowing that you are as much a part of God as God is part of you. I believe that is true of all of us, but few are given the absolute proof that you have been granted."

Leo turned away and took a few steps to put some distance between himself and Eric. He had the most extraordinary control of the javelin, moving it from side to side, over his head, smiling like a stage-magician. Eric watched the flashing disc of light, starting to respond to it as a subject to hypnosis.

"God loves the being of all creatures, yea, all men are alike to him, and have received lively impressions of the divine nature," Leo sang with the airy intonation of a choirboy, "though they be not so gloriously and purely manifested in some as in others, some live in the light side of God, and some in the dark side; but in respect of God, light and darkness are all one to him; for there is nothing contrary to God, but only to our apprehension." He paused in his parrotry, grinning impishly. "Wonderful men, the old Ranters!" he called out. "Great rebels!"

Seizing the tapered end of the javelin he began whirling it around his head; then, using the technique of a hammer-thrower, he span a couple of times on his toes and hurled it upwards at an angle of forty-five degrees.

The javelin soared in a huge arc across the graph-line of the fells. It was a very long throw, sticking into the earth a good hundred feet beyond the limits marked for the funnel.

"A completely illegal technique, of course," he said, rubbing his hands as he strode off to retrieve it. "Banned and outlawed. Most of the best things are."

That night, having got permission to stay at the curate's house from the Reverend Salmon, he had dinner at Leo's with Pauline. Afterwards they played cards for half-an-hour then Leo announced that he had an appointment and left the house. They went up to the attic room and found the covers on the bed already drawn back on both sides. When Eric awoke in the morning Pauline had gone, but Mrs Ackenthwaite was there to cook his breakfast. As he left the house he heard the bells of Saint Mary's ringing to call people to holy communion. They continued to ring as he mounted his bicycle and headed back towards Kendal.

Upon his return he went into his room and became very low in spirits, feeling lost and confused with it all again. Daniel came in and, finding him in this morose state, suggested a picnic in the ruin of Kendal castle with a few bottles of beer and a couple of meat pies. Sitting inside the broken walls with the sun beating down overhead they ate and drank, then lay back on the grass, replete. After several belches Daniel made a few mild interrogations about Pauline.

"I'm asleep," Eric murmured. "Leave me be."

"Have you fucked her yet?"

"Have I *what*?" Eric replied.

Daniel raised himself on one buttock and farted loudly.

"That on your taciturnity."

"You're disgusting."

"An explosion between the legs, according to the dictionary."

There was a pause while Daniel ruminated over the tactics for his next approach.

"Do you know what taciturn means?" he asked finally.

"No, I don't."

"Do you know what a fuck means? Don't bother to answer. It comes from the Latin *fugare* to cudgel, so the dictionary says."

Eric rolled over and got to his feet in order to escape from Daniel's relentless badgering. Walking to the jagged shell of the castle he climbed up and sat on top. Below him a gang of boys played french cricket. He watched them, trying to ignore the scrabbling sounds as Daniel clambered up after him. Once he had arrived and ensconced himself on a piece of broken wall nearby Eric turned and pointed a threatening finger at him.

"If you mention her again I'll throw you off here," he said fiercely. "It's private! Okay?"

"God's blood, nothing was further from my mind," Daniel replied lightly. "Your sex life or lack of it is your own affair."

"Remember to keep it that way, then," Eric said heatedly. "I've had enough of your prying."

"Scout's honour, you'll never be bothered again," Daniel chanted, his hand raised. "I abjure the literature of passion whether it be Boccaccio, Rabelais, Dante, Shagsper or Eric. Look at this bloke!" he added hastily as Eric turned and bared his teeth. "What does he think he's doing?"

A fair-haired, spindly young man clad in flimsy white running kit had emerged from the grey housing-estate that abutted the playing-fields. He ran up the steep grass slope to the hollow of the moat then ran back down again, repeating this several times.

Daniel pointed to the south where a large municipal cemetery lay spread out under evergreens.

"It's a corpse trying to get home," he said. "Perhaps a disorientated vampire."

"Don't make pathetic attempts to get in my good books, you shit," Eric snapped.

"You're being very difficult today, Romeo. Let's not talk about it though. Look at that maniac. I find him disgusting. Why does he expend so much energy on his body? Is he creating anything useful? Why is he burning himself up?"

Daniel waited for a reply, tossing a stone from hand to hand. He raised his arm as if to hurl it as a missile at the runner who had now broken from his routine on the slope and was tearing across the sward inside the ruined walls of the castle.

"I'd like to hit him with this. You're a better thrower than me. Have a go, go on. He deserves it. See if you can get him right between the eyes." He paused but upon being ignored again continued animatedly. "Shall I explain this man's behaviour? He lives in that housing-estate with his mum. Every day he comes out and works off his frustrations running up and down this hill passing through ruins, age, then down to death and corruption yonder. None of this goes through his mind consciously, but subconsciously, another matter. Then, once a year, when he's superbly fit but little more than a mechanical contrivance at best, his mum drives him out to the mountains and she lets him loose in a fell-race, which he doesn't win. He comes home, looks at himself in the mirror, and decides he's been a dickhead. From then on he pursues a life of dissipation, catches the clap and dies." He paused again, blinking like an owl behind his distortive glasses.

"I'm sorry, have I upset you with this tragic story?" he added.

"You don't upset me at all," Eric retaliated. "It's you I feel sorry for having nothing better to think about."

"You'd better think about what will happen if you have to do your National Service and you have to tell the army doctor you're a virgin. They can tell at a glance, you know. I hear they put you in a cage with a female gorilla and they make you do it at gun-point. Do let me know when you get your leg over, please."

"I'll keep you fully informed." Eric said, nodding grimly.

"If you're going to be a vet you'll have to understand these things. Didn't your mother ever tell you about . . . you know, how it all works? Ovulation, tumescence, ejaculation, marvellous words! Eric, old son, tell me, are you really interested in the subject at all? Perhaps you're asexual?"

"Perhaps I wish I was," Eric retorted.

"Oh, don't say that. I wanted this to be a therapeutic visit to give you your confidence back. Listen, she'll surrender some time, I promise you. Just keep pegging away at it. You need a tonic. Now this castle should be doing a great job on your male hormones. It's ancient emotional reverberations should be getting through to your cortex of male pride right at this moment. Surely you know to what I am hereby alluding?"

Eric glanced at Daniel's face. After a quart of beer it was flushed and his eyes were sparkling with satanic glee behind his glasses. The nostrils of his large, heavy nose were as flared as a hound's scenting game.

"Don't say that I have to point out that this castle was the home of the most sexually apprehensive woman in English history? I

95

brought you here for a purpose, my son. Switch on! Respond! Feel the vibrations!"

Still Eric refused to be drawn. He lifted one shoulder and glared out over the landscape of low, swelling hills.

"This Pauline must be about as anxious about you as the lady of this castle was in fifteen forty-three when she went down to London to marry. . .? Who? See, you've been living here for two years with your head stuck up your arse. Catherine Parr was the lady, and she was the sixth and last wife of that misogynistic psychotic Henry the Eighth. She must have had a few anxious thoughts about it, as Pauline must when she contemplates the latent power of your repressed id. Henry the Eighth was all id. It's the id that has shaped English history. . ."

As Daniel rattled on, enjoying his own volubility, Eric hunched forward, clinging to his spire of broken wall, a gargoyle overlooking the Devil's domain, and vomited.

13

Eric contrived to keep the different streams of his life separated from that time on; being as close-lipped as he could with his mother while appearing to be a dutiful son; keeping Daniel at bay, carefully restricted to Kendal and the school. It was impossible for Eric to imagine an existence where all parts could come together in peace because Pauline was so dominant and Leo and Deidre so demanding that there was no room for any other authority. For his own will and ambitions to remain intact and active while dealing with the new power over his life was enough of a task. If all the pressures had been allowed to join forces then disintegration was a real danger. He was no fool. In the ensuing months he was able to recognise the full impact Pauline had made upon him. He was drunk on her; to be with her meant that they had to make love no matter what obstacles or hindrances: her periods he overrode, undisturbed by the mess, lost in her beauty. He amazed her with his relentless appetite. She coped with his exhaustive hunger by never saying no or playing the coquette. His passion was his right, as was her surrender to it. As they descended through the layers of their closeness, often blinded, often bewildered, they clung to each other, asking questions to which the answer was always more, more. Protected from the dangers of too much thinking and too much planning by the knowledge that Leo was shepherding them through this magical vale so that they could love without fear of the future, they came to look upon restraint as an enemy. All the vitality and excitement of life were present in their private world which had its own laws that were not the same as those governing other people. They were, in Leo's words, the Elect. What he had guided them into was, after all the metaphors and scriptures had been pushed aside, the original Eden.

That a certain blitheness and good-nature should appear in Pauline as a result of this was no surprise to Leo, nor to Eric who could feel the reason rather than work it out with any pretence at psychological insight; but it upset her perverse mother who accurately guessed that its source was in no way connected with her influence. Having, until then, discouraged Pauline from making friends and kept her few acquaintances out of the house because, as she claimed, other people's children were not used to their ways, she now began to invite girls of Pauline's age from her school and the neighbourhood to visit. Most of them survived only one encounter with Deidre's hospitality but the daughter of a local farmer persisted and made a bid to become part of Pauline's circle. Her name was Esme and she attended the Queen Elizabeth School but was in the form below Pauline. Although not intelligent she did have an appreciable charm based upon a compact, rounded body and long, jade-green eyes which gave her a prettiness which the world could admire without affording it awed respect.

Esme had had lots of boyfriends by the time she was seventeen. None of these relationships had attracted any scandal to her reputation in the district. If there was a commonly held opinion amongst her ex-admirers it was that she was a prick-teaser but that she managed it all with an alluring, merry style which did not offend yet efficiently deflected serious ardour.

Her first visit to Pauline's home coincided with an unscheduled arrival by Eric who had called in on the off-chance that Pauline might be able to go out for a cycle-ride. Over the last few months, Deidre had become tolerant of Eric's relationship with her daughter and he had been invited to tea a few times, but she remained cool with him. On this occasion she let him know that she did not like him to arrive without prior arrangement and kept him waiting on the step. While she explained to Eric what the correct procedure would be in future — a 'phone call asking permission to see Pauline being a prerequisite — Pauline went out of the back door, wheeled her bicycle round to the end of the terrace and rang her bell to let Eric know that she was ready.

"Come back here!" Deidre shouted. "You can't go out when you've got a friend visiting you."

Pauline laughed and wheeled her bicycle further down the lane. She knew Esme and had little time for her.

"She can't go out. I forbid it!" Deidre snapped at Eric. "This is your fault!"

"No it's not, Mrs Nash. I've stayed too long. My mum's expecting me home."

Esme looked over Deidre's shoulder as she spoke, weighing Eric up with a muted, approving impudence. He was hot from his ride, his shirt open in the late autumn sunshine. Every part of him shone with urgency and Esme could see that he had no fear of Deidre whatsoever. All he was interested in was getting Pauline out of the house.

Esme stepped past Deidre and put a hand on Eric's handlebars.

"My brother's got the same model of bike as you. They're okay. The colour suits you," she said cheekily. "I'm Esme Clark. What's your name?"

"That's Eric and he's a nuisance," Deidre seethed, going in and slamming the door.

Eric hesitated. He could see that the small, blonde girl was challenging him with her sharp eyes, testing him out to see if she could raise a response.

"I'll walk down with you," Esme said, her hand still on the handlebars. "I might even go and get my bike and come with you. Should I? Would you like that?" She paused and grinned, show-ing very good, white teeth, then asked, "Are you Pauline's boy-friend? I mean, *the* boyfriend everyone's talking about?"

Eric looked at Pauline who had her back turned as she pushed her bicycle further down the lane. He wanted to escape from the girl and join her but he could only do so by being abrupt and as Esme was hanging on to his machine and trying to peer into his face, it was difficult for him to get away.

"Well, are you *the* boyfriend or not?" she demanded. "Own up!"

Eric nodded and pushed the bicycle forward, hoping it would loosen her grip but she held on, trotting by his side.

"Do you know Keith Johnson? He's in your form at school, I think. I went out with him for a while. He had his own motorbike but my dad wouldn't let me go on it."

Eric pushed the bicycle so hard that she was forced to release her grip. He ran a few steps and mounted, shouting goodbye as he pedalled off down the lane. Esme stopped, folded her arms under her breasts and pulled a tongue after him. By the time she had walked to the top of the rise Eric and Pauline were far down the road, cycling shoulder to shoulder.

"What did she want?" Pauline asked after a while. "I can't stand that girl."

"Oh, she was just asking questions."

"What kind of questions?"

"About a boy at school she used to go out with."

"She's been out with so many I'm surprised she can remember any of them individually," Pauline retorted, cycling ahead.

Deidre's social strategy for Pauline did work once Leo decided to put his weight behind it. Pauline had always been a singular child, never prone to loneliness; coping with her mother and struggling to accommodate her bond with Leo in her understanding was enough to fill her need for close human contact until she met Eric. A part of her nature which had been closed off until then opened up to receive him, but it did not sweep the rest of her peers in with him. There was nothing to attract her in the friendship of other girls; their small-mindedness and silliness offended her and she had kept aloof. As she had grown up in the community this caused resentment; she was thought to be stand-offish, even a little superior because of her beauty, but this criticism was moderated by the knowledge that her mother was part-mad and her circumstances so pinched that the Church had to take a protective interest in her welfare.

When Leo and Deidre began to surround her with hand-picked companions who would provide a more balanced environment for her relationship with Eric, Pauline did not protest but continued to hold these newcomers in mild contempt. Having known them all since childhood and kept her distance from them, to expect her to treat them as equals when she was enthralled by Eric's love was asking too much. All she could manage was toleration and politeness: as these were the qualities which Leo had decided were essential if the passion was to be kept under control, the experiment with new friends dragged on longer than nature would have determined, but it did throw up Esme Clark.

Pauline's arrogance had been hard-won inasmuch as she had been forced to battle with a contorted adult world from an early age but she did make the elementary mistake underestimating the skill of another girl who knew boys far better than she did. Esme had developed the knack of attracting males, playing with them, delving into their strange clockwork and finding where they could be wound up, and satisfying them without giving anything of herself but her nymphish talent for flirtation. To date she had not encountered serious trouble. There had been no explosions of grief, no tragic consequences, only regrets as if her light-heartedness with love had become generally understood. And she found that this suited her; it was enough: until she stumbled upon the real basis of Pauline's relationship with Eric.

Leo's influence over Pauline had irked Eric from the beginning but he had seen that there was no point in challenging it until he was in a strong enough position to do so. The fact that Leo took an interest in him and acted as his tutor and mentor did not ingratiate him with Eric because it was plain that it was not done for Eric's benefit, nor for altruistic reasons, but in order to smooth Pauline's path towards Leo's idea of her proper fulfilment. To Eric, this was a mystery which he was excluded from even though he appeared to be an essential part of the process; and the whole design seemed to take no account of him as an individual with his own plans and needs. But he put up with Leo, as he did with Deidre and her frequent deliriums, paranoias and dementias, because it paid him to appease rather than oppose. At the back of his mind was the hope that one day Pauline would fight clear of these influences.

It was this optimism which had made Leo's most inflictive interference bearable. On the day when he had first coached Eric in throwing the javelin he had put a coda on the lesson by taking Eric into a pub, sitting him down in a dark corner with a pint of bitter, and giving him a lecture on the use of contraceptives. Eric had been acutely embarrassed, staring at the floor, his ears burning red, but Leo had not allowed the boy's shame to deflect him from his purpose. His guidance, he had said, was to be law in this matter. He had studied birth-control techniques, bought books and pamphlets, consulted doctors in the field, and it was better that Eric and Pauline come to him for advice with any problem of this kind. Then he had leant forward and slipped a folded brown paper bag into Eric's jacket pocket, indicating that the discussion was over.

When Eric had left Leo that evening he had stopped at a gate and propped his bicycle up against it while he opened the brown paper bag. There were twenty packets of contraceptives inside, each containing three. He suddenly found himself laughing but he did not throw them away. Leo had accurately guessed that Eric was not capable of negotiating such a purchase himself.

A year later, Leo alluded to the matter again while he was alone with Eric. He mentioned casually that he had heard that research was about to produce the first oral contraceptive pill for women and how much more aesthetically pleasing that would be for all, as well as being less prone to error. What had occasioned the comment was the handing over of another folded brown paper bag containing another sixty condoms, a gift which Eric could now accept without blushing, it being the third he had received.

Esme Clark made several attempts to become friends with Pauline after her first meeting with Eric. The gossip about the pair in the district and at school was scant but straightforward: Eric was a Kendal lad, deliberately encouraged by Deidre because he was an outsider and not as aware of the family's reputation for oddness as he would have been if he had lived locally. Behind Deidre, the local sages spotted the figure of Leo, rumoured by the disrespectful to be Deidre's boyfriend but by others to be merely Pauline's adopted uncle, a rôle which earned him praise when people considered how aggressively protective Deidre was of her daughter.

But Esme had a feeling about Pauline. She had watched her grow to be more beautiful than herself, heard the valley's women brooding over her as she passed, caught the admiring but cautious glances of the boys as they looked at her, and had had to confess that she did not understand how a girl with such good looks could be so strange and distant, so lacking in enjoyment of her natural advantage. If Esme had had Pauline's extraordinary loveliness she would have used it to create a court of gallants. The more Pauline had pushed away attention and kept to herself, the more Esme had become intrigued. Now that there was a male attached to the enigma she was determined to find out why and how he had broken through Pauline's reserve. Her guess was close to the truth: that Eric had discovered that with Pauline there was no game, no caprice, no playing with sex for fun. It was serious because it had to be; the skills of the teenage tease having passed her by and her responses being urgent and direct.

After meeting Eric she began to talk about Pauline behind her back. Her gossip was light-hearted as that was her way, but it started to become obsessive and her friends accused her of fancying Eric herself. Whilst denying this, Esme became excited at the thought that she might tempt Eric away from the most beautiful girl in the valley and prove herself to be supreme. She invited Pauline to her home several times and was rebuffed. Swallowing these rejections she accosted Pauline at school and strongly indicated to her how much she would like to be friends. Pauline failed to respond, showing by her reaction that she had no interest in Esme and possibly found her to be a nuisance. Esme then asked her father if she could take extra Latin tuition from Leo.

By the time Esme made this approach, Leo had garnered enough information from his parishioners to make him suspicious so he put together a plan that was both decoy and test. He thought that Esme had a schoolgirl crush on Pauline because of the very reasons that had made the girl decide to compete with her for Eric's attention: her aloofness, her beauty and her refusal to join in the juvenile scramble for sexual reputation. He told Esme's father that he was too busy to take her on as a pupil himself but recommended that he should approach John Salmon in Kendal who had recently started taking on private pupils in both Greek and Latin to supplement his retirement pension. Esme's father put this suggestion to her and she balked at it as it did not fit in with her purpose, but her father's interest had been aroused and, thinking that she needed the extra coaching, he insisted that she go to Kendal once a week to improve her chances of passing Latin at Ordinary Level.

Her first lesson with John Salmon took place six weeks after her first encounter with Eric at Turner Row. She went over to Kendal on the bus on a Thursday evening in early July and spent an hour with the old clergyman. John Salmon found her to be a difficult pupil and soon diagnosed her lack of enthusiasm. After the lesson was over and Esme had gone back to Kirkby Lonsdale, John Salmon rang Esme's father and told him that he was wasting his money as his daughter had no real interest in improving her Latin. When Esme got home she was faced by her indignant parent who demanded that she ring John Salmon up immediately to apologise for her attitude and to arrange her next lesson.

Esme had to obey. When she rang it was Eric who answered, giving his name. Without a pause, or any indication that she knew who she was talking to, she asked to speak to John Salmon and was passed over to him. Her apologies were profuse. She told the old cleric that she had had a headache but that next time he would find her very enthusiastic and attentive. Mollified by her rapid and wholehearted response to his criticism, John Salmon agreed to give her another chance.

When she came over for her second lesson Esme was fully prepared. She was experienced in charming old, academic men — there being three sixty-year-old part-time teachers at the Queen Elizabeth School—and she used all her brightness and gaiety on John Salmon until, by the end of the period, he was eating out of her hand. It was no difficult task for Esme to extract from him the information she needed to confirm Eric's presence in the house as a lodger. Indeed, such was her success with the old man, that he insisted on her having coffee with him in the sitting-room and meeting his two charges, Daniel Fleck and Eric Sherwin.

When Eric was called down he did not immediately recognise Esme, a failure which piqued her but she made a joke of it. She was so inwardly dismayed by Eric's lack of reaction to her that she ignored the other boy, Daniel, who sat in a leather armchair with his cup and saucer on his knee, shooting nervous glances of admiration at her.

"Have you seen Pauline lately," Esme asked Eric with an arch display of innocence.

Eric frowned as he saw John Salmon prick up his ears.

"Not for a while . . ." Eric replied unwillingly.

"Pauline?" John Salmon said. "Do I know her?"

"She's a mutual friend. Mr Midgely knows her very well. People say she's very pretty."

"Oh, I wouldn't know about that, would I?" John Salmon murmured grumpily. "I hope you're behaving yourself, Eric. Remember you've got your mother to answer to."

"He behaves himself, Mr Salmon, I know he does," Esme said with a curl of her lip. "He's a good boy, aren't you?"

"There's no such thing as a good boy," John Salmon chipped in, eying Esme with faint distrust as he caught the provocative sarcasm in her tone. "Surely you've learnt that by now, young woman?"

Eric stood up and excused himself, avoiding Esme's direct, confrontational gaze which, she imagined, would convey her interest in him. Normally, her approach was gentler and more winning but there was something in Eric's demeanour, his surly separateness, and in the amount of trouble she had already taken to meet him again, that made her more daring.

"Are you going somewhere?" she said.

"We've got to go to the Debating Society," Eric replied briefly.

"What are you debating?"

"I think it's something about the Atom Bomb."

"'Is the Atom Bomb the only real guarantee of world peace?'" Daniel told her, his eyes flickering behind his glasses. "I have to second the motion."

"The only guarantee of world peace is common sense," John Salmon said, supplying the young people with a sigh, "but no one listens. Off you go. Miss Clark, you must go straight to the bus. I promised to ring your father once you've left."

"Eric and . . . his friend, will walk me down to the bus stop. It's on their way," Esme replied, giving the old man a smile. "We can talk about the Atom Bomb. You never know, I might come up with something interesting for them to say."

Daniel Fleck courteously opened the door and ushered her out, revelling in the fragrance which trailed behind her as she tossed her blonde hair back over her shoulders on her way. Eric followed gloomily, knowing what was in store. His only hope of extricating himself from Esme's obvious designs was to shift her sights on to Daniel who was already wildly enchanted by the girl's looks.

As soon as the three of them were in the street, Esme pushed between Eric and Daniel and linked arms with both of them. She felt the tremor Daniel gave as her skin touched his and the definite hitch which Eric made to ensure that her arm lay against the sleeve of his jacket and not against his flesh.

"He's a sweetie, isn't he?" she said conversationally, skipping her shoes along the pavement. "What's it like living there"

"Like being in a monastery," Daniel responded, his face grave as he struggled to hold down the huge excitement that was rollicking around in him. "He's from another age, old Salmon."

"But he's a good sort, isn't he, Eric?" Esme insisted, giving his arm a squeeze. "He can't be too strict. He doesn't mind you having a girlfriend and spending all your time over at Kirkby."

She felt the muscles of his arm tense under her hand and gripped harder in order to stop him taking it away.

"What about you . . . oh . . . I'm sorry, what's your name again?" she said to Daniel, putting her head appealingly to one side. "I'm sorry I've forgotten. I'm hopeless with names."

"Daniel."

"Dan?"

"No, Daniel. I prefer Daniel."

There was a pause in which they seemed, to Eric, to walk a mile through mud. He could see Daniel's chagrin and disappointment and he felt for him. If Esme had not been so skilful in switching her full attention to Daniel by the end of the pause she would have alienated him for ever.

"Who do you go out with then, Daniel," she murmured, her eyes roaming all over his face as if searching out the information. "Come on, tell me? I bet I know her."

"I don't have a girlfriend," Daniel blurted, his wrist now burningly sensitive to her touch. Glancing at Eric he saw that his worst fear was not realised: he was not smiling. "I don't seem to have the time," he added with a half-hearted attempt at coolness.

"Are you a swot, then?"

"Yes, I am," Daniel replied. "I can say that I've got a brain."

"You wouldn't be a swot if you went out with me, I can assure you," Esme riposted, breaking her arm-link with both of them. "There's a bus coming. I'll run for it. See you."

She crossed the road, aware that Daniel would be watching her as if she had become an angel in flight. What thoughts Eric might have about her were suggested by the view of the two boys she had as she sat down at the rear of the bus and looked out of the window.

Daniel was walking sideways, his eyes fixed on the bus, one hand clutching the upper part of Eric's sleeve as if to steady himself. But Eric was looking straight ahead, his head raised and his bearing military as if he desired to shut out all frippery and nonsense from his mind.

"She ran like a gazelle," Daniel whispered as the bus disappeared round a bend in the road. "That was an invitation she just gave me. She made a pass. Don't you think it was a pass?"

"She's a tart!" Eric snarled.

"Hey, come off it, she's not a tart just because she likes me. At first I thought it was you she fancied but now I think it's me. She couldn't remember my name because of the powerful effect my personality and stunning physique had upon her. I literally bowled her over."

"If you don't mind dropping the subject," Eric said, increasing his pace, "I'd rather contemplate the Atom Bomb."

Eric went over to Mansergh the following weekend and stayed at Leo's. On the Sunday afternoon he went for a long walk with Pauline and they lay down in a wood to make love. He was so lost in what he was doing that it gave him a severe shock when Pauline stiffened and clutched him close, hissing, "Don't move, don't move whatever you do!" into his ear.

He asked her what was the matter and drew his head back to look at her. Her eyes were fixed on something over his shoulder. Turning, he saw a white horse standing a few yards away and the rider staring down at them with a pale, fixed stare.

"Go away!" he shouted, his voice shaky with angry shame. "Leave us alone!"

The rider did not move but allowed the horse to lower its head to graze by letting the reins slip through her fingers. Beneath the riding-cap Eric recognised the face of Esme Clark.

Eric groped for his clothes and pulled them across his backside to shield his nakedness from the girl's protracted, catatonic gaze. Her features were expressionless, her mouth slightly open as if frozen in the initial moment of a surprise.

"Get away, will you?" Eric roared, his head lowered, the whole scene dissolving into excruciating humiliation as Esme kept staring. When she still did not move or turn to go he called to her in a voice edged with pleading:

"What d'you want?"

That broke the spell and Esme yanked up the horse's head, long grass festooning its mouth, and urged it across the clearing, its hooves coming down close to where Pauline's and Eric's feet lay crossed together. As she went past, Esme whipped the horse's rump with her riding-crop so it bounded forward, crashing through the bushes, taking her away.

Swearing and cursing under his breath, Eric immediately started to get dressed but Pauline put a restraining hand on his arm.

"Esme Clark is never going to spoil anything for me," she said. "She's not worth it."

"Oh, God, she'll tell everybody. . ." Eric raged.

"So what? D'you think I care?"

"Your mother will."

"My mother ignores gossip. Come back. Forget it."

Pulling him down beside her she held him in her arms, feeling the panicked beating of his heart.

"She followed us," Pauline whispered, "and she's been watching me at school. I'm not imagining it. I know you think I do dream these things up but I don't."

"What does she want?"

"I don't know. Perhaps you should have asked her?"

"It's not funny," Eric fumed. "The bloody little spy!"

"She can't help being nosey. She's a peasant," Pauline said into the flesh of his shoulder. "Listen, I never want to hear about Esme Clark again."

She kissed him and he clung to her, impressed and a little frightened by her strength, then his own, as he felt his body unstintingly returning to the power which had filled him before the interruption.   *

When Esme came over to Kendal for her next lesson she made no attempt to contact Eric but saw to it that she encountered Daniel who was studying in the garden. While they talked, Esme took some interest in the house and found out from Daniel which room he occupied. He offered to take her up to show her, his mind already racing ahead in dreams of fantastical debauchery, but she declined, casually enquiring whether Eric's room was close to his, whether they spent much time in each other's rooms, could they be private when they had to lock the door and do revision for exams, and, finally, whether Eric was around on that day? Daniel was convinced that the reason for these questions was to ascertain whether it would be safe for Esme to come to his room and he was forthcoming with his answers. When Esme said that she had to go, and asked Daniel to give her regards to Eric who, as she had discovered, was doing his prep in his room, Daniel promptly suggested that he should walk her to the bus stop. Esme refused, saying that her father was picking her up in his car and it would be inadvisable for Daniel to be seen with her *just yet*.

Daniel watched her go, entranced. Although he looked at his books, wrestling with optical physics and concave and convex lenses, he could not concentrate on anything but the fresh memory of Esme's female presence. In this dream-like state he remained in the garden, doodling in the margins of his notes.

Esme went round the side of the house and re-entered it by the front door which she knew was kept off the latch. From John Salmon she had discovered that he was due to go out once the lesson was over, and that it was the housekeeper's day off, the old man having had to make their coffee himself.

Going straight up the stairs she went to the door which she had worked out from Daniel's description must be Eric's, and knocked. She heard him call out, "Come in," and opened the door. Eric was lying on his bed with a book propped up on his raised knees, a pencil in one hand. He had to turn his head to see who it was, and when he did so his face froze into a grimace of shocked embarrassment.

"Before you say anything, I'm sorry," Esme said quickly, closing the door behind her. "Please forgive me. I didn't mean to be there."

Eric gripped the book, struggling to stop himself from turning crimson. After what had happened, he was astonished that the girl could have the gall to confront him in this manner, tactless and, apparently, fearless. But when she spoke, his indignation and confusion evaporated and the words on the page of the book danced before his eyes.

"Do to me what you were doing to her," Esme said. "I won't tell anyone, I promise."

Eric's legs shot out as if they had been beaten down with a club. He could not avoid looking at her, his startled glance wide-eyed and amazed.

"What?" was all he could say.

"I want to try it, but I musn't get pregnant. Dad would kill me." She grinned nervously. "That's all, honest. Only once." Sitting on the edge of the bed she put her flat hand on his chest. "Don't be shocked. No one need know."

"If this is your idea of a joke?" He choked. "I'm not just. . ." He groped for words, trying to steady his reeling thoughts. Leo loomed suddenly into his mind. "I can't. It's sacred."

"Oh, come off it," she replied, baring her perfect teeth, "It's not, you know that as well as I do. Not when you use French letters. I went back and found the packet where you'd thrown it."

Eric groaned aloud, knotting his fists between his knees.

"Why don't you ask Daniel?" he said in desperation. "He thinks you're great. I'll give him some Durex."

"I don't fancy him."

"Well, if it's just to get it over with, does it matter?"

She nodded, her mouth framing the words, "Yes, it does." Patient and alight, sitting next to him, her hand firmly pressed against his heart, her rapt features had the cast of a jungle idol which awaits a sacrifice that is only its due.

"Go on, Eric," she murmured, putting more pressure on his chest.

"I can't!" he said with sudden violence. "I just can't."

"Yes, you can. If you can do it to her you can do it to me. You shouldn't knock around with her, anyway. She's a loony."

"Don't talk about her like that!" Eric flared.

"Well, she makes me sick," Esme muttered, her colour high and her breathing uneven, kneading his chest as if she were making bread, sweat dewing her lip. "She really fancies herself. Anyway, I know all about her. You weren't the first."

Eric felt the anger surging up and knew that he must, at all costs, avoid hitting the girl. Her closeness and immovability made the temptation much greater, and, he noted fearfully, her stupid, virginal selfishness at close quarters was a provocation which had its own sexual appeal.

He sat up and leant his head against the wall.

"Esme. . ." he began.

"Don't try to talk me out of it. I've made my mind up," she replied, a warning light in her eyes, "and I can cause trouble."

"This is all to hurt Pauline, isn't it?" he said.

"No, I don't care about her. You'll find out what a cow she is soon enough. If you can do it with someone who's mad then you can do it to . . . well, someone who isn't mad . . ." She hesitated, the progress of her argument getting twisted in her own mind. "Well, what's all the fuss about, anyway?"

"You tell me," Eric countered harshly.

Esme paused, her reasoning in shreds. Her lower lip trembled and tears welled into her long, jade-green eyes.

"Please," she whispered, lowering her head for the first time. "Don't make me keep having to ask."

"But why don't you wait until you meet someone?"

"I just want to get it out of the way. It's a nuisance."

Eric sat up, brushing her hand aside, and went to stand by the window.

"And if I say no you'll tell everyone what you saw on Sunday; is that the idea?"

Esme kept her head down and shrugged.

"Wonderful," Eric sighed. "What a life."

"I'll pay you if you like. I've got a fiver in the post-office."

When he heard this, he lightly banged his head against the wall. In the garden he could see Daniel bent monkishly over his books. It made him want to laugh at his own predicament and the absurdly outrageous logic behind the girl's demand. As soon as Esme heard the dark note in his chuckle, she swiftly started to undress.

*

The next time he went over to Mansergh, he told Pauline exactly what had happened. She took the news very calmly and only showed her disappointment and resentment by being wooden and distant when they were making love, which she still allowed. But she turned from his kisses, shrank in his embraces, cut short his caresses, forcing him quickly into the basic act as if it were something which she wanted to get over with. When he returned to Kendal it was with the knowledge that he had been punished. When he saw her again he found out how slow the process of her forgiveness would be.

At school, Pauline had to endure the triumphant, mocking smiles of Esme Clark for the rest of that summer. She bore the girl's malice bravely, steering a course around her, until they were both cast in the school's production of *The Merchant of Venice* that Christmas. Pauline was given the part of Portia and Esme Clark had to play her waiting-maid, Nerissa. During the entire rehearsal period, Pauline performed the long Act 1 scene two between Portia and Nerissa as if she were completely alone on stage, while the director went mad trying to make her relate to Nerissa. Nevertheless, there was no overt conflict, only a permanent frost from Pauline who was also struggling with her dislike of being in the play at all, having been dragooned into the production because the director thought she would look right.

Once the play had opened and had been declared a success by the Head, Esme began to find a way of delivering her speeches to Pauline which implied all the taunts and jeers which she had kept bottled up while the play was under rehearsal. She twitched Pauline's costume, pulled her hair while she was supposed to be dressing it, and generally indicated to the audience that her subservient rôle on stage was not one that she found congenial. Pauline allowed her to persist in these displays, only showing her displeasure in the condescending and restrained manner appropriate to the part.

On the final night of the show, Eric came to see it with Leo and Deidre. They sat in the third row from the front and Esme had Eric in full view. Her jibing and sneering became cruelly obvious as the long scene progressed and Eric was forced to look away in horror. Pauline had not mentioned to him that Esme was in the play as her servant, nor had she told him that there was a long-running problem which had been caused by his infidelity.

Towards the end of the scene, having run through a list of all Portia's suitors, Nerissa reminds her about Bassanio. Esme changed all the rehearsed moves and came to the front of the stage so she could look directly at Eric and say:

". . .he, of all the men that ever my foolish eyes looked upon, was the best deserving a fair lady," adding her own unscripted line, "But he's anybody's."

Esme Clark had her back to Pauline. If she had not broken the set moves she would have had a chance to see the transforming rage at work in her victim's face. Before the first blow was struck, Leo and Deidre were on their feet, recognising the spectre of Pauline's black, terrible anger. She only had time to strike three times before the backstage staff pulled her off Esme and the curtain was brought down. When Esme was carried weeping, bloody and hysterical into the dressing-room it was discovered that she had a broken nose.

The incident was talked about for a fortnight and not everyone was unsympathetic to Pauline, Esme's wilful provocation having been noticed by many people who had been to see the play. The school chose to believe that Esme had been eaten up with envy because Pauline had the leading rôle and that Esme thought, with every justification some said, that she should have been given the part of Portia as she was the better actress. As the gossip died down and the New Year filled people's minds with thoughts of times ahead, it was the consensus view that, if blame had to be apportioned, it had been six of one and half-a-dozen of the other.

Neither of the girls concerned ever owned up to the real cause of the attack and, from the night it had taken place, entered into an unspoken truce to ignore each other. This decision was easier for Pauline to abide by than Esme, as the latter had to live with a disfigurement which spoilt her looks for the rest of her life.

14

In spite of the damage which Eric's tangle with Esme Clark had done to Pauline's confidence in him, she became aware that it had made her love him in a more sympathetic way. That he was vulnerable to such obvious stratagems temporarily put him back into his original context; the boy who had followed her round the playing-field like a dog, someone who could pursue his quarry, overcome fear, make blunders then correct them, and learn to learn. The revulsion and rage that she felt when visualising him in Esme's arms was alternately soothed and inflamed by his claim that he had only been able to get into bed with her by pretending that she was Pauline. Knowing Eric's imagination to be severely limited, and not being flattered by any comparison with her rival, Pauline soon stopped bringing the matter up when they were together. It was better for her, she decided, to accept Eric as he was, with all his faults, rather than force him to attempt the construction of complicated untruths in order to placate her pride.

What she did learn from the betrayal was that she did love Eric in a completely natural way and any suspicion that she had had that her emotions were solely the raw material for Leo's machinations was dispelled. This relief was strengthened when she realised that the bitterness she had felt at his unfaithfulness to her had not only been suppressed by forgiveness, but had actually gone. What she was left with was a lover who had many windows to him, all his strivings, defects of temperament and mind, foibles and strengths being clear to her. What was surprising was that she should not only continue to love him while having this knowledge, but should then love him more. There seemed to be no need for mystery; a point which argued against allowing Leo to continue to pontificate over the relationship.

However, it was now Eric who appeared to need Leo's support. He felt guilty for months and Daniel was no help as he blamed Eric for spoiling his own imagined chances with Esme, even though he was the one person, other than Leo, who had guessed the truth about the débâcle at *The Merchant of Venice*. As far as Daniel was concerned it had been Eric's responsibility as a friend to handle the matter to better advantage and pass the unwanted attentions of the sparkling blonde on, not sit back and allow the whole situation to degenerate into mayhem and waste. Affronted by this brutal admission of self-interest and made scornful by the weakness it showed up, Eric turned his back on Daniel and a period of coolness followed; but, as the spring came and the common foe of the A-Level examinations appeared on the horizon, the two boys slowly re-adjusted themselves to friendship, but with scars to show.

In these months it was Leo who nursed Eric back into being able to trust himself. The boy's mortification had been much more severe than Pauline had thought possible: to her, he had behaved as a male animal behaves, and she had said so. Eric had never seen himself as a stud. Love was all that mattered. If he had traduced love then he was evil. When Pauline had told him that what had hurt her most had been the knowledge that he could actually, physically *do* it without love, that had slain his self-respect. He began to languish, disgusted by what he had done. He could not make love to her. In panic she tried to undo the harm but the forgiveness which she eventually gave him was not yet fully formed and he knew that she was still in pain, so he took no comfort from mere words.

Appalled by the destruction, Pauline left it to Leo to sort out because she had lost the touch. It seemed to be a completely male matter to do with inner disgrace and a moral pride which was a contrary notion to the idea of Eric as a farmyard lover with a facility for instant sexual service. Within what mockery she had allowed herself to make of him in this capacity, she had always left room for him to explain just how difficult it was to be a male of the species and always in the thrall of indiscriminate desire cursed with dumb, natural peccability. But he had refused to use this get-out, preferring his guilt, which was, at least, honest, and left him in possession of his own spirit rather than having it chained to a mindless sexual drive.

When Eric did recover it was questionable whether it was Leo, Time, Nature or the school work which he threw himself into in order to forget his sin, which effected the cure; but Leo took the credit as his ministrations had convinced Eric that Pauline's forgiveness was sincere and that he could now abandon his remorse with honour and accept a full pardon. This was a boon that only Leo could grant as priest of the moving spirit which existed between them.

The person who was left out of these rehabilitations was Deidre. When Pauline had publicly assailed Esme Clark, Deidre did not guess the real reason behind it and, indeed, never tried to find one. To Deidre it was only another clear manifestation of Pauline's profoundly unusual psyche, the vital forces of which would project her into that greater, richer, better world. When Deidre looked at Pauline in that last year of her secondary schooling, she saw someone who was already in full bloom. The distinctiveness of her mind, her behaviour, the very curves of her body, showed the mother that her daughter had entered into a state which was rapidly moving away from her control. Her own madness seemed to abate in the face of this estrangement; she relaxed into a gentle melancholy, talked reminiscently about her own youth and her dead husband and his work, and took far less interest in what went on around her. Occasionally the old firebrand would rear up, her ire raised, but in between these upsurges she was a more easy-going, though regretful, woman. This did not mean that she lost sight of the outline of Pauline's future; although in all other practical matters she became more slipshod and neglectful than ever, her wishes and opinions on her daughter's expectations became increasingly emphatic.

As she looked at her eighteen-year-old daughter on the eve of her A-Level examinations, she did not see a schoolgirl but a woman who knew her own power and had been well-loved by man, woman and child, and whose beauty was not her own any more but the torch of all Deidre's grief burning with a painful glory, ready to be carried into the arena.

On the day that Pauline and Eric received their A-Level results in August, nineteen-fifty-eight, Leo took them both out with Deidre to a remote hotel in Ribblesdale. They had driven there in the early afternoon, parked the car, then climbed part-way up Ingleborough from the north side. The sun had shone brilliantly all day, the curlews had been fluting and bubbling over the ascension-songs of skylarks, the views over to Pen-y-Ghent and Malham had been magnificent. They sat in the hotel dining-room that evening, easily mistaken for a family.

"Are you sure that going to Liverpool University is such a good idea, Eric?" Leo asked casually as he looked over the menu. "It's often advisable to keep well away from old stamping-grounds and associations when one goes to college."

Eric shrugged, his eyebrows raised as if he had never considered the question.

"It's one of the best veterinary departments in the country," he replied. "I'm lucky to have got in."

Leo smiled thinly and bowed his head to indicate a measure of doubt. Eric had not consulted him on the choice of university because it never seemed to be part of Leo's province; the entire question was to do with earning a living and the compromises one made with the social machine. The only connection which Leo had with this other dimension was the Latin which Leo had taught Eric in order that he might enter it. The archaic, recondite quality which this language retained for Eric only increased the alienation between Leo and this pragmatic world.

Unable to disguise his resentment at the realisation of how free Eric had remained, and how equipped he seemed to be to juggle with two kinds of truth, Leo did something which he had privately decided not to do.

"Are you sure that you still want to be a vet?" he said, lowering the menu.

"What else could I be? I've never considered anything else," Eric protested.

"It's a very noble profession, easing the suffering of animals," Deidre chipped in, fiddling with the cutlery. "Oh, I do wish they'd hurry up and take our order, I'm starving."

"It's easy to get oppressed by a job," Leo said thoughtfully. "I don't mean to disparage veterinary science but it's quite similar to the priesthood really. Your patients tie you down."

"Oh, come off it, Leo," Deidre scoffed, "stop being such a

martyr. He can go where he likes if he becomes a vet. They have vets everywhere."

"One becomes enchanted by suffering," Leo said with a lopsided smile. "The best jobs are those to do with making things out of non-human material. The manufacture of garden gnomes is a business I'd recommend."

Eric began to feel angry at the drift of Leo's irony. He could see that Deidre would never be liberated from her dependence on someone who had become her confessor, nurse and pseudo-husband for so long, but he had reached the point of hoping that Pauline would soon escape from Leo's peculiarly clinging oppressiveness. As far as he was concerned, Eric had Leo ready to be shoved into the background once university had started.

"I'm talking about making mistakes at crucial moments," Leo continued smoothly. "I should know plenty about that. I made a huge mistake choosing the Church. Why? Because I was drunk on ideas; I saw the world as a machine run by ideas. That was an error which no one took the trouble to point out to me. My best bet would have been commerce."

Deidre threw back her head and laughed.

"Rubbish! You couldn't sell water in the desert!"

Leo gave her a look which was intimate and ominous, silencing her noise. He unfolded his napkin and stroked out the corners.

"Your friend Daniel is going to Liverpool to study geology, John Salmon tells me," he said. "Have you discussed that with him?"

"Not really. I'm just glad we're going to the same place."

"A trifle odd. Your friend has chosen the subject which he has come to find the most difficult. Daniel has a very versatile and capable intellect with many strengths but he has selected the discipline which has proved hardest for him to master. Why do you think he has done this?"

"He's like that."

"You're not? You don't create challenges for yourself? Would you agree with that analysis of Eric's character, Pauline?"

"I don't know," she retorted, "nor do I care."

Pauline gave her order to her mother then went out of the dining-room. A minute later Eric saw her in the hotel garden, standing by a bush of white roses. He excused himself and went out to join her.

When the waiter came, Leo ordered for him, guessing what he might want to eat.

"Are you glad that Pauline failed to get into Liverpool?" Leo asked when the waiter had gone. "I thought it best."

Deidre smiled warmly and tapped her nose.

"Thank you for arranging that," she said. "You're a dear."

Pauline had applied to study English. Her A-Level results seemed to be more than adequate but she had been marked down on her interview, so the head of the school had told her. Her second choice had been King's College, London, which had accepted her.

"They will go on seeing each other," Leo said soberly, "be prepared for that. That love will not die."

"I don't mind," Deidre asserted cheerfully, glancing out of the window to where Eric and Pauline were standing in the garden, "as long as she gets the chance to meet other people; and she'll get plenty of opportunity to do that in London, won't she?"

"And you've definitely decided not to move down to be with her?"

Deidre nodded sedately.

"I have taken your advice. To begin with, she is going to stay with her grandfather. He knows a lot of interesting and influential people who will extend her horizons."

Leo grimaced, unable to hide his misgivings.

"That their love needed to be tested is one thing, but not destroyed. It is the most beautiful thing I have been close to since my own youth. You must promise me. . ."

Deidre unfolded her napkin and tucked it into the neckline of her summer dress as the waiter brought her soup.

"I promise you nothing from now on, Leo," she said with a toss of her rust-coloured hair, "and now's the time to remind you who her father was. Not you, by a long chalk."

During the past two years Eric had spent very little time with his mother and brother in Liverpool but his short visits had been spread over the period so the impression was avoided that he was deliberately neglecting them. His mother had no wish to visit Kendal and there was no room in John Salmon's house for visitors anyway. Eric's brother had been up for the week-end a few times when Daniel Fleck had been away and his room had been free, but Eric had not let him meet Pauline. To deal with Pauline's mother was enough of a problem; once his own got wind of a steady girl-friend he knew that she would start hoping that he would get married and have children. If she had ever been allowed to meet Pauline this desire would have increased.

Deidre had agreed that Eric and Pauline should have a holiday together before going up to university. She had given Pauline fifty pounds for doing well in her A-Levels and Eric's mother had at last relented and bought him a motor-scooter, a black NSU 150cc Prima, to get around on. In addition she had authorised an allowance for him that would be paid until he graduated. His father's estate had been bequeathed to Eric and his brother John in equal parts but until his mother's death it was to be for her use and management, though not disposal in terms of capital. The allowance was five hundred pounds a year, nearly twice as much as he would have got if he had been eligible to receive a grant from the county education authorities to go to university.

They decided to accept Leo's suggestion that they should go on a Grand Tour, following the route of the young English poets, artists and noblemen who had gone to the Continent to see the remains of the classical world. It meant taking the scooter and flying from Lydd to Le Touquet, then to Paris, Brussels, Aachen, Cologne, Munich, Salzburg, Geneva, Turin, Milan, Cremona, Bologna, Venice, Florence and Rome, where Leo would meet them and show them the Eternal City. He had a conference to attend and they scheduled their arrival to coincide with its final day. When Eric enquired what the conference was about, Leo told him that it was a get-together of alternative theologians from all over the world who were meeting to discuss the validity of egotheism as the basis for a new ecumenical incentive.

"The actual chamber where we will debate this issue is in the shadow of the Vatican," he told Eric with sardonic glee. "We are hoping that *il Papa* might drop in and give us his views."

In the final days of August Eric and Pauline rode the scooter down through London to the south coast at Lydd, loaded it on the Silver City twin-prop aircraft, and flew over the Channel in fine weather to land twenty minutes later at the French resort of Le Touquet.

When they disembarked it was to set foot for the first time outside their native country; and to be together for the last month of the idyll. They both knew that beyond this time, once they had gone to their separate universities, what they felt for each other would be tested.

As they rode off on the road to Paris both of them had no doubt their love could survive all the knocks.

At Frévent, thirty miles along their way, they were stopped by a police car and taken to the local headquarters where Pauline was informed that her mother had hanged herself from a bedroom window.

15

Deidre was cremated a week later and, in accordance with the stipulations of her will, no service was held and her ashes were thrown into the River Lune at Mansergh by her daughter to whom she had left little more than the fearsome legacy of her self-slaughter.

During the few days that it took to put her affairs in order and sort out her effects, Pauline stayed at Turner Row, refusing Leo's offer to stay with him in Kirkby Lonsdale. She remained alone in the house until her last walk down to the Underley Hall Bridge with her mother's ashes then took a taxi to Oxenholme and caught the train to London.

From the time that she heard the news in France to when she left Mansergh, she hardly spoke to Eric at all. The tragedy seemed to have scythed through their relationship as far as she was concerned; he could only be attentive and sympathetic, biding his time for when the wound would heal. Sure enough, a fortnight later he received a letter at his family home in Liverpool providing him with an address and telephone number for her in London. The tone was cool and polite and there was an absence of endearments, but it served to comfort him in his confusion. He had begun to feel that Pauline blamed him for her mother's suicide but Leo told him that it had been a threat Deidre had made many times but which he had never seen reason to believe, and the only way it could be accounted for was to agree with the coroner in his verdict that Deidre had killed herself while the balance of her mind was disturbed. By what? was a question Eric chose not to enter into, assuming that Leo was more able to answer this than he could ever be.

With his holiday plans in Europe ruined Eric went to Ireland with his mother and brother. They stayed in a farmhouse on the coast near Wexford. During the fortnight they spent there he sent Pauline one postcard and was surprised how little he thought of her. His mind was not occupied; all his time being used up on walking, swimming and talking to his mother, whom he had to get to know all over again as both of them had greatly altered. What he discovered on their re-acquaintance was that he could now perceive her as a woman. Freed from his father and any shadow of Pauline she emerged as unexpectedly feminine, scattering all his childhood notions about her. He became interested in the way she dressed, the way she saw herself, her opinions, her view of him. One morning when they were walking along the two miles of white sand which was the eastern boundary of the farm, his mother asked him about Pauline. Before he answered he was forced to remember with considerable shame how little of his immediate past he had shared with his family and it made him hesitate.

"Is something the matter?" his mother asked. "Don't tell me anything if you'd rather keep it to yourself."

Eric found himself on the verge of tears. When he tried to speak his lips were so numb that he could not frame the words.

"Do you miss your girl?" his mother's voice intruded.

He nodded but checked himself, wondering if this were true. On this strange shore, surrounded by the unfamiliar and his mother shining with a new light, he could not be certain. After everything that had happened, it could be dying. The whole thing had been a dream, a phase, a convulsion of youth. He asserted control over his speech, determined that the doubt should not visibly discomfort him.

"I've got a lot of thinking to do," he said carefully.

"Can I help? I know what it feels like to have your emotions knocked about. No one's life is straightforward, son."

He was able to smile at her. Ahead of them he was glad to see his brother John astride the dappled grey carthorse being led along the water's edge by the farmer. For the moment he could retire from the conversation, knowing that should he wish to start it again and ask his mother for help, the offer was there.

That night they went to the village dance with the family at the farm, all of them riding on the milk cart. There were only a dozen young girls in the hall and they were naturally interested in a stranger. One of them was bolder than the rest and after Eric had sat out several dances she came over and asked him to dance, glancing triumphantly over her shoulder at her companions to confirm that she had carried out the dare. Eric got up and danced a quickstep with her, chatting easily enough, but his relaxed attitude was a mask to cover the shock he felt at holding another woman in his arms. Until now that experience had been monopolised by Pauline and it had created a shape within his mind, a mould into which only she would fit. Now there was someone else edging into that space, a girl he had met a few minutes ago. As she pressed herself against him and he felt the flesh move under his hand, the first surge of desire he had ever felt for a woman other than Pauline moved him, leaving an aftertaste of self-disgust, recalling his guilt over the Esme Clark affair.

The girl's name was Bridget. She was the niece of another farmer in the district and she had come down from Dublin for a holiday with her uncle. She was direct, sure of herself, pretty enough to sustain it but he knew that there was an underlying practised urban coldness there. It was this he found most attractive. When he asked if he could take her for a walk down to the strand, she agreed.

Looking round for his mother to make his excuses for not going back to the farm with her, he found that she had already gone.

Bridget was a small, neat girl with slightly protuberant blue eyes and a head of billowing brown hair. She walked a few steps ahead of him, her white skirt swinging in the moonlight, frequently glancing over her shoulder to check that he was following. As she went down the lane she talked, raising her voice so he could hear but never allowing him to get close enough to chat. By the time he arrived on the shore Eric was exasperated.

"If you'd wait a moment then you wouldn't have to shout," he chided her.

"Oh, I like shouting at men," Bridget called back.

Eric broke into a trot, overtook her then blocked the path with his arms held wide.

"You don't have to worry. I'm not going to attack you," he said sourly. "I'm not a maniac."

"Oh, what a pity," she replied, teasing him. "A fine young man like yourself going to waste on a Saturday night."

Skirting round him she walked on for a while, then headed for sand dunes which ran down to the strand. Eric turned his back on her, staring out along the ribbon which the moon made over the incoming tide. When he looked round she had disappeared. He shouted for her a couple of times then shrugged and began to retrace his steps. As soon as he did so a piercing whistle came from the shadows of the sand dunes.

Walking over he found her sitting on the top of a dune between spiky grasses, hugging her knees.

"You'd given me up as a bad job, had you?" she said as he sat down beside her. "You've obviously got no patience at all."

"I thought you'd gone back."

"How could I possibly go back through the countryside alone? I'd be abducted."

"If you say so."

"I do say so. What did you say your name was again?"

"Eric."

"Well, Eric?"

She put her head to one side and regarded him with a knowing smile.

"Well what?" he riposted.

Bridget laughed derisively. He noticed how, in the moonlight, her pencilled eyebrows had disappeared giving her a doll-like blandness of face. Lying back on her elbows she thrust her legs out, ploughing up the sand with her sandals.

"You're all the same," she averred with a worldly-wise sigh. "Get yourself over here."

Eric remained where he was. The girl's crude, back-street coquetry had not offended him, but its rawness was new. With Pauline he had always been enfolded by her solitary beauty in a landscape which had no reference to an outside world: there was nothing of the city and its reduction of everyone to the same level. No one assumed knowledge of the other nor insisted upon such desolate rites as these were.

"I don't feel like it," he said flatly.

Bridget sat up, a retort on her lips, but she thought better of it and relaxed back on her elbows.

"Well, I suppose I might have deserved that," she said with a sniff of disdain which could have been aimed at herself; then, with a toss of her hair, "It's the wrong time of the month anyway."

Eric was silent, not daring to give way to the laughter rising to quell his revulsion. He suddenly experienced an immense friendliness towards the girl.

"Would you like to go somewhere tomorrow?" he asked impulsively.

"Are you pulling my leg?"

"No," he responded. "I just thought we could find something to do. I'm here with my mum and little brother and there's a limit to what you can get up to round here."

Bridget got to her feet and shook the sand off her skirt. Beyond her Eric could see the wide mirror of the moonlit sea and it made her body show in a silhouette, round and clownish. Raising his hand he asked her to pull him up. She did so with an angry jerk.

"Got that all wrong, didn't I?" she said, then turned and ran down the side of the dune.

He walked her back to her uncle's farmhouse and arranged to call for her the following morning for a bus trip into Wexford. When he arrived to pick her up he was invited in by the mother of the family and given a cup of coffee while he sat and waited for Bridget to come down. Sitting in a chair by an oil stove on the other side of the big kitchen was frail old woman wrapped in a plaid shawl. Her hair was snowy-white and tied back in a bun and she held a basin in her lap. Hanging from the arm of her chair was a rosary. As the old woman sat gazing at the stove she muttered to herself in rapid, irritated bursts, shaking the basin. The farmer's wife had failed to introduce Eric to the old woman so he thought it best to keep quiet.

When Bridget came down she was dressed casually but her hair had been pinned up and she wore shoes too elegant for wandering around a town. Also he noticed how much jewellery she was wearing: bangles, ear-rings, a necklace and a decorated brass buckle on her broad belt. The old woman chortled as Bridget entered the room and waved the basin at her.

"Nana is waiting to peel the potatoes, aren't you?" Bridget explained with indulgent brightness. "She's a clever old thing."

Embarrassed, Eric was glad to have his attention drawn to the window. A heavy shower had started. Bridget frowned at her shoes.

"I was determined to wear these damned things. I've had them three months," she complained. "Why does it have to rain today?"

"You'll have to wear your wellies!" the old woman said with vicious clarity. "Those'll be no use in the mud."

They sat at the kitchen table and waited for the shower to pass. Bridget's aunt came in and gave Nana a couple of potatoes to peel. She attacked them with vigour.

"Now, now, careful, Nana," Bridget said, getting up and standing next to the old woman. "Don't go so fast or you'll cut yourself."

"Don't you try to tell me how to peel a potato. I've peeled millions of potatoes!" Nana exclaimed indignantly.

Bridget returned to her seat at the table.

"Guess how old Nana is," she said with a rueful grin.

Eric hesitated, watching the little knife in the old woman's blotched claw.

"I wouldn't know."

"Go on, she doesn't mind. You don't mind, do you Nana?"

The old woman shook her head and examined a peeled potato, putting it carefully into a small saucepan of water.

"He won't believe it but I can show him my birth-certificate," she said proudly. "No one can argue with a birth-certificate issued by the British government. They should never have left Ireland. We were happier then. After they went it was all downhill."

"Nan is a hundred and two," Bridget announced, "and all there."

"That's right. God is looking after me. Get some more potatoes, I've finished these," Nana declared. "I don't know what I've done to deserve it."

"You've been a good woman, that's why," Bridget cajoled her. "You did your duty."

"No, no," Nana said, stabbing a potato, tears gathering in her sunken, monkey-like eyes, "God doesn't want me."

Eric made every effort to adjust his expression to the correct one as Bridget went over to the old woman and knelt down to embrace her. He was aware that Bridget was watching him to see how he would respond.

"There, there, you'll be with the angels one day, Nana," she crooned. "Don't worry about it."

"I've been a sinner . . ." the old woman said with a rattling sigh.

"Oh, come on now, we all have."

Bridget got to her feet and winked at Eric as she sat down again at the table.

"It's all right. This happens every day. She's amazing really. Nine children, thirty-four grandchildren, two husbands — takes it out of you, you know," she whispered.

"I can hear you, Bridget!" Nana cried out. "You're talking about me."

"I was telling my friend here what a wonderful woman you are, Nana. We're all very proud of you."

Nana turned and scrutinised Eric, leaning over the side of the chair as if she would like to touch him.

"Is this your young man?" she demanded.

"Oh, one of them, Nana. You know I have hundreds," Bridget replied, giving Eric a playful nudge.

"Can you trust him? He looks a bit of a devil to me, to be honest with you. Is he a farmer?"

"He's nothing at all yet, Nana. Tell her yourself, go on, she won't bite."

Bridget went and turned Nana's chair to face Eric then presented her with a magician's gesture.

"Your public! Tell her what you're going to be. You haven't told me yet."

"Ah, the Army will have him. They get all the ones which look like him, unsure of themselves, a bit lost. There'll be another war soon enough. . ."

Eric did not have to open his mouth. Nana did all the talking, meandering through opinions, memories and her moments of doubt.

The shower became a downpour and soon other members of the family came into the kitchen, driven off their jobs by the rain. They sat around the table drinking tea, chatting amongst themselves, taking no particular notice of Eric. He had the feeling that he had simply been incorporated into their lives rather than ignored or neglected. He had come, he would go. The same applied to Nana in spite of her great age. Time had the use of them all.

16

Everything in Pauline's life had taken place on the rim of a void since her mother's death. She was unable to relate to any person or event beyond obeying the simplest rules of existence. She accepted the advice of everyone, disputed nothing, but acted only at the instruction of her inner emptiness.

Deidre had left strict instructions about the future. It was all to be conducted according to the plan which she had outlined during the previous year: Pauline was to go to her grandfather in London. From her will it was clear that she assumed he would take on all parental control and responsibilities. Leo was not mentioned in the will at all; not a word of gratitude, friendship or explanation. It was as if Deidre had taken his influence and expunged it with her death.

Joe Nash, Oswald's father, was approaching seventy. He had had a profitable but undistinguished career as a solicitor specialising in industrial and patent law. He lived in a large modern house in Kew, close to the gardens. His wife had died of a blood disease five years before and, since then, he had lived the life of a club bachelor, having many friends but seldom bringing them home. Oswald had been his only child and since his death Joe Nash had not found it possible to be close to Deidre or Pauline, partly because of Deidre's eccentric behaviour but also because he found it painful to contemplate the girl's predicament in having such a mother. He had offered to adopt Pauline at one stage but had been savagely rebuffed. Now, when his proposal had been implemented under the worst circumstances possible, he had become alarmed at the idea of having a beautiful young woman about the house. He was not sure how he would be able to cope with her.

Joe Nash was a short, stocky man with a stiff brush of iron-grey hair. His pink complexion and light-blue eyes gave him an appearance much younger than his seventy years. He was semi-retired but still active, alert and in good health, taking frequent holidays, playing golf and reading widely and enthusiastically; but his main pleasure was his friends. Over a long working career and as a man-about-town he had garnered for himself a host of companions. Most of them were in the City and finance and the law, but there were others in politics and diplomacy. It was this breadth of contacts which had caused Deidre to put such faith in him as middleman for Pauline's future. As usual, however, she had made inaccurate deductions from a mistaken impression; for although Joe Nash had many friends they were mostly of his own age, many were bachelors or widowers and those who were not kept family and the club as far apart as possible. He knew few young men and fewer young women.

When Pauline came to live with him he gave her a bedroom and sitting-room of her own and the use of the kitchen. He had an aversion to domestic help and did all the housework and cooking for himself even though he could well have afforded servants. For a couple of weeks he cooked for the two of them, aware that Pauline was still in the grip of grief, but after that he left her to find what she needed for herself in the refrigerator and pantry.

One morning a postcard arrived for her from Ireland. The ink was smudged but the crosses after the signature were clear enough. Joe Nash felt his spirits lift. He was glad to discover that she had a boyfriend. A few days later he mentioned to Pauline that she could have friends to stay whenever she wished. His offer appeared to arouse no interest.

"Wouldn't you like your boyfriend to come and stay?" he asked jovially. "He's perfectly welcome."

"I haven't got a boyfriend," Pauline replied levelly.

"I couldn't help seeing the postcard."

"He's just someone I knew."

Joe Nash lapsed into a disappointed silence. He had to admit that he found it hard to believe that his granddaughter had no man in tow.

"Well, I expect you'll make plenty of new friends once you start at King's College," he said cheerfully. "You'll be beating them off with a stick."

Pauline made no reply except to make a small grimace of disapproval. That night, for the first time, she made dinner for them both. He noticed how unusually attentive she was to his needs and comfort, even to the point of emptying the ash-tray for his cigar.

The following day he took the vacuum-cleaner up to her room while she was out. Beside the window he found a plastic bag from a local hardware store containing a length of blue nylon rope. On his way out of the room he noticed a small brass bolt which had been fitted to the inside jamb of the door.

On registration day at King's College, Pauline encountered the mass of her peers. There were thousands of them in the university buildings which she had to enter; they thronged the halls, the refectories, the union cafeterias, the library and bookshops. London's crowded streets had spilled into a place that she had hoped would be a sanctum. She returned to Kew that evening in bewildered misery.

Her grandfather had booked a table at a local restaurant to take her out and celebrate the start of her university days, but she asked to stay in. When he went up to her room half-an-hour later to see if she had changed her mind, he knocked then tried the door, expecting to find it bolted: but it was not. When he entered the room he discovered her in bed, her back turned towards him. He went over and sat down, laying a hand on the swell of her hip.

"D'you want to tell me what happened?" he asked deferentially. "Or is it just over-excitement?"

"I have a headache, that's all," Pauline murmured.

"Have you taken some aspirins?"

"No, it will go away."

"I'm just facing up to cooking dinner," he said with a sigh. "Are you sure you won't change your mind and come out? It's a very good little restaurant, Italian, very cheery. . ."

She turned over and gazed at him wearily.

"Grandad, I don't want to be looked at ever again," she said.

Joe Nash hesitated. When she had set out that morning he had imagined how much admiration she would get and he had assumed that she would enjoy it. The way she dressed and held herself was not that of a shrinking violet, in fact he judged her to be advanced for her age and well able to look after herself. The notion that the scrimmage of student amatory advances was too much for her made him want to laugh.

"They don't mean anything. It's all in the fun, isn't it?" he said, patting her flank.

"Not for me it isn't," she replied, raising her head from the pillow. "I'm a very private person. I find them insulting."

"Oh, come on, they're only boys. . ."

"They're animals! I want nothing to do with them!"

Her voice was so charged with loathing that it silenced him. Of all the problems that he had anticipated having with Pauline this was the most unimaginable. When he had contemplated the practical problems of having her living in the house the major one he had foreseen was that her beauty would make her too popular — his home would be overrun by callow rowdies chasing a good time and abusing his hospitality. He had found the prospect sufficiently humorous to share it with his friends who had advised him to be stern and strict about such matters, many of them having had their home lives plagued by juvenile mayhem. As he looked down at her angry, hunted countenance, and saw the real damage that had been done, the good spirit and optimism he had felt growing after Deidre's death were withered again. The dreadful thought struck him that the girl might be as impossible as her mother.

"Surely you're used to receiving attention," he said with fatherly calm. "Mansergh might have been a bit in the backwoods but there must have been lads around."

Pauline sat up and shook her head.

"No, I have to learn. You teach me. I was dedicated to Mummy, you see. There was no time for anything else. Will you show me how to behave?"

She held out her arms to him for the first time since she had come to London. He took her head on his shoulder and let her weep.

"You'll have to learn how to handle such attentions," he said. "Men are like that; they've always been like that."

She pushed herself away and dried her eyes on a corner of the pillow, then announced that she wanted to go to the restaurant.

"You'll have to watch the waiters, my love. You know these Italians," he said with a chuckle, touching her damp cheek. "My, you should be glad to be so lovely. Has no one ever told you that it's a gift from God?"

Pauline smiled. Her grandfather's commonplace dropped into a matrix made at Mansergh in a manner far more refined and ornate than an old man's cliché. But this had more power because it lacked complexity and guilt. The earnestness and emotion behind the remark lifted her heart. She saw the wonderment in her grandfather's eyes as he looked at her: in a ghost behind the aged but lively features she espied Eric, Eric entranced, Eric enraptured. What the ghost communicated was not only its familiar adoration but a reflection of her own, an exchange of secret, joyful information which cured the disease of her day. When her grandfather left her room, Eric's imprint remained behind.

The dinner at the Italian restaurant was a success. Pauline was relaxed and happy and Joe Nash enjoyed all the cracks, compliments and comments of the waiters who knew him well enough to go far in their badinage. He basked in her loveliness, boosted by the awakening she had given him. Emerging from the unruffled male equilibrium of his friendships and club society into her youth and insecurity had been a mental proposition until now; but it had happened. What he had not bargained for was the shock it would give to his system.

He walked her home past the great gardens. Scents came over the wall in the October air. They were both quite drunk, arm in arm, feeling very pleased with life, aware that there had been a change for the better.

After she had gone to bed he stood outside her room and looked at the thin line of light between the door and the jamb. His heart moved as he saw that she had not shot the bolt. He coughed loud enough for her to hear then put his hand on the doorknob. A moment later he heard a click; the bolt went across and the light went out.

Three days after he started at Liverpool University Eric rang Pauline at the number she had provided. It was Joe Nash who picked up the telephone. When he realised who it was at the end of the line Joe Nash was perturbed to discover how hostile he felt towards the owner of that dour, northern voice with its inbuilt truculence, devoid of respect or courtesy. He imagined his interlocutor to have a chip on his shoulder, an aggressive, uneducated youth who had difficulty stringing a coherent sentence together. Actually, Eric's pauses and grunts were the result of the clipped, chilly responses he was getting from the London end. After sparring for a few exchanges, Eric asked if he could leave a message for Pauline to ring him. Two days later she had not returned his call so he tried again and got her. When he asked why she had not rung him as requested she told him that her grandfather had not passed on the message.

They chatted for a while, avoiding any mention of Mansergh or Deidre. Eric talked about what it was like living at home and having Daniel Fleck staying there; about his mother and brother, the Irish holiday, the department of veterinary science, anything rather than what was on his mind. Pauline made hardly any contribution to the conversation at all. As the call dragged on she became increasingly reticent until he was forced to ask her if something was the matter. She denied that there was. In desperation he followed this up with the suggestion that he should come down to London to see her the next weekend. She demurred, saying that she had a lot of reading to do and it was, after all, the first weekend of the term and it might be better to wait a while. Eric relented but succeeded in persuading her to let him come down the weekend after that. This negotiation was so thorny for them both that by unspoken agreement they did not raise the question of where he would stay, or whether further telephone calls were in order. When Pauline finished the call she felt drained. Returning to her room and her books she sat down and tried to take up her work again, reading and making notes on Joseph Conrad's novel, *Nostromo*.

She could not concentrate on the text. Conrad's dark, tense language repelled her. When she attempted to make a note it petered out before the sense could be established. She doodled, allowing her mind to drift. The street lights went on beyond the garden wall and the pure evening blue was discoloured.

She gave up trying to study and went out for a walk. People were hurrying home from work. They ignored her, passing on the pavements, heads down. The roads were full of traffic stopping and starting, the exhausts pouring vapour into the cool evening. Ahead of her she saw the blood-red spots of the lights at a major crossroads.

There was a telephone box on the corner. When she got close she saw that it was occupied by two girls who were passing the receiver back and forth and laughing. Deciding to wait, she leant against the high wall of the gardens. The girls put more money in and continued, glancing defiantly in her direction.

"Waiting for someone?"

The man who had accosted her had a broad accent which she thought might be Australian. He was tall, broad, with a ginger moustache and moist, brown eyes. She could smell the beer on his breath.

"I'm waiting to make a call," she said.

"I thought you might be waiting for me," the stranger replied with a grin. "Fancy a drink? There's a pub just down the road."

There was a tapping from the telephone box. When Pauline turned to look she saw the two girls frowning and pointing.

"Looks like they think you're muscling in on their patch," the stranger remarked, "but I guess they've got you wrong. My name's Greg. Any time you want work, though, my number's scribed in the box."

Pauline brushed past him and walked towards the traffic-lights. They were blood-red with warning again as if they had never changed. Although she had found the man's assumption that she might be prepared to sell herself crude and offensive she had to admit that it was strangely comforting that a stranger could guess from her appearance that she was capable of such a thing.

Pauline did ring Eric before the weekend agreed upon for his visit. The only person in the house at the time was Daniel Fleck who immediately recognised her accent and knew, even before she introduced herself, who she must be. He took her message for Eric with great precision and politeness and spoke smoothly and fluently

135

as he had trained himself to do when addressing women. During the long summer holidays he had attended a course in Leicester on self-improvement and techniques of personal communication. A married woman called Rita who lived in Islington had been on the course. She had seduced him and, at a stroke, altered his personality. He was now so confident as to be overbearing and every woman he encountered had to endure the full brunt of his newly-minted charm. By the time he put the telephone down Daniel had invited himself along on some later visit, discussed *Nostromo*, swopped notes on university organisation and given Pauline a considerable amount of advice on how to handle Eric.

When Eric came in later that evening and returned Pauline's call he was overjoyed to find her in a much better mood than the last time they had spoken. She was humorous, relaxed and generous, giving him the impression that she was looking forward to his visit. She had arranged for him to stay at the house and her grandfather was pleased that he would have the opportunity to meet him. One change of plan was proposed: she thought it would make things easier if Eric brought a friend. As yet, she said, my grandfather doesn't know how close we've been.

"Been?" Eric echoed in alarm. "Don't you mean *are*?"

Pauline left a short silence before she replied, "He thinks you're just a boyfriend. Look, I'm only starting to get to know him all over again. He couldn't stand Mummy so he never came up to Mansergh. He doesn't know anything about life up there." She nearly said, "He's never even met Leo," but hastily thrust the thought back down from whence it had risen.

It was the first time Leo had come into Pauline's mind since she came to London. The mere mention of him aroused a heavy, complex force in her and she struggled to suppress it. Eric did not pick up the allusion, preferring to leave Leo where he was laid, safely in the past.

"I thought your friend Daniel sounded so interesting, perhaps he'd like to come? Joe is going to have a party for me," she continued. "It will be more fun if you bring someone."

"Is Joe your grandfather?"

"Yes, he likes me to call him Joe," she replied. "Is that all right?"

Eric was forced, against his better judgement, to agree to Daniel coming down with him. When he heard that this had been arranged Daniel was delighted as it gave him an opportunity to see Rita again a week earlier than he had planned.

Eric and Daniel got a lift from a fellow-student who was driving down to London to see his girlfriend, and there were two other passengers on similar missions, all of them having left home for the first time and not yet hardened to the break. The car was an old hump-backed Standard Six that was heavy on petrol and the five of them shared out the cost. At the end of the seven-hour journey Eric and Daniel were dropped off at Highgate station on the Northern line of the Underground and had to travel right across London to Kew which took another hour-and-a-half. By the time they found the house it was ten o'clock, two hours later than they had estimated their arrival.

There were expensive cars parked in the drive: Jaguars, Rovers, a couple of Aston Martins and a Rolls Royce coupé. All the lights in the large house were on and they could hear music. Standing in the impressive porch with their rucksacks they exchanged sardonic looks.

"D'you think the butler will let us in?" Daniel said. "I didn't pack my evening suit."

Eric rang the bell. He had to repeat the process three times before anyone came to answer it. When the door opened it was a portly, red-faced old man with an ice-bucket in his hand who received them. He had been on his way to the kitchen when he had heard the bell over the din. Initially he was unsure about letting them in but once Eric explained that they were friends of Pauline he stepped aside and waved them through.

"Come in lads, go through," he boomed cheerfully. "I think you'll find her surrounded by a lot of old buffers like me. Get in there and liberate her, poor wench."

Leaving their rucksacks in the hall they followed the bearer of the ice-bucket into the crowded lounge. It was full of men; the sound they made was a profoundly male noise, crashing laughter, rumbling sonorities. Eric peered through the squareness of their shoulders and the whiteness of their shirts, searching for Pauline. As he went from face to face he realised that all these guests were over fifty; their spectacles, mustaches, beards, hearing-aids, bald pates, scrawny necks, bloodshot eyes, yellowing teeth and, most of all, confident, arrogant eyes, radiating the success of age. He stopped, looking over his shoulder to find Daniel who was his only ally. Behind the door, tucked as far out of sight as he could manage, was Daniel talking to the only woman visible in the room. She was a tiny, bird-like creature with big, anxious eyes and she appeared to be upset. Unable to face barging through the crowd to find Pauline on his own, Eric retreated to the door and slid in beside Daniel who looked embarrassed at his arrival.

"I can't see Pauline anywhere," Eric said.

The woman fiddled with an evening bag and tossed her head.

"Aren't you going to introduce me to your friend?" she asked Daniel petulantly. "After all, I've been standing here for an hour being ignored before you came. Why did you ask me to come here? They'd never heard of me. It was so humiliating."

Daniel kept his eyes lowered as he introduced the woman as Rita. As Eric had been regaled with many chapters of Daniel's lubricious adventures in Leicester he was fully *au fait* with the background. Unable to rebuke Daniel in front of her he offered his hand instead.

"Well, you've got more manners than he has," she twittered. "I should think you're a very nice boy. You'd think Daniel would have taken the trouble to get things right, wouldn't you? He knows I've got enough rejection problems without adding to them."

Before she could continue with her plaint a chorus of "Happy Birthday" came from the other side of the room. Eric's mind raced as he tried to remember if it was Pauline's birthday and he had forgotten, his memory clotted with recent happenings. But he remembered her birthday was in June. Relieved in his mind he heard her singing above the basses and baritones of the old men and this time he burrowed through their packed ranks to be with her.

She was standing beside a buffet table holding a sabre over a chocolate birthday-cake made in the shape of a fort. Beside her was a short, brown, bald man wearing a white dinner-jacket with a carnation in his buttonhole who was chatting to Joe Nash. As Pauline began cutting the cake the man in the white jacket beamed and laughed.

Eric watched, open-mouthed. He hardly recognised Pauline in the evening gown she was wearing. Her hair was swept up and held with glittering combs, her white arms and shoulders were bare and as she cut the cake her breasts swelled against the low neck of her gown with a brazen nakedness that affronted him.

When she turned and saw him he could not help cringing inwardly. He was not only a stranger at this feast but a boy once again. She had moved on.

"Oh, this is Eric," she said off-handedly, waving the sabre vaguely in his direction. "I told you about him, Joe, remember?"

Joe Nash stepped forward. He took in the crumpled shirt and trousers, the shifty, averted eyes, the flush on the boy's cheek. Suddenly he felt ashamed that a child should feel so obviously out of place in his home. He took Eric's hand and put the other on his shoulder.

"Welcome, Eric. An old friend's birthday, one of the most fascinating chaps, a good sort, old Bruin. You'll meet him later," he said cordially, "but first you must have a drink."

As he was led away to the bar Eric looked over his shoulder. Pauline had put the sabre down on the table and was talking to the man with the carnation then listening attentively to his replies and smiling at him. Eric knew that this must be an act for his benefit: she was deliberately being cruel, but for what purpose he could not imagine.

"Hope you don't mind all these fellows hanging round my grand-daughter," Joe Nash murmured with mock-affability. "It does no harm for her to meet accomplished people, I believe. Spending time in their company could be looked upon as an advantage, depending on one's point of view. Did your mucker come along, as arranged?" he asked as he presented Eric with a glass of red wine, neglecting to enquire as to what he would prefer. "Tell me his name again."

"Daniel," Eric replied stiffly. "Yes, he did come with me."

"A woman turned up for him, rather a neurotic one, I thought. Not his older sister. Perhaps his mother?"

To his horror, Eric found himself blushing again under the sardonic, supercilious gaze of the older man who took encouragement from his discomfiture and pressed ahead.

"You might have asked if he could bring guests along. This was planned as an all-male affair," he stated aloofly. "Next time, if there is a next time, please remember not to take my home for granted."

"I'm sorry," Eric stammered, "I didn't know he'd invited her."

"Then I'd be more careful how I chose my friends, if I were you," Joe Nash said, giving Eric's elbow a squeeze. "If you can't cope with people, avoid them, that's my advice, young fellow."

He strolled off leaving Eric alone with the glass of wine in his hand. Without tasting it he put it down on the table and forced his way back to the door. When he found his rucksack in the hall he saw that Daniel's had gone. Letting himself out he went back to the station, took the Underground back to Highgate and started hitching on the Great North Road.

17

It took Eric all night to hitch-hike back to Liverpool, zig-zagging over the country with eight different lifts, hanging about in roadside cafés with the long-distance lorry drivers and their strange whores of the road. As Eric looked at these women, guessing at the mysterious urge that kept them wandering from man to man and city to city, he never saw them as anything but a completely separate breed. In their wariness and ferocity, their mad humour and lewdness, they were like soldiers. By the time he reached home, it was nearly ten o'clock, but his mind had not wasted the hours. Pauline had been reinstated, his anger and resentment had gone, he blamed himself, he had decided to be worthy of her, she had all the things he wanted, without her life was impossible.

Incoherent with remorse, desperate to apologise, he let himself in to the house and went straight to the telephone to ring her up and beg forgiveness. As he dialled the number his mother came into the hall and took the instrument out of his hand.

"Never mind that now," she said forcefully. "Go and sit in the kitchen and I'll make you some breakfast."

Eric protested and attempted to recover the telephone.

"Do as you're told, you bloody idiot!" his mother shouted, clutching it to her breast. "Haven't you caused enough trouble? Her grandfather's beaten you to it. He was on the 'phone to me at half-past seven this morning!"

Eric trudged into the kitchen and sat down at the table. He felt all the strength go out of his limbs. Lowering his head he rested it on his arms.

"What did he say?" he asked his mother as she started to clatter pans on the stove in her temper.

"He wanted to know if you were all right. He said you'd just walked out of his house without a by your leave, not a word. That's not at all like our Eric, I said to him. Oh, I'm sure it's not Mrs Sherwin. . ." She turned and slammed a bowl and spoon down on the table in front of him. "What the hell did you think you were doing? He's had the police out looking for you, he says."

"No he hasn't," Eric muttered. "He's just saying that to frighten you."

"Well, he succeeded. And I heard all about our Pauline, our precious Pauline, the dark horse you've never seen fit to introduce me to. I suppose we're not good enough for her?"

Eric shook his head, refusing to meet his mother's furious eyes.

"You've got it all wrong . . ."

"Don't you touch that telephone until I've rung him back to say you've arrived safely home. He says that this Pauline is very upset by your behaviour — she must be sensitive, it strikes me, though she can't be too much so if she goes around with the likes of you, Eric, you bloody numbskull."

"Don't go on, Ma . . ."

His mother threw a packet of cereal at him across the table and crashed a bottle of milk down under his nose.

"He made me feel that big," she said, showing him the gap between her thumb and forefinger. "I've never been so ashamed. My son not knowing how to conduct himself at a social event; my son a bloody hooligan."

Eric reared up indignantly.

"I didn't do anything. All that happened is I didn't feel welcome so I walked out," he said.

"You were drunk when you arrived."

"I was not! I hadn't had a drink at all!"

"He says you were, and you were dressed like a scarecrow."

"Ma, they were all in evening dress. I haven't even got evening dress. She didn't tell me . . ."

"Did she tell you that it was all right for your friend Daniel to take his girlfriend into the bedroom?"

Eric sat frozen. He quailed under his mother's triumphantly vengeful gaze.

"Oh, no," he groaned.

"Oh, yes. Mr Nash himself caught them at it. The final straw he said. Well, you have my total support, Mr Nash, I told him. I'm as disgusted as you are with these lads. And I am, Eric, I am. We never brought you up to behave like this."

"Ma, it wasn't me who was in the bedroom!"

"It might just as well have been. And she was twice his age, Mr Nash said, and she made a scene, an hysterical outburst calling Mr Nash and his guests names and swearing." She suddenly sat down at the table as if the thought had become too much to bear standing up. "I'm not having Dan back here. He'll have to find other lodgings, I'm afraid."

There was a pause. Eric could not find the courage to say anything in Daniel's defence. Taking the cereal packet he poured some into the bowl. His mother opened the bottle of milk and handed it to him.

"Ma, it's the first time Daniel's had a real . . . well, a woman friend . . ." Eric explained lamely. "You know what he's like. It's all or nothing."

"I've a good mind to write a letter to his mother, I'll tell you that. I bet she has no idea what he's getting up to, poor woman." She left the table and took bacon and eggs out of the refrigerator. "I feel very sorry for Daniel's mother, I do really."

"We weren't all to blame. Her grandfather made the party formal so we couldn't fit in, and he didn't tell us that we were expected to dress up. He rigged the whole thing to embarrass me."

"Do you think a man in his position would go out of his way to make your life difficult? Why? He expected that you'd know how to conduct yourself, and you failed. Don't make excuses for yourself, it makes me feel worse."

As his mother started to fry the bacon Eric decided to keep quiet. While he ate and his mother fumed he was surprised to note that he could only smile every time he imagined the discovery of Daniel *in flagrante delicto*.

In spite of Eric's protests his mother rang Joe Nash and apologised on his behalf, saying that he had no excuses to offer. This made it impossible for him to talk to Pauline so he had to write. He was employed on this delicate task when Daniel made his return late that Sunday evening, hollow-eyed from lack of sleep. Eric's mother had been into Daniel's room and packed all his things, putting the cases in the hall and locking the door of the room so he could not get in, and had then gone to bed.

"What's all this?" Daniel said, staring at the suitcases.

"She's chucking you out," Eric said flatly. "Mr Nash rang her up."

Daniel threw down his rucksack with a curse and went through to the kitchen, slouched with fatigue.

"Make us a cup of coffee, will you? I'm absolutely knackered," he sighed, slumping into a chair.

"I'm not surprised," Eric replied grimly as he filled up the kettle. "You've been very busy ruining my life."

"Oh, come off it. They deserved everything they got. What do you want with people like that? It was a homos party as far as I could see so I redressed the balance."

Eric bit his lip. It was not the time to explain to Daniel how much damage had been done. In his present state of exhaustion nothing would sink in, anyway. Besides, it had been his own action in walking out of the party that had made the rift. Daniel's catastrophic *faux pas* had simply made the crevice into a canyon.

He gave Daniel his own bed to sleep off his exhaustion and stayed up in the kitchen himself, penning the letter to Pauline. It was two o'clock before he crept into the sitting-room and lay on the sofa, the letter inside his shirt in case his mother should find it.

The following morning he woke early and went out to post the letter. When he returned he noticed that the cases had gone out of the hall. Going into the kitchen he found Daniel and his mother having a cup of tea and a conversation.

"Well, if she's that old, Daniel, then she should have known better. It strikes me you've been misled."

"I think it's the divorce that's done the damage, Mrs Sherwin. She's very insecure. Does everything on the spur of the moment . . . she's very impetuous."

"Sounds like it, son."

"Anyway, I've learned my lesson," Daniel asserted gravely.

"Good, I'm pleased to hear it."

144

Eric did not interrupt. Leaving the kitchen he went upstairs and looked into Daniel's room.

The cases were on the bed, open, half-unpacked.

With a sense of rueful admiration for his friend's powers of pleading, Eric went to his own room, got his books and went out of the house to catch the bus into university.

Three days later, on the date when he would have anticipated his own letter's arrival at Kew, he received one from Pauline. When he began to read it was clear to him that these correspondences had crossed. He was depressed by this: he was being thrust back into a situation which he had hoped to remedy with the arguments and explanations he had offered in his own letter. All the benefits of his abject apologies were dissolved and his expression of them, as he remembered, was paltry and inadequate. However, he was able to glean some hope from her letter, once he had read beyond the rebuke in the first paragraph:

> 27, Mariner Drive,
> Kew,
> Surrey.
> 20th October 1958

Dear Eric,

So, what happened to you? One minute you were there, the next you'd gone. I had to spend some time with Joe's friends, especially old Bruno who'd bought *me* a present on *his* birthday! Do try to give Joe a chance, for my sake. He's very good to me.

Your friend Daniel made a complete fool of himself and I don't think it can be excused. Joe blames the woman he was with but that's too easy. Daniel virtually invited himself anyway so it was his duty to be reasonable. None of that was your fault, darling.

My first couple of weeks at King's College have been very hectic and I must admit that I'm a bit confused. There does seem to be a lot of disorganisation and my tutorial groups don't offer much. Anyway, I must give it all time to settle down.

How's the department of veterinary science? (Had to look that spelling up in the dictionary.) Have you started dissecting things yet? I don't like the thought of you messing about with dead things, I must say. Not that I've got any room to talk. All the writers I have to study are dead as well. What is disturbing me is the thought that English isn't a real academic subject at all, it seems to be all made up for the purpose. Not a discipline. I mean, if someone reads books and goes to plays, they should have a degree as much as someone who goes to university. I haven't discussed this with anyone yet but I might have to.

I know this is a long way off but Joe wants to take me to France at Christmas. We are going to stay with a friend who has bought a chateau and retired there. Joe would like you to come over, if you can, so he can get to know you better. If you have to spend Christmas with your family I'll understand but do try to come. It could be wonderful fun.

I'm always thinking about you.

love,

Pauline

When he had finished reading it he fervently kissed the paper. There was more than enough in it to console him. He was bewildered by the tone, shaken by the distance, but she had forgiven her darling, love had been mentioned, and she had confessed to thinking about him *always*: these were not crumbs of comfort but potent signs, declarations to be treasured and venerated. They made him feel happier than he had done since they had set off on their Grand Tour together.

He put the letter in the breast pocket of his shirt: a talisman of her enduring magic. It was only later when he read it again that he realised she was telling him to stay away from her till Christmas.

That night he went out drinking with Daniel. They got home past midnight, taking care not to wake Eric's mother. Daniel went to bed and Eric sat down in his room to write a letter in reply to Pauline's, his head teeming with all the advice which Daniel had given him during the evening. After a couple of attempts to make a start he was forced to abandon it: all the points which he had accepted from Daniel clashed with what he wanted to write.

Daniel had urged him to get tough with her, to be scathing about her life-style, her condescension, her assumptions, and to attack the grandfather who was engineering a split between her and her own generation. Daniel had outlined what was happening, drawing on new skills in psychology he had recently acquired from his reading and the experience of dealing with a girlfriend who suffered from the malignant effects of paternal autocracy.

"Rita's the way she is because of her father," he had confided over his sixth pint of bitter. "Even though he's dead she still has to confront him. That whole business at Kew was all her idea. She was challenging her own father's totemic authority."

"Pauline's father's been dead since the war!" Eric had protested.

"That can make things even worse. The grandfather figure has an extra dimension inasmuch as he represents ancestor authority *and* paternal authority when the father is absent. I'll give you a book to read."

"But she's not resisting him, she's going along with it, as far as I can see."

"Until you wake her up and show her what is happening! Tell her! Warn her! Say, look, you're going to be gobbled up. She's only eighteen, for God's sake, and those old buggers are going to make her into a plaything. She'll lose her youth. They'll destroy her. She'll be old before her time. . ."

Eric had interrupted the enthusiastic flow of Daniel's prophecies with the solemn, sentimental declaration that, to him, Pauline would never be old. Daniel had leapt on this, waving his arms around as if to frighten away a host of female demons.

"No wonder she's got you by the balls, you romantic old tosser! You should have fucked her when I told you to then all this wouldn't have happened. She would never have got interested in those plutocratic old farts if you'd done your stuff."

Eric had kept silent. To have told Daniel the truth at this point would have been tantamount to breaking the dam wall and allowing the mighty waters of popular contemporary psychology to inundate the conversation.

"Answer me this: whose behaviour is basically more youthful — Pauline's or Rita's?" Daniel had said slyly, stroking his upper lip and sitting back, his pint glass cradled to his chest, bottle-end spectacles picking up all the light in the dim corner of the noisy pub.

"You know it's Rita's," he had said smugly, "and I'll tell you something: she's twice Pauline's age. It's all in the mind, how you see yourself. If you see yourself as a failure then that's what you are. Go out and fight! Take that old bastard on! Drive him away from her. Conspire, cheat, assassinate if need be."

He had paused, his features alive with brotherly sympathy.

"Tell me something. This has been going on for a long time. Do you love her?"

Eric had nodded miserably and kept his eyes down. As soon as he had made the admission he had regretted it. He had felt Daniel's attitude shift with all the unrejectable impetus of a plate movement in the earth's crust.

"Then that's a different matter all together. With Rita and me it's completely physical. That's what we've agreed. But in your case . . . well, we're on serious ground. We have to be careful."

For the next two hours Daniel had given Eric the full benefit of his musings on love. In essence they boiled down to his original thesis that the experience was everything and the consequences nothing. Without this total commitment to it, love was not worth having. It had to be shit or bust.

Sitting in his room, Eric made a third attempt at the letter. Everything that had been implanted in his mind by Daniel in the pub was jettisoned. He wrote to her straight from his drunken heart:

> 46, Westbourne Street,
> Walton,
> Liverpool
> October 24th 1958

Dear Pauline,
            I received your letter today and you probably got one from me as well. I'm writing back immediately

because I can't keep anything but you in my head at the moment. Why I bother to go into the department, I don't know. I'm deaf to everything the lecturers are saying, and the whole place and the atmosphere seem very alien. From what you said in your letter about King's College you are probably feeling the same. Perhaps we should think the future out again? Some people do get married while they are at university and they make it work. The thought of being apart from you for the next three years at minimum is just not on.

I want us to be together now. If it means giving up university then I'm ready to do it, though it might be possible for me to transfer to the Royal College, London for next year. I could find a temporary job and we could get a flat somewhere. When I'm twenty-one I get some family money from my father's will which will help out. If studying to be a vet for five years is going to get in our way I'm quite happy to give it up and go into my family's business which is a ready-made job. We could live up here.

Think about all this. All that matters to me is being with you. I will do anything to make you happy.

I don't feel that it's a good idea for me to ring you up at your grandfather's house, so you'll have to ring me and let me know.

I love you.

Eric

The next morning he woke up with a hang-over. Lying in bed he read the letter through and was surprised to find that it accorded with what he wanted to say. There was nothing that he wished to change, or retract.

He had breakfast with Daniel who was free of any ill-effects from their night's drinking, then they went out together to catch the bus into university. On the way Eric slipped the letter into a pillar-box.

"Is that to Pauline?" Daniel said. "Hope you got it right."

"No, it's my ma's. She's writing off for a mail-order catalogue," Eric replied, quickening his step. "Come on, I'm going to be late."

18

The letter was waiting for Pauline when she returned from
college one day later in the week. Joe Nash had taken it up to
her room and placed it on her pillow, the address and postmark up.
It was his way of letting her know that he was aware that a
communication from Eric had taken place and they would need to
discuss it. Once she had read the letter she bolted the door. It was
her turn to cook dinner that night but she made no attempt to start
preparing it. At half-past eight Joe Nash knocked on her door.
When she opened it he was standing there with a tray.

"Room service," he said. "I thought an omelette aux herbes
might be in order."

He entered the room and put the tray down on her desk, his eyes
scanning it for the letter.

"You shouldn't have taken the trouble, Joe," Pauline said
nervously. "I'm not really hungry."

"Has that lout upset you again?"

"He's not a lout," she retorted.

Taking her by the shoulders Joe sat her down on the bed and
pulled up a chair to sit facing her.

"My darling, it was all on such a small scale up there. You knew
nothing. Both of you were only kids," he murmured. "You have to
put him in perspective. Everything has changed. You've left that
world."

Pauline groaned, "Not again!" rolled over and curled up on her
bed, turning her back on him. Joe Nash saw the letter crumpled up
in her hand and tugged a free corner.

"Let me read it," he begged.

"No!" she yelled fiercely, pulling her hand away. "It's private!"

"I thought you said that you were getting over him," he replied in the most reasonable tone he could muster from his own emotional tumult.

"I'm never going to get over him!" she raged back. "I don't want to get over him!"

"Well, that's a very different story from the one you've been telling me so far," he replied falteringly, his disappointment showing through. "Last time we spoke on the subject you said that there was no future in it."

"Then I've changed my mind, haven't I?"

Straightening herself out on the bed she lay like an effigy on a tomb, the letter clutched in her big hands, an emblem of her salvation. Joe Nash got up from the chair and stood over the tray of food he had prepared.

"May I ask what he has put in that letter which upsets you so much?"

"Something you wouldn't understand."

"Because I'm too old?"

"No, because you're too . . . everything."

He snorted softly, lifting an edge of the omelette with a knife and grimacing. Out of the corner of his eye he saw her looking at him. There was the ghost of his son in her defiance; eyes confused, pleading. It brought him up with a jolt and he hardened his heart against the memory.

"When you can talk sensibly I'd like to discuss the whole matter with you," he coldly chided her. "If you don't know your own mind it often helps to share a problem with someone else."

He lifted up the tray and headed for the door, his back as erect as a professional waiter's.

"I'm assuming that you don't want any of this," he said without looking over his shoulder.

"Oh, come back, Joe and stop playing games," Pauline sighed, getting off the bed and taking the tray. "We'll talk if you like. I suppose there's no one else I can go to except my Moral Tutor. Ha! A lot of use he'd be."

With a relief which he failed to disguise, Joe Nash turned from the door and sat in the chair again.

"Well, I'm all ears," he said with a grin.

She shook her head and pointed at him.

"No, you say what's on your mind first."

He thought for a while then made a gesture of humble oblation.

"I suppose I believe that there should be a certain equality in what people can offer each other. You have great beauty."

Pauline sighed and put the tray down on top of her study papers which were strewn all over the desk, then remained by his side for a moment, a hand on his shoulder, in a pose which was suggestive of an old family photograph.

"Did you love my gran?" she asked.

"Of course I did."

"Was she beautiful?"

"I thought she was," he replied, shifting his feet and watching his shoes move over the carpet.

"When you married her did you have any doubts?"

"No, I didn't."

"Did she have any?"

"Not that she mentioned to me."

Pauline walked away. Joe Nash watched her hips pass him by, the stateliness of her slow movement raising his blood.

"I don't believe you," she said with a flash of irritation. "No one can be that sure. Or were you both doing what your parents wanted?"

Joe Nash shook his head and put on a knowing smile.

"You won't catch me out, Pauline. I know what my feelings were."

"So, some marriages are made in Heaven?"

"No, the good ones are organised down here." He stood up, his eyes on her level. "If this boy really loves you he'll want your happiness. He knows that you come from a very different family background, talented people. Why not ask him to give you some time?"

Pauline laid her large hands, one on top of the other, over a stack of text-books. Joe Nash's eye followed the straight lines and corners of the volumes up until they ran into the deep swell where her solar plexus became her breasts. He hoped that she would stand there and continue talking to him until his heart flowed over.

"Could we have a bottle of wine?" Pauline asked.

"The very best, my darling," he replied.

He left the room and she heard him running down the stairs. In a few minutes he was back, slightly breathless, clutching an opened bottle from which he poured a dark, heavy wine.

"Can't beat Marsala. Kills the appetite dead. Forget dinner. Here's to The Temple of Concord!" he said, chinking his glass with hers. "I'll take you there one day."

"Where is that?"

"Agrigento, Sicily. When people get married in the local church they go to this old Greek temple afterwards and ask for —harmony? Peace? A settled way of life? Understanding? Whatever concord is, they know that they need it."

"What an old diplomat you are, Joe."

"If you had had to deal with someone like your mother at my level for all those years, you'd put a value on diplomacy too," he replied with a brash laugh, then froze into a mock-cringe. "Shouldn't I have said that?"

Pauline lolled back against the wall, the glass in her hand. "My mother proves that people shouldn't marry the people they love. It ruined her life. She never got over losing my father. Perhaps she should have married someone else, coldly, in an *organised* sort of way, and kept him as a dream. He became a dream, anyway, when he died," she said with a strange sneer. "You were all against her marriage to my father."

"That's true, I was."

"You wanted a nurse for him, not a wife."

"That's your mother talking."

"Even when you knew how much he loved my mother, you kept on telling him that she was unstable. That was very cruel."

Pauline looked at the letter in her hand and squeezed the ball of paper harder. Tears sprang into her eyes.

"Do you really think he's a lout?"

"I'm afraid I do."

"But I know that I love him."

He fought for control of his features, anxious that she should not witness the impact of this statement on him; but when he spoke it was not his voice that he heard but the cry of the wounded.

"That might have to change," he said. "For your own good, for your sanity's sake — and you must remember that you are your mother's daughter, and that your father was an epileptic — whoever becomes your husband must be a man who can look after you . . ." He hesitated, searching for words. "He must, well, be exceptional."

"Are you saying I'm abnormal?" Pauline demanded, her eyes wide.

"No, only abnormally beautiful," Joe Nash averred, his colour rising, "and whoever has you must deserve you."

Pauline took agitated sips at her wine, unable to meet his earnest eyes.

"I'm not epileptic. My mother had me tested," she said after a while.

"I know she did. It was my suggestion. But I also know that the tests are unreliable. They can tell you that you *are* definitely epileptic but not that you're not. It can develop later on in life."

"Eric's training to be a vet. He'll be able to look after me," she said bitterly. "Oh, this is nonsense, Joe. You're just making excuses. You don't like my boyfriend, that's all, admit it."

Joe Nash finished his wine at one draught and firmly put the glass down, squaring his shoulders and walking across the room so there would be enough distance for his declaration.

"In every family, in some generation, a child will be born with extraordinary qualities. Most of the time, because family life can be full of envy and oppression, that child will end up being smothered. That is what has been happening to you: your mother, that wretched con-man Leo, and this Eric fellow, have all crushed you. But you are my blood, Pauline. I won't stand by and see your qualities squandered. I want you to be nurtured, not get buried under a pile of nappies by the time you're twenty."

Pauline shrieked and threw the crumpled ball of paper at him.

"You read it!" she snarled. "You disgusting, interfering spy. You steamed it open. I hate you!"

Joe Nash had managed to catch the crumpled letter. He tossed it back to her and went to the door.

"I didn't have to, my darling," he said. "You're so transparent it hurts. And don't forget that I've been around. I know the signs of a second-rater on the make."

"He's not on the make. He could have any girl he wanted."

Joe Nash smiled, his poise completely recovered.

"That makes no difference when the only girl he wants is you. And do you know why? Because you're beyond his reach. Eric knows himself, and why he wants you. I could see it in his eyes."

"What d'you mean?" she cried, helplessly.

Joe went over to her bookshelf and took down a volume which had a slip of paper sticking out between the pages.

"You're the student of literature. See what you make of that with your adoring Eric in mind," he said, dropping the book on her pillow. "I marked the place for you. Being so old and inarticulate means I have to get help in my arguments from sources you might respect. Will you listen to Shakespeare?"

He left the room, closing the door behind him. She went across and bolted it, then returned to examine the book. Her grandfather had lightly pencilled a question-mark alongside the opening lines of sonnet fifty-seven:

Being your slave what should I doe but tend,
Upon the houres, and times of your desire?

The same evening Joe Nash waited for Pauline to come down to talk again but by ten o'clock she had not appeared. Going up to her room he knocked on the door and got no reply. Upon trying to open it he found that it was bolted. He knocked a second time but there was no response. Panic welled up in him and he began to hammer at the door and shout. When he paused there was only silence from the other side. In his mind he saw a repetition of Deidre's terrible act of self-destruction. Guilt overwhelmed him. Shoulder-charging the door he burst it open and stepped into the room, his heart beating frantically. The window was open. A length of blue rope hung over the sill, tied to a leg of the bed. Shaking with fear he stumbled over and thrust his head out, knowing what he would find.

The rope was neatly tied to a drain-pipe next to a clump of pampas-grass. He could see how the stalks were trampled where she had got down. Thanking God, delirious with relief, he ran to the telephone and rang Eric's number. Mrs Sherwin answered.

"Is Pauline there?" Joe asked tremulously.

"Pauline?"

"Yes, this is Joe Nash, Mrs Sherwin. I thought Pauline was coming up to see Eric."

"First I've heard of it. Eric's at the university. I don't think he's expecting her."

"If she turns up would you be so good as to let me know? I shall be in all day tomorrow."

"Maybe she wants to surprise him?" she suggested helpfully. "Eric will be pleased if she does come. He thinks the world of her, you know."

"That's very kind of you, Mrs Sherwin. You've got my number, haven't you?"

"Yes. Pauline will ring you if she arrives. Everything all right? Our Eric has been very locked into himself these last few days . . ."

"Thank you, Mrs Sherwin. You've been most kind."

He put the telephone down and returned to the window. The lawn was moonlit and webbed with moisture. He saw her footsteps crossing the lawn to the garden gate, and swore under his breath. Wandering around the city at night! The fool! Turning away from the window he searched the room for any note which she might have left. There was nothing.

He sat on her bed. On the floor beside it was the tray he had brought up to her earlier in the evening. She had eaten everything that had been on it and the bottle of wine had been emptied. As he ran his mind over what had been said and done he remembered the sonnet. That had been a sharply-plotted stratagem, one over which he had preened himself. He had made himself thoroughly miserable by reading the whole sequence through a few months before, noting down the numbers of those which touched upon his own experiences in love. In their darkness and groping sadness he had found an echo of the last years with his wife: their vitality had not passed him by, merely exercised his disbelief. When Pauline had moved into Kew he discovered the poems resurfacing in his thoughts, becoming new-formed islands in the sea of his polished pragmatism. With many sonnets he began to see what they were about, feeling his way through their coiled and complex passions. As he sat on her bed, looking at the dent which her head had made on the pillow, he was forced to remember his age; at seventy he had started to understand those poems, but the first use he had made of his new wisdom had been to employ a sonnet as a weapon.

He searched the room from top to bottom, but could not find the book of sonnets. Wherever she had gone, Pauline had taken his question-mark with her.

Drunk on Marsala, raging against her grandfather's emotional cupidity and meddling, Pauline had gone to the telephone box and rung the number written in felt-pen on the inside. A woman answered, said Greg was out, and told her to wait in the box. The 'phone rang a minute later, it was the Australian on the line. "Glad you're on," he said. "Nice to have a bit of real class with us for a change. Car's coming. Here's the registration number . . ." When it arrived the passenger door was opened and she got in. The driver was a young Arab with a moustache who was clearly nervous and anxious. He introduced himself as Feisal, then chattered excitedly about a course he was on as he drove to Kensington where he parked the car in an underground garage and took her up to a flat on the third floor of a block of apartments. The rooms were barely furnished but carpeted from wall to wall. Beside the double-bed was a table of drinks; at the foot of the bed a television-set. Suitcases lay open against the wall.

As the man got into bed beside her he was trembling like a dog. He clutched at her as if he were drowning. From the time he had picked her up she had not said a word, or been asked to do so. Beneath the bedclothes, in the darkness, the youth climbed on top of her, whimpering. She helped him all she could, but although the act was performed, she was as inviolable as bronze.

Afterwards, the Arab was very courteous. He gave her forty pounds, which was the price agreed with Greg, plus an extra five for herself, then he called Greg to send a car for her. When the driver arrived he demanded Greg's half of the money but Pauline gave him the whole forty-five pounds, with her best wishes, then asked to be taken to an underground station, where she caught a tube to Euston. When she arrived there it was eleven o'clock and the concourse was an infernal landscape peopled by beggars, vagrants, alcoholics, prostitutes and policemen. There were few travellers waiting at the big northern terminus; most of its denizens were

157

predatory but, unlike her, they had not made a strength out of their fateful weaknesses.

She bought a ticket and boarded the train which was dirty and smelt of its last load of passengers. Choosing the carriage next to the guard's van, she sat down in a compartment with two other women. Opening the book of sonnets, she began to read. As the train left Euston a wild group of boy-soldiers came roaring down the corridor.

Pauline raised her head and looked each one over, her book a fortress against them. They shouted and pointed, smacked their lips and banged their heads against the windows, but they were held. Not one tried to enter. They scuffled amongst themselves then, with lingering, infantile glances of lewdness at Pauline, crept away down the corridor.

She watched them go, unable to mask a superior, elated smile. For the first time since her mother's death she felt cleansed and secure. From now on she was indemnified against all her old self, the innocence and dependence gone. There was no pain she could not endure.

She was capable of anything.

19

The train got her into Oxenholme Station at three-thirty in the morning. There was no taxi waiting so she rang Leo and asked him to come and fetch her. He did not sound surprised to hear from her; when she queried his coolness about being woken up in the middle of the night he explained that Joe Nash had rung and told him about her disappearance, asking if she had been in touch.

"Since then I've just been lying here reading, waiting for your call," he said with a light laugh. "I'll be with you in about half-an-hour, if the car will start."

It was a clear night with a half-moon. From the station platform she could see the rim of the Lakeland fells. As she sat waiting, freight trains thundered up and down the line, shaking the platform. The air was cold but she did not notice it.

Returning to the telephone box she rang the house at Kew. Joe Nash answered immediately.

"That was quick," she said. "It hardly had time to ring."

"Where are you?"

"I'm not going to say. All I'm ringing for is to let you know that I'm safe."

"I have a right to know. I'm your legal guardian."

"Phooey."

"Pauline, I've been out of my mind with worry. Why did you run off like that?"

"I have some sorting out to do. When I've finished, I'll come back."

"How long will that be?"

"I'm not sure."

"A week? A month?"

"Not as long as that. Will you ring up my Moral Tutor and tell him that I'm ill, please? Say I've got 'flu, or something."

There was a dark pause at the other end of the telephone.

"I don't like telling lies, even for you."

"Phooey again."

Another freight train came down the line, roaring between the platforms at high speed.

"What the hell was that?" Joe Nash squawked.

"Oh, nothing," Pauline replied, "in my life it happens all the time. Good night, Grandad."

Laughing, she put the receiver down. Through the glass of the telephone box she had seen headlights approaching the station entrance. Leaving the box she went over towards the car. The lights were flashed and the passenger door opened. When she got inside she saw that Leo was wearing his dog-collar. This struck her as ludicrous and she giggled.

"What's so funny?" Leo asked calmly as he reversed the car round. "Are you drunk?"

"No, I'm not drunk."

"Why have you come like this, in the middle of the night?"

"Spur of the moment."

Leo thrust the gear-stick into first and accelerated, winding the engine up more than was needed, raising his voice above the noise.

"I had the impression that I had become *persona non grata* as far as you were concerned."

"That's something I hadn't thought about, to be honest," she replied, countering his annoyance with blandness. "Have you been well?"

"Very well. And you?"

"I'm just fine."

"But a bit tired," he said with practised gentleness. "Just relax now and we'll talk tomorrow."

She obediently lapsed into silence. As he drove along the twisting road to Kirkby Lonsdale he stole glances at her profile, hoping to catch an expression which might give him a clue about the reason for her visit. There was nothing: her eye was dry, her mouth was firm, her chin was raised, her arms were folded under her bosom as a woman does when she waits.

"Is there anything you'd like to tell me that I can be thinking about?" he said after a while.

Turning away from him she crossed her legs to get more comfortable and rested her forehead on the cold glass of the window. He looked at her for a fraction too long, nearly running into a bank on a bend.

"Sorry about that," he muttered. "My night-vision isn't all that good."

"There is something I'd like to say, Leo," she said with a sigh, then, mischievously, "just in case you kill us both with your bad driving."

"And what can that be, I wonder?"

"You were wrong."

Seeing a farm-track turning ahead of him he drove the car off the road and bumped a few yards up the ruts, turned off the lights and engine and sat back, staring out of the windscreen at the half-moon.

"That will need explaining," he said frigidly.

"You did ask. Can't we go and have a cup of tea in the kitchen and talk rather than sitting out here?"

"Wrong about what?" he demanded vexedly. "You create this silly drama then have the cheek to say I'm wrong. Wrong? You're being absurd."

A car came along the road and caught them in its headlights. They turned and watched through the back window as it slowed down then turned into the same farm-track they had parked along, and stopped. A door slammed and a figure came towards them shining a torch. When it reached the driver's door they saw a hand rapping on the window.

"Oh, God," Leo breathed, "it's the police."

He wound down the window and the torch was flashed over their faces.

"Hello, Mr Midgely. Everything all right?" said a man's voice in a strong Westmorland accent.

"My car started losing power so I thought I'd better pull off the road," Leo said glibly, opening the door and getting out. "I'd just been to pick Miss Nash up from Oxenholme Station."

"Have you been here long, then?"

"No, it only happened a minute ago."

"What train comes in at this time of night?" the policeman said with a hint of doubt. "I didn't know they came in this late."

"Then perhaps you'd better read the timetable," Pauline retorted acerbically. "It's the midnight train from Euston."

"All right, all right, young lady. We can't know everything like you students," the policeman replied. "If I was a young woman I wouldn't travel overnight, alone. But then I'm old-fashioned."

Leo broke the interchange by starting the engine of his car. The lights flared up on the hedges ahead and the policeman wandered down to the front of the car, putting his hand on the bonnet.

"Well, whatever it was seems to have cured itself. I hope we haven't upset you, Reverend. Only doing our rounds. We were on the look-out for sheep-rustlers, which is what we thought you might have been, parked here like this. A natural enough mistake, I think you'll agree."

The policeman walked back to his car and reversed out of the track and back on to the road. Once he had gone, Leo followed suit. As he drove off towards Kirkby Lonsdale he saw the police car come up behind him. The headlights glared into his rear-view driving mirror all the way to his house.

"No secrets in the country," Pauline said as Leo cut the engine and watched the police car drive off into the night. "By lunch-time everyone round here will think we're having an *affaire*. What will the Bishop of Carlisle say?"

Leo slammed his door shut, glaring at her over the curved, moonlit roof of the car.

"I'm not sure I like this new Pauline," he said darkly.

"Pity," she snapped in return, "because this is the one you've got and the other imbecile isn't coming back."

Pauline found unpicking her old theology in front of its creator a laborious but liberating task. He offered no arguments because her nihilism permitted no refutation. She was, she said, much happier believing in nothing because it accorded with her resolution about her accursed beauty, which was nothing also, thus providing her with some integrity, at least. And wasn't integrity the only quality of value in anyone's life? Oneness? Body and spirit? The unity of these lay in nothing.

Leo stemmed the flow of her heresy at this moment, pulling out his cuffs like a man who is entering a banquet-hall full of notables.

"Do I detect a bit of Buddha here?" he said, giving her a keen, intellectual look. "What kind of company have you been keeping down in London?"

"I hope Buddha didn't go through what I've gone through working it out. If he did, I don't trust a thing he says because he must be as unreliable as I am."

Leo smiled, glad to have established the required distance between the girl and her problems. She had created an objective sense which would be useful. Also he had to admit that the tragedy of Deidre's death and the tautening power of grief had only accentuated her beauty. What she had described as nothing had increased. She had grown closer to the completion of her loveliness, bringing all the promise of her girlhood to fruition. Pauline was the creation of his best years when he had been able to see into the nature of the sensual universe and God's genius.

"From this *nothing*, these ashes, you will rise," he assured her. "This was all necessary."

"Do you know what I've done?" Pauline asked him, using the unspoken answer as a threat.

"It doesn't matter what you've done," he replied smoothly. "It's what you are that matters. You are alert to the world. It is a reality to you, not a routine or a chore. Every experience you have will be vital. My dear girl, you are only at the beginning. Now, isn't it time you went to bed?"

She made no protest but followed him up the stairs to the attic. When they lay side by side in the bed she looked up through the dormer window and saw the half-moon shining down on them.

"It's good to know that you still trust me," he said quietly. "When I think of all the times we have lain here and talked; how long must it be? Ten years, at least. You were just a little girl when you first came. Do you remember? You'd run away from home. Deidre had frightened you. Can't recall exactly what she'd done that time. There were so many . . . fracas . . ."

His voice tailed away. Pauline stole a glance at him to see if he had

163

gone to sleep but his eyes were open and he was smiling, gazing up at the October moon.

"You know, I do believe it was being able to come here that saved you. If you hadn't had me to run to, Deidre would have destroyed you. I'm not speaking ill of the dead. I was Deidre's best friend, as you know. She knew herself, anyway. Why do you think she tolerated the situation? If it hadn't been me who offered you refuge it would have been someone else, some social worker or the police."

He left a long silence which she recognised as her cue. Over the years this had been the pattern of their discourse. She would arrive, exhausted and upset. He would calm her down by talking, lying beside her, releasing all his thoughts and ruminations, letting the language flow softly over her. After the shouting and screaming of her mother this mellifluous stream of words had been soothing, acting as a lullaby, putting her to sleep. As the years went by she had started to listen, then to get involved. By the time she had reached pubescence she was responding. When she had been too fatigued and anxious, or the subject he had chosen (or his approach to it) was slow to stimulate her mind, he had left these long pauses pregnant with encouragement for her to make her contribution.

"Nothing to say?"

The phrase was like a bell in her brain. It repeated her own crude, come-lately credo, but with separate sense. Even juvenile nihilism had its origins in a line of Leo's. She lay and wondered whether there was any thought she might have which would be truly her own.

"This is all to do with Eric, I suppose?" Leo said when it was plain that she was not going to speak.

She nodded, knowing that his eyes were on her.

"You will always love each other."

"Why?"

He gave a little grimace of satisfaction at having succeeded in making her say something.

"Oh, Pauline, how many times have we discussed this? You should feel privileged. How can one get closer to the eternal love of God than to love someone absolutely?"

"But why does it have to be Eric?" she said exasperatedly. "Why shouldn't it be . . . anyone . . . an Arab?"

Leo chuckled and put his hands behind his head, tensing his lean muscles.

"From the beginning it was Eric. For him it was always you. He will always love you. It is magnificent."

"Well, it doesn't feel magnificent," she replied sourly. "It's making both of us unhappy."

"Then try to break it. Don't see him. Tell him you don't love him."

He paused but this time she knew that it was not an opening which he had left for her. There was more to come.

"But I bet you end up going back to him," he added smugly.

"That's cruel."

"Cruel?" Leo laughed as he echoed her accusation. Raising his knees he gripped them, staring up through the dormer window at the stars. "You don't know the meaning of the word."

"And you do, of course."

"Yes, I do. One day you might understand."

"What's the matter with now? We don't seem to have anything better to do," she countered sarcastically, then, with a sudden surge of anger said: "This all seems so obsolete to me now. I shouldn't have come. What the hell am I doing here?"

"Pauline, this has been your home," Leo said reprovingly. "You lived here, virtually. When you needed comfort, some kind of security, someone to talk to, you came here."

"Only because there was nowhere else to go," she replied, "and you had a use for me."

Leo was silent. She could sense his fury at the accuracy of her rejoinder.

"That's not fair," he said finally, his voice filled with bitterness. "I never exploited you."

"You took a lot of risks with me, Leo."

"I never touched you."

"You're a homosexual so why should you?"

Leo released a long, shuddering sigh, turning his back on her.

"I didn't say that to hurt you," she whispered after a while. "I just think you ought to face up to it."

"I'm not a homosexual," he said hollowly. "I wish I was. Life would be a lot easier."

"Then what are you?"

165

"Nothing. That's why I can't bear to have you believing in such a thing. Nothing is emptiness. I'd rather have a life full of agony than a vacuum. Physical love is a stage I cannot make. Once, I nearly did cross the barrier."

"With a girl?"

"Yes, but I failed. There was always this great space between us and my body seemed to be indifferent. At the time I thought this was a sign of my spirituality, a kind of numbness which religious people suffer. It will break down, I told myself, and I will feel desire. But it didn't and the numbness remained which I chose, in retrospect, to identify with the love of God."

"What happened to the girl?"

"She got bored waiting. With her beauty there was no lack of admirers and off she went. I felt a complete fool, quite unmanned, but as far as she was concerned I'd rejected her."

Pauline laughed softly and put her hands behind her head.

"And you never tried again?"

"Never. I knew I couldn't respond."

"A clever prostitute would have made you. Didn't you ever think of going to one?"

Leo got up off the bed and walked to the far wall holding his head.

"Who is this I'm talking to?" he moaned. "What's happened to you?"

"I've woken up, Leo. And don't think I've swallowed that story wholesale. You've been playing a game with Eric and me . . ."

"It is not a game!" Leo hissed.

"That's what it feels like now."

He came back to the bed and sat on the edge of it, staring at her, his eyes so wide that she could see broad scimitars of moonlight across them.

"You must never accuse me of that again!" he said passionately. "Anything else I can take, but not that, not from you. I have loved and cherished you, in many ways I have saved you, I believe. Can you imagine what your life would have been like if I hadn't taken an interest in you?"

"You got something out of it," Pauline protested, unable to stop herself cringing like a child in the face of his wrath.

"Yes, I did! I got the satisfaction of seeing you survive! No one understood you better than I did. Are you telling me that when Eric came along you didn't *need* him?"

"Only because you'd been playing about for so long," she insisted. "I didn't know what to think."

He stiffened, drawing away from her in disbelief.

"What are you trying to say?" he asked incredulously.

"You know very well what I'm saying"

"No, no . . ." he groaned, shaking his head. "You never wanted me. I would have known."

"Of course I did. Before Eric came along who else was there for me? All the boys I knew couldn't compete with you. I couldn't spend any time with them, be in a bedroom with them. . . What did you expect? Sex is very simple, really."

Leo bowed his head and pondered. She could see that he was half-pleased with her admission that she had found him attractive but the looming blame contingent upon it had to be avoided. When he looked up and smiled at her she knew that it meant he was busy in his mind shedding all responsibility for what had happened.

He wagged his finger at her.

"No, no, Pauline. I'm not falling for that," he chided her with an attempt at fun. "With you it has always been Eric, purely Eric, your natural mate. I believe in that: one phase of eternal life in love which takes place in this world. Paradise is only an extension of it."

"Then Paradise is a place of suffering," she said. "And if I'm in it I want to get out of it."

"Of course Paradise is a place of suffering. I thought we'd always agreed on that. But through suffering we find God's will, and our destinies. Now get some sleep. You must be very tired."

Within a few minutes he was asleep. Pauline lay seething beside him, her mind unable to come to rest. She had felt repelled before but never with the revulsion which she now had. To abandon her malformed, perverse past was essential, she decided. Once it had gone and Leo's influence had been exorcised, she would find the means to live a normal life.

When she heard Leo's breathing deepen and knew, from experience, that he was asleep, she got off the bed and crept out of the room.

In the morning he found her curled up on the sofa in the living-room. He brought her a cup of tea and put it beside her, ruffling her hair with what he considered to be a mild, forgiving rebuke.

To her it was the touch of the enemy, but she still had a favour to ask of him.

"Leo, I've decided to do something which will hurt Eric very much, but I have to go through with it. I want to write to you now and again so you can pass on certain information to him which would best come from you," she said, staring up at him from the sofa. "Will you do that for me, and not ask any questions?"

"Another man?" Leo asked, smiling. "You can handle that."

"As I said — without asking questions?" she retorted severely. "Do listen when I talk to you."

He nodded meekly but there was amusement in his eyes.

20

Eric received letters regularly from Pauline over the next eight weeks, but no 'phone calls. She wrote about all sorts of topics with warmth and humour, replied to his questions with interest but distance. By the middle of December he knew that their future depended upon how he would conduct himself in France over Christmas. It was a test which Joe Nash had set him. If he could come up to the mark and behave properly in that kind of company, Joe Nash would remove, or at least reduce, his opposition to their relationship.

He had waited patiently for two months, losing himself in his work when it became obvious that his proposal of marriage had been absorbed without producing an answer. Pauline managed to convey to him that she had received and understood the letter without replying to his specific questions. His transfer to the Royal College, the idea of the flat they would share, all these were left in abeyance as if they were suggestions which had been fed into a cloud.

It was fortunate for him that his own anxieties became overshadowed by a crisis in the life of Daniel Fleck who had discovered his mistake in selecting geology as his degree course at the same time as he had fallen in love with another married woman, Hennie, a Dutch post-graduate student in suffragette history. After weeks of frenzied adultery he had discovered that Hennie was a sadist whose chief pleasure was not sex but torturing him with accounts of her other love-affairs, past and present. Totally enslaved by now, with his university career on the verge of dissolution, Daniel flew into the arms of the dark angel administering mental breakdowns. The collapse was sudden and severe. Before all others — psychiatrist, mother, father, the Dutch demon herself — he turned to Eric for help. With only time and waiting as his own problems, Eric could not deny his friend the full support which he needed. When he witnessed the terrible pain that Daniel was in, and the cause, he was not inclined to press his own passions to the furthest limits in case he became similarly afflicted. When Daniel was put into a mental hospital and subjected to electro-convulsive therapy and a course of heavy sedation, and all for love, Eric shrank from the power which was as active in his own life as that of the patient he went to visit. On one such occasion he met the Dutch paramour; a slight, wispy woman with small, dark eyes and a sallow complexion. As they sat by Daniel's bedside together Eric could not keep his eyes off her, marvelling that such an insignificant and drab creature could have attained such sway over Daniel's intelligence. But when the patient was discharged and sent back to live his life, he immediately went to the university authorities and managed to persuade them to allow him to change his course to his first love — Clio, the muse of History, who now looked suspiciously like a post-graduate student from the Netherlands.

When Leo turned up at Eric's home one Friday evening in mid-December, both Eric and Daniel were out at an end-of-term party. Eric's mother immediately recognised him and was embarrassed, knowing that he would be able to remember the time during the war when she had fallen by the wayside. Leo skilfully avoided the past during their conversation as they waited for Eric to return, concentrating on Mrs Sherwin's other son, John, and his prospects, as well as praising Eric.

"I had to come to Liverpool on business," he told her. "Since Eric disappeared from view a few months ago I must confess that I've missed him. He's such a challenging companion. Always kept me on my toes. You know that I gave him extra lessons in Latin, which he passed, I'm pleased to say?"

Lily Sherwin looked at him cautiously. It was difficult to believe that anyone could age as little as he had. Her memory of him went back nearly twenty years, over a time in a man's middle life when his surfaces change. Those years had not touched the Reverend Midgely's exterior image and, from his speech, she could not detect any alteration within.

She still did not quite trust him. Her opinion was rooted in that of all the parishioners at Mansergh long ago: the man with his long, lean, quizzical presence was not a comforter.

"Eric will be late," she explained. "You know these student parties. They can go on all night."

"It would be such a pity to miss him," Leo said, re-crossing his legs with great care. "Do you know if he has kept up with the javelin?"

"The what?"

"I trained him to throw the javelin. He was quite good. When he came down here he promised me that he'd keep it up."

"I don't know anything about that," Lily answered with a hint of chagrin. "Our Eric doesn't tell me much that he doesn't have to."

Leo looked at his watch. It was nine o'clock.

"You're right, Mrs Sherwin. Waiting would be pointless. You wouldn't know where this party is being held, would you? If it's the usual student thing they're not going to mind me dropping in, as long as I bring a bottle, of course."

She did know the venue. It was Hennie's flat in Hope Street. Daniel did not spend much time with the Sherwin family these days and was virtually living with the Dutch woman, in spite of all the misery she had caused him. Thinking it could do no harm for the clergyman to call round — perhaps it might even be enjoyably mischievous in a light-hearted way to send a churchman to such a gathering — she provided him with the address and when he said that he would rather leave his car parked outside and, in case he got lost, go in by taxi, she called one for him.

The flat was on the ground floor of a large Victorian house. When the door was answered Leo found himself looking down at a child, a boy of about ten with blonde hair in a basin-cut. It was not until Leo got into the light of the hall and the boy turned from shutting the door that Leo could see that he was mongoloid.

"*Hierheen*," the boy said and went down the passage, his gait wide-elbowed like a wrestler's.

"*Dankie*," Leo replied, but the child did not turn to acknowledge the use of his own language. When they reached a door covered by a curtain on a rail, he dragged it back and opened the door, holding up his hand to show Leo the way through.

There were no more than ten people in the high-ceilinged room, all sitting or squatting. They turned and looked at Leo, reacting to the sight of his clerical collar with bemusement. Leo took the mongoloid boy by the hand and bent down to whisper in his ear:

"*Ek is onbekend hier.*"

"*Kan u Afrikaans prat?*" a woman said, rising from a chair.

"*So'n bietjie,*" Leo replied.

"My son lives in South Africa with his father most of the year," the woman said, stroking the boy's head. "Are you sure you're in the right place? Jan brings anyone in he can find."

Leo smiled, watching the woman's sharp eyes as she examined him.

"I'm looking for a friend of mine, Eric Sherwin," he explained. "I hope you don't mind me dropping in like this?"

"Not at all," she replied, showing her teeth in a curious grin. "I didn't know Eric had a friend who was a pastor."

"He is probably ashamed to admit it. But I have brought a bottle, which proves I can't be all that bad."

Hennie took the bottle off him and poured a glass of white which was open. As Leo was sitting down to talk to her the door opened and Eric arrived with Daniel carrying bottles and cans. In these first moments he did not notice Leo who was thus able to fleetingly study him without the inevitable shrouding of character which would follow the discovery of his presence.

Eric had a waxen, unwashed pallor in the yellow-shaded room lights. His hair was long and lifeless, hanging down to his collar. As he entered the room there was no response to the action in his eyes as if all places were the same to him. There was jocularity from the other guests to greet the fresh supplies of drink but it did not raise an answering smile from Eric. It was only when he almost tripped over the long, black-trousered legs of Leo who had thrust them out from his seat on the sofa that he recognised the stranger. Then there was life in his face as he recoiled.

"What are you doing here?" he demanded, unable to suppress the hostility he felt.

"I called round to see you while I was in Liverpool on business. Your mother kindly told me where you had gone. Aren't you glad to see me?"

Eric had enough poise left to adjust his reactions. Everyone else in the room was observing the confrontation and Leo's hand was out to be shaken. Taking it, Eric made the handclasp longer than usual, giving himself time to control the turmoil Leo's apparition had caused.

"Sorry, Leo," he said, "I couldn't believe it was you. Not here. You gave me a shock."

"Well, it was meant to be a surprise. How are you, my dear friend? Working hard?"

Eric sat down next to him but immediately got up again to get himself a drink. When he returned, the mongoloid boy was on Leo's lap and they were conversing in Afrikaans. Eric did not interrupt but sat listening, determined that Leo should not see how afraid he was. He had a sense of something being very wrong. Leo was here for a reason; a reason as tangled as a thorn. When the boy got off Leo's lap and wandered off, Eric put his glass on the carpet and sat with his hands together refusing to make small talk, making his act of waiting obvious.

"Is there another room we could go to?" Leo said after a while.

"Why?"

"I'd rather we were in private."

"I'll be all right. It doesn't matter what it is, I won't disgrace you."

"To be honest, Eric, you do look as though you've been under a strain," Leo said concernedly, "and what I have to tell you is quite a shock."

Eric got up and walked out of the room. When Leo followed him out into the passage he found him already putting on his coat.

"Let's go out into the street if you're so scared of what I might do!" he said vehemently. "Fucking hell, Leo, I'd hoped never to see you again as long as I lived!"

"Later on you might explain why, but, putting that aside for the moment, let's go out, if that's what you want to do."

Eric was already in the hall, opening the door. Leo hurried to catch up with him and they walked off into the night. It was the far end of Hope Street before Leo could keep alongside him long enough to talk.

"Would you slow down?" he asked. "You're making me quite breathless."

"Give me the good news," Eric said, quickening his pace even more.

Leo stopped on the pavement. The street was deserted and it was starting to rain. Up the hill he could see the lights of the Anglican cathedral; the thought of its great, rosy, twentieth-century pomposity up there in the darkness filled him with bile. For Eric to be cleansed, cruelty was necessary. He called out his message and was satisfied to see his quarry stop and turn.

"What did you say?" the boy yelled.

"Pauline has got married!" Leo repeated, his voice carrying down the canyon of the glistening street. "She sent me a letter from Cannes. D'you want to see it?"

Leo's hand went to his inside pocket but there was no need for proof. From the note of Eric's cry he knew that the dart was home and the wound, eternal.

They did not go back to rejoin the party but returned to Eric's home instead. His initial reaction had been a stunned, silent misery which persisted for all the time it took to find a taxi and ride back to Westbourne Street. Leo was forced to treat him as a farmer does a bullock, leading, nudging and guiding the animal because it doesn't know where it should be. When he attempted to comfort him it produced no response; words and gestures were repelled by the sheer density of unhappiness.

When they arrived back at the house they found that Eric's mother had gone to bed. After they had had a coffee in silence in the kitchen Leo said that he had better start driving back, which prompted Eric to speak for the first time since he had been given the news.

"Do you have to go?" he said dully.

"I have a service at seven-thirty."

"Couldn't someone do it for you?"

"I'm afraid not," Leo replied. "Don't you want to be left on your own?"

Eric blinked as if he were waking up. When he looked at Leo there were tears in his eyes.

"Why did she do this to me?" he said numbly. "I've never harmed her."

"We should have a long talk about it but I don't think now's the time."

"Do you know who she's married?"

"I don't know him personally but I have some information," Leo affirmed. "Look, Eric, why don't you come back with me now and spend a couple of days getting over this? It'll do you good. Has the university gone down yet?"

"Yes, but I'm not sure that I could stand being up there with everything that's happened."

"Better to face it there than here. It's not all bad news, I assure you."

"What d'you mean?" Eric blurted out, suddenly animated. "Is there something you haven't told me?"

Leo smiled and washed up their cups, speaking to Eric without looking at him.

"It will take all your powers of understanding but, in the long run, I know you'll win. Come up with me and we'll sort it out."

Eric tried to write a note to leave for his mother but he found that he could not make the simplest sense so he abandoned it in favour of a telephone call he could make later. Only minutes afterwards he was in Leo's car, heading north.

Leo fed him the information piecemeal: some in the car, some the following morning after he had returned from celebrating Holy Communion, and some in the afternoon when Eric accompanied him on a pastoral visit to an old people's home on the coast at Arnside where four ex-parishioners of Kirkby Lonsdale had ended up. The tide was in and the estuaries of the Rivers Kent, Bela and Gilpin were flooded, branching the sunlight out over the dykes and sea-meadows. While Leo did his duties at the home, Eric walked along the rocky path towards Blackstone Point and the wider bay, his head running with ideas. He was still confused and hurt but Leo had nursed him back to a more positive attitude, explaining Pauline's motives and how they had arisen from her peculiar history. As he skirted the sea and the silent fishers for flukes who stood gazing out to the distant Cumbrian mountains he struggled to think his way constructively through the calamitous change which had taken place.

According to Leo, she had married a man whom she did not love; his name was Bruno Wegelius, an international financier who was the son of a Swiss friend of Pauline's grandfather. Wegelius was about forty, had been married once before but his wife had died in a 'plane crash. He had met Pauline in London shortly after Deidre's death. His proposal had come out of the blue but, in Leo's opinion, it had been prompted by Joe Nash's anxiety about Eric's pressure on Pauline to marry him. She had caved in, guilt-ridden about her mother, unhappy at university, unable to cope with being so much apart from her lover, and assigned herself to another life; a life which appeared to fulfil all her mother's wishes for her, mad though they might have been, and allow her to be at peace. But this life, Leo argued, was a superimposition which lay over her true existence like gold leaf on a piece of hewn stone. It was not reality but a glittering show, a livable mirage of wealth behind which she could shield herself.

Eric followed the reasoning but balked at the answer to his question as to what he should do next. Leo had advised him to continue loving her (as if he could help it), and to follow wherever she went.

"It may take years," he had said, "but she will always be yours at heart. I know it. This marriage is no more than a place to hide."

A flight of gulls swept along the edge of the grey water, searching for the same prey as the fishermen. Further up the neck of the bay a diesel train slid across the long railway bridge, its motion smooth as an oiled bolt. Behind it the fells were darkening, the firm line of the tops undulating as randomly as the worm-casts on the uncovered sand, curves within chaos.

The only certainty he saw was man-made. If he was on that train it would connect with another train, to another train, and so on until he was where she was. Wherever she had gone he had the power to find her. From the stem of the branching estuaries he took a truth: without her he was *nothing*.

He strode back along the limestone which had been worn smooth by the feet of aged men and women from the many retirement homes taking their daily promenades. Some of them were out looking at the high tide and the sunset. They stepped aside to let him pass, whispering about his lack of manners, but he was a train going over a bridge, thoughtless except for his decision to get to the country on the other side.

21

Eric heard nothing more from Pauline about Christmas and the invitation to go to France. When he asked Leo if he knew where she was living now she was married he told him that it was impossible to find out because Wegelius had many houses in different countries but at some time, so Leo guessed, Pauline would settle down in one of them; that could be in France, Mexico, the United States, Switzerland or England. When that happened Leo would find out and pass the location on to Eric. He suggested that there should be no attempt to discover Pauline's whereabouts from Joe Nash who would be sure to be hostile to any protraction of Eric's interest now Pauline was safely married.

"As far as he is concerned, you're over and done with, I'm afraid," Leo had said as they drove back to Kirkby Lonsdale from Arnside. "The old boy has never really approved any part of your relationship; and that's probably because Pauline never told him the truth about what it meant to her."

It was this behaviour of hers that troubled him all that Christmas: she had put him in a compartment in her life, a place where he ruled completely but which had no links with the normal world. After the collapse of his plans to go to France he had accepted an invitation to take his brother and mother to Daniel Fleck's home in Yorkshire for Christmas. It was a good house to be in, full of hard-drinking Poles and sturdy, sceptical mining-folk, all determined to enjoy themselves through the length of a cold, rainy week. They made a fuss of his mother and spoilt his brother but he was left to his joint devices with Daniel whom they treated with some delicacy because he had had a breakdown. Two satellites, they orbited the festive world, able to mock it, or reflect it, and this was the position they preferred while they both made plans to recover their dignity: for the Dutch post-graduate had ended her affair with Daniel and put him in the same position as Eric, smarting with rejection. But whereas Eric intended to fight back and remedy the situation, Daniel had given up.

"I don't think it's worth your while," he advised Eric one night as they were walking back from a pub on the top of a hill. "Write her off to experience. Carry the scars, find someone else."

"I don't want anyone else."

"You will if you get rid of her," Daniel assured him. "You'll get involved with another woman in three months, given the chance. Though why anyone should want to bother I don't know. I can't imagine going through all that again. For what? I'm sure procreation wasn't intended to be such a melodrama. Perhaps that's the real difference between human beings and other animals? A propensity to painful complication which produces emotional agitation which creates intellectual stimulation which brings about civilisation. How about that for an idea? The meaning behind human history can be divined from coital conflicts. Politics is the problems of inter-party and international coitus, try studying foreign policy, rapprochements, détentes, French, you see, language of love . . . Hey, are you listening?"

Eric nodded.

"Then why aren't you laughing?"

"Because I'M FED UP!"

Eric's bellow rang out over the hill. In the valley the colliery lights snaked over the vast, rambling structures around the pit-head and they could see the sheave-wheels turning as the afternoon shift came up at ten-thirty.

"You've got no right to be miserable," Daniel said after a few steps to recover his composure. "I have. It's me who should be doing the shouting. I've been through hell. My woman's left me, the sadist. She poisoned my existence for six months, drank my life's blood then ran back to her husband in fascist South Africa. But you wouldn't care about politics, would you? Not you and Pauline. You couldn't care less what's happening in the rest of the universe. Perhaps both of you weren't actually born into this life at all but emerged into some philosophical bubble of your own, the divine twins of gender, Adam and fucking Eve!"

178

It was the first time that Eric had ever hit his friend. It was a hard blow to the side of his head and it sent Daniel reeling into a hawthorn bush at the side of the road. Before he had time to extricate himself Eric had run off down the hill. When they met up again in the big kitchen at the house Daniel sat at the other end of the table to Eric and stared gloomily down at his friend through his misted-up spectacles. His grandmother, a small, stout woman with a fuzz of white hair in a net, was baking, preparing dough to rise overnight.

"Eric clouted me just now, Gran," Daniel said, "it didn't half hurt. And it was all for nothing."

"Somebody should have done that to you years ago," she replied with a sniff, her tiny hands kneading the dough with increased energy. "It might have made a man out of you."

For want of anything better to do while he waited for Leo to come up with Pauline's whereabouts, Eric went back to university in the middle of January and worked hard. During this time he made a couple of visits to Kirkby Lonsdale and kept in touch with Leo by telephone. As spring approached, Leo began to eke out news of Pauline's movements around the globe: confirming his claim to have special knowledge, one week she would be in California, another in Hong Kong. While he did this he encouraged Eric to be active in his studies and also to take up the javelin again to keep himself interested in things other than Pauline. Eric's response was automatic: as Leo had the life-line then his advice was sacred. He drove himself to keep up and even exceed his work schedules at the veterinary department, and joined the athletics club. Three days each week he went down to train at the gymnasium and he signed on for special javelin coaching over and above that which Leo continued to give him on the occasions when they were together. At the same time, he moved out of his family home and took a flat with Daniel in the Everton valley. At the back of his mind was the moment when he would have to tell his mother that he was abandoning his degree course and any hopes of becoming a vet and he knew that this would upset her. Although he had not told his mother about Pauline's marriage he knew she had guessed that there had been a great disappointment in his life connected with this girl whom she had never actually met. When he gave everything up to be with this mystery it would be much more difficult if his mother knew the true cause.

As and when Leo fed the treasured information about Pauline to him, Eric found himself sharing it with Daniel. There was no one else who could understand. Daniel's indignation at the extent of his friend's commitment to a woman unworthy of him was therefore fuelled at regular intervals and he did not hesitate to criticise what Eric was doing to himself. As the picture of Pauline's life-style was assiduously filled in by Leo, Daniel responded to it from within his flourishing political consciousness. She became an inflatable symbol of everything he was coming to detest. But the more he railed against her, the more Eric descended into subjugation at her feet. As Daniel hurled his invective against international capitalism and the betrayal of the masses, Eric sank deeper into his own form of slavery. This provoked many arguments but they were tireless in pursuit of their points: the one for the general truth, the other for the solitary illumination which comes from particular feeling. Day after day, night after night, they toiled through their disputes, addicted to the excitement of the clash between these forces. But as Daniel persisted in his campaign and he was faced by the resolute determination of his friend to give up everything for this one woman, he began to admire the nobility of the enterprise. This did not mean that he surrendered his right to disapprove and censure the woman and the system which she had espoused, but it did mean that he treated Eric with more compassion as one might a man who has been unjustly condemned to lose all his goods and life for an act of insane charity.

At the end of the spring term a pattern had emerged in Pauline's wanderings between the great cities of the world but Leo had not yet been able to provide an address where she could be said to live. Eric was thwarted and his frustration was increased rather than decreased by the success which he had begun to achieve in his studies. The improving quality of his work seemed to imply a future triumph for him whereas he knew that it was fated not to be so. When his mother enquired how he was getting on at the university he was forced to scale down the level of his achievements in order to reduce the shock she would inevitably receive when he relinquished his place at the veterinary department. But he could not do without the work. It was holding him together. The more he burrowed into his books the less the horror of losing Pauline haunted him. Moreover, it gave him the impression that his intelligence was such that he would eventually be able to outwit Wegelius and get her back.

It was the figure of Wegelius in his imagination which gave him nightmares. Under Daniel's constant assault on the financier's character — all surmise though it was, and culled from the man's occupation rather than any precise knowledge of the subject — he began to see him as a cartoon, someone who was all function with no living face. This disturbed him because his memory of Pauline was so strong and absolute that the caricature of her husband disintegrated whenever he thought about him. Wegelius had to be real because she had made him so.

After the first week of the spring vacation Daniel rang him from London. It was mid-afternoon and Eric had been in his room doing his daily system of exercises which the athletics coach had devised for him. When the telephone rang he ran down the stairs and picked it up, still panting.

"You been wanking again, Sherwin?" came the familiar voice. "I thought I'd warned you against all forms of self-delusion."

Eric wiped his face with his singlet and smiled. He had to admit that he had found the last week difficult with not having Daniel around.

"What else is there to do?" he said. "There has to be something else in my life other than anthrax."

"Well, I can give you something to keep your mind occupied," Daniel replied ominously. "I've found something out about Wegelius"

Eric's heart speeded up again half-way in its descent to a more restful rhythm.

"Don't you want to know what it is?" Daniel said irritably from the other end of the line. "I've done a lot of research work in Companies House on this."

"What have you found out?" Eric managed to say.

"He peddles military equipment. The bastard's an arms-dealer."

There was a long, troubled pause.

"Are you sure?"

"Sure I'm sure. He's involved with everything from aircraft to artillery. He sells obsolete ex-War Department stock."

"How do you know something like that? Companies House won't tell you that sort of thing, will it?"

"That's my business. All I'll say is that history isn't a science, it's an art-form made out of information. One of my tutors knows this area of international trade. Didn't you know that the First World War was started to save Birmingham's screw-makers from bankruptcy? Heh-heh. See you soon."

Eric put the 'phone down and went back upstairs to finish his exercises. As he drove himself through the routines he found new strength that enabled him to go beyond his old physical limitations: whereas he had only been capable of fifty of one, now he could a hundred to celebrate that his hatred of Wegelius was justified. His own jealousy and enmity had been exonerated from blame. With enthusiasm he doubled the speed of the exercises and ended up spent, gasping on the bed.

As he lay there in a fog of physical exhaustion he could not keep one question at bay, and it bored into his brain and laid its eggs.

Why had she married such a man when her only knowledge of love had come from him?

22

It was May before he received the information he needed from Leo. They met at an athletics match on Tyneside when Liverpool, Durham, Newcastle and Edinburgh universities competed against each other in track and field over a weekend and Eric was throwing the javelin. His distances had been steadily improving and he was now the best thrower in Liverpool's string of three. Leo drove over the Pennines from Kirkby Lonsdale and, after the match, took Eric back to stay over Sunday night with him. They had dinner at The Royal Hotel then returned to Leo's house and sat by a fire in the sitting-room drinking whisky. As Eric relaxed, his right shoulder began to trouble him. He had torn a muscle during training and it was still liable to give him pain. Going up to the room which Leo had prepared for him, having bought a camp-bed in a sale as the frequency of visits had increased, Eric took off his shirt and started to rub embrocation into the sore part of his shoulder. The door opened and Leo entered, holding out his hand.

"Here, let me do that for you," he said. "Come and sit by the fire downstairs."

Eric obediently handed over the bottle. The thought of being massaged by Leo troubled him but the man had good reason for wanting to help. He had a vested interest in Eric's continued progress as an athlete and seemed to take great pleasure in his achievements.

Eric sat in a chair by the fire while Leo warmed his hands.

"I'll just take the chill off them before I attack you," he said with a grin. "Is your back all right?"

Eric nodded. As his training had got more strenuous and frequent, three points of strain had emerged: the throwing shoulder, the elbow of the same arm and the base of the spine where the final twist of power came from for the javelin's flight. Keeping control of the stress on these three areas was part of the skill in personal physiotherapy which he had learnt from his coach.

Leo poured embrocation on to his hands and began to massage Eric's shoulder, gently at first, loosening up the muscles then driving his finger-tips deeper.

"Say if I'm hurting you," he murmured.

"No, that's all right. I felt a twinge when I was throwing but not much."

"I should rest it for a week. Don't put any strain on it. I used to get exactly the same problem in the old days. It was probably that winning throw — phenomenal upthrust you got. I felt very proud." He paused, then said, "She's at a place called Churt," gripping Eric's shoulder-blades as if to steady him. "The butterfly has settled." Leaning over he examined Eric's face, his own a mask of questioning concern, but he could not disguise the triumph he was enjoying in his revelation, and its effect.

"Where?" Eric asked stupidly.

"Churt. It's a small village on the border between Hampshire and Surrey. Lloyd George lived there with his mistress. In fact, I think he died there. There's a pub called after him, if I remember rightly. . ."

Eric stood up, rapidly pulling on his shirt as if he were about to set off for the place immediately.

"That's going to be their main base, apparently. The house is called Fenlon Old Farm," Leo said smoothly. "Don't get upset."

"He'll be living there?" Eric demanded fiercely.

"He's her husband, after all."

Eric tucked his shirt in and stood with his hands gripping the mantelpiece, trying to control his anger.

"She writes to you but she won't write to me!" he raged. "Why?"

Leo put a comforting hand on his back.

"She knows that writing to me is like writing to you. Whatever she tells me I'll pass on. Don't forget, she is married. There's her grandfather looking over her shoulder as well. She has to be careful."

Eric turned, his face savage.

"You know he's an arms-dealer?"

Leo sank his long chin into his throat and chuckled.

"That's going a bit far," he said reprovingly. "Bruno Wegelius is a man of many parts I know, but I hadn't heard that was one of them."

"Well, that's what he is. A man with the moral conscience of a vampire."

"Not one of your *bons mots*, I suspect. Was Daniel the author?"

"The man's a total shit. He sells arms to anyone who'll pay for them . . ."

"So does the British government," Leo said with a smart grin. "No, I'm teasing. It is an unethical business."

Eric sat down and picked up his glass of whisky, swilling the golden liquid round. Leo could see that he was trying to keep still, to discipline his anger. Sitting down opposite him, Leo leant back in his chair, signalling that he was ready to discuss the matter further.

"Whatever you do, let it be for the right reason," he counselled. "Don't imagine that you can brush aside Bruno Wegelius. He's a very influential man, and he has his rights, after all. Concentrate on Pauline. She is still yours, at heart."

"I'll go to Churt," Eric declared.

"Work out what you're going to do before you go. Think about it. One thing: abjure confrontation. Your world with Pauline is an interior one, a secret. Keep it that way and it can survive anything. If you bring it all out into the open it will be fatal."

Eric suddenly let himself go and laughed, then drained off his glass.

"What's the joke?" Leo asked.

"I'm going to see her again!" Eric replied, his face full of rejoicing.

"Of course you are," Leo responded, raising his glass and regarding the young man through the distorting lens of his whisky. "To ineradicable love."

Eric returned to Liverpool the next morning and rode south on his scooter that same afternoon, travelling through Birmingham, Oxford and Newbury to get to Farnham, the nearest town of any size to Churt. It was a journey of over two hundred miles and he arrived too late to start looking for Fenlon Old Farm so he found a bed and breakfast and stayed in Farnham. He was up at seven and shared the breakfast-table with two commercial salesmen who knew the area. When he mentioned that he was going to Churt they told him that it was an enclave of very wealthy people, a reservation for the ultra-rich, the kind of place any man would dream of having for his home. They travelled in security alarm systems and knew the district well. Although they could not recall Fenlon Old Farm in any detail they were both fairly certain of its whereabouts just over the bridge across the stream that serves as the Hampshire/Surrey border, about half a mile from the Old Mill House which they had fitted out with an alarm system the year before. They were able to draw Eric a rough sketch-map to enable him to find it.

"Not a burglar are you, son?" one of them chaffed him as he handed over the drawing. "That wouldn't do at all."

"I'm an old friend of a girl who lives there. We were at school together. She gave me directions but I lost the bit of paper," Eric said steadily. "She's expecting me."

"Well, I should keep in there if I were you. Use your head, son, marry a rich woman. It's much better than working."

Eric took his leave of them, paid the landlady, then took the road towards Churt. It was hilly, wooded country broken by stretches of sandy heath and ponds, the road winding into small valley bottoms dense with beech then rising up to silver birch and gorse. It was a sunny morning with plenty of birds about and he felt his spirit rising from the depths which Pauline's marriage had cast it into. His mission filled him with an optimism that he recognised as unreasonable but it was based on a shared past, presided over by Leo and his passionate, well-made logic. Pauline was much more a part of that than he was and her true self must still be rooted there if she placed any value upon integrity.

The sketch-map provided by the commercial travellers was not completely accurate. Having arrived at the village, which was surrounded by deciduous woodland, he found the church of Saint John, which they had mentioned, the Working Men's Club (which they had thought to be a joke in this area), the post office, butcher's, newsagent's, garage and pub. Turning right at the crossroads by the primary school he rode down a deep lane to a road bridge over a narrow stream then, following the instructions on the map, turned right along an unmetalled track. In the position which should have been occupied by Fenlon Old Farm was a small white house but the track went further north so he followed it and eventually came out into a clearing and broad turning-circle amongst huge beech trees. There was a pair of open ironwork gates set on red-brick pillars and surmounted by acorns carved in grey stone. A high wall went both left and right, ducking under the trees and disappearing. Throttling back his scooter he paused by the gates and found a small sign with the name of the house cut into weathered wood. It was Fenlon Old Farm. He cut the engine and stood the scooter on its stand, took off his crash-helmet and gauntlets and put them in the well of the machine, then prepared to enter the gates. He would have done so, devoid of plan or subterfuge, so excited he was, if a man had not wheeled a large wooden wheelbarrow out of the gates just as he was going to enter. The man was about fifty, bald except for a half-circlet of short grey hair, and neatly dressed to a point where he looked rather ludicrous wheeling a barrow-load of rubbish. He eyed Eric, carefully put the handles of the wheelbarrow down, rubbed his hands on a cloth tied to his belt, and asked him what he wanted.

Eric replied with the first thing that came into his head, prompted by the man's forthright gaze and businesslike manner.

"I'm looking for work."

"No work here," the man assured him in a clear south-country voice which was friendly enough. "I'm the only one who works here and I'm temporary."

"Oh," Eric said, struggling to think what he could say next. "I'd heard that it was a big place."

"It's big enough but there's no one here at the moment. Mr Holt used to have me as his gardener but he's sold up and moved to Cornwall. The new owner hasn't arrived yet."

"When do you think they'll be here?" Eric asked.

"Any time, but when they do arrive I'll be first in the queue. Mr Holt gave me a good reference after twelve years of being his gardener and I've still got my family in the house you passed back there." The man adjusted his cuffs and picked a few pieces of twig off his shirt-front. "What's your line then? Indoors?"

"Anything."

"Anything? Well, who knows, the new owner might want someone to do anything."

He walked over and looked at Eric's scooter.

"This any good?" he asked. "I've been thinking of getting one. What kind is it?"

"It's an NSU Prima."

"Is that Italian?"

"No, it's German."

"Christ, you can't get away from them, can you? If it's not Eyeties it's Krauts. Where's the British scooter, then? Why hasn't someone made a good British scooter?"

"D'you want a go on it?" Eric said.

"I can't ride one yet. If I get one I'll sort myself out." He touched the handlebars lovingly and turned the throttle. "Tell you what, though. I have to go into the village to get something. You could give me a lift, if you like."

Eric immediately agreed and put on his crash-helmet and gloves, straddled the scooter and started it up. The man cocked his leg over the pillion and mounted. As Eric pulled away he was forced to put his arms round Eric's waist because the track was so bumpy.

As they passed the small white house the man waved at a woman in the kitchen window.

"That'll set her thinking," he shouted to Eric, "she'll wonder what's going on!"

Once in the village the man went to the big, white Thirties-style garage and picked up a part for a lawn-mower from the workshop, then returned to Eric who was waiting on the forecourt astride the scooter.

"Tell you what, it's my tea-break now so we'll drop in at my place on the way back, if that's all right? You can come in and have something if you like."

Eric drove back and parked the scooter by the fence of the small, white house. As they went in to the kitchen the man introduced himself as Len, then his wife as Barbara. She was a plump, chatty woman with round spectacles and crooked teeth who had a habit of laughing at everything whether it was funny or not. Her value to Eric was that she knew all the local gossip about Fenlon Old Farm and its new owners.

"The name is Wegelius," she said, "but you don't say it that way. What you say is *Vedgelius*, like vegetable, that's what his secretary rang and told Cynth at the newsagent's when he was ordering his papers. What kind of a name is that?" She went off into a long, slithering buzz of laughter.

"Well, it's not English, whatever it is," Len retorted. "and what you've got to do is hope he wants me to do his garden or we're all in trouble."

"I don't want to leave this little house. We've been happy here, haven't we, sweetheart?"

Len put his cup down on the table and signalled to Eric that the tea-break was over.

"Better get on with it," he said to his wife. "I'll be back at half-past one not one because I want to get that mowing done."

He ushered Eric out and stood by the scooter, obviously wanting to complete the ride back to his work. When they reached the gates Len leant forward and gestured that he should ride through.

Eric drove down a long looping track through an orchard of apples, pears and plums in blossom with gooseberry and red and blackcurrant bushes alongside the track. The ground fell away steeply beyond the orchard, revealing the house which was an agglomerate of many styles built over the previous three hundred years, the central part being seventeenth-century and crowned by six great ornamental chimneys of extraordinary height. There was a main courtyard of orange pea-gravel and an arched access to the front of the house which faced over a large flower and herb garden to a meadow going down to the stream. Len signalled to Eric that he should drive off to the left and guided him along a narrow path between herbaceous borders and flowering shrubs to a modern brick building set behind a small plantation of fir trees. There was a concrete standing with a large green motor mower on it and a shed with its doors open.

Len tapped Eric on the shoulder and told him to stop. When he had got off he invited Eric to park the scooter and have a look around.

"This is my province, or used to be," he said with rueful pride. "Tucked away nicely, no one breathing down your neck. Not a bad little set-up."

189

Eric spent the next hour with Len going around the garden. He had a key to the house but he thought it better that they did not go in as Wegelius could turn up at any moment.

"It's a warren, that place," he said, "room after room, none of them the same, all shapes and sizes. You can get lost in there. When Mr Holt was here I had the run of it, really. I used to be one of the family, you could say. What this new bloke will be like I can't say. But I'll tell you what, Eric. If he does keep me on one of the things he'll have to learn straight away is that this garden is too much for one man. This was a source of disagreement between myself and Mr Holt. He was a bit tight, if you know what I mean, used me for everything. My wife tells me this Wegelius is a very wealthy man so he might be more open-handed. If he does have me, and he agrees that I have an assistant, I'll put a good word in for you. How about that?"

Eric's mind had not worked as fast as Len's in this respect. He was so involved with imagining Pauline living in this place, seeing her moving about this garden, that he had not yet applied himself to the problem of how he could become part of her new life. But he had the sense to thank Len for his offer and to provide him with his address and telephone number. When Len looked at the piece of paper he raised his eyebrows.

"Liverpool?" he said quizzically. "You'll have a long way to come to work."

Eric smiled and got astride the scooter.

"I'll move down. There's nothing for me up there. You will keep me posted, won't you?"

Len nodded, folded the piece of paper and put it carefully into the fob-pocket of his neat, black waistcoat.

"And if you do get the job you can teach me to drive that thing," he said, touching the scooter's front wheel with the polished toe of his boot. "Then we can say that we're quits."

Eric returned to the village and filled up with petrol at the garage. He had not planned to leave but he could see no point in remaining at Churt. Nonetheless, it was the only contact he had with Pauline and he was loath to leave it. Leaving the scooter by the church he climbed a fence and cut through the woods to the stream then walked along the bank until he was opposite the house. He could hear the motor-mower working but could not see Len behind the shrubs which shielded the lawns. Sitting at the foot of a tree he studied the house in all its details, each window and drainpipe, each door and corner, storing it away in his memory. Soon she would be living there, moving from room to room, going into the garden, strolling across the meadow to the stream, looking across to the woods where he was sitting.

It was a beautiful place, he decided. He could endure the thought of her living in it, provided he was there.

All he needed to do was become an acceptable part of it, someone as naturally fitted to the area as the people in the village, and she would understand. There could be no confrontation as Leo had pointed out, because he would inevitably lose. To win all he wanted at one blow was impossible. Now he had seen what Wegelius had given her, this house which even he admired, he knew that love would not be enough to bring success. From now on he would have to find some cunning.

Returning to the village he looked up the telephone number of Mr Holt in the book in the box and found it listed. As he wrote it down he was aware of how his perception of himself had shifted: now he was spy, stranger and conspirator with his own feelings, having to guess how she would respond to his machinations.

He drove back to Liverpool that day. The following Saturday he sent Len a postcard signed Eric Mullins, reminding him that he was waiting to hear. As a result of his lack of foresight he had not been able to use an alias for his Christian name when first meeting Len at Churt but, as Leo said, there were loads of Erics about and the surname mattered most.

23

Eric waited for a fortnight before trying the telephone number he had got from the Churt directory. It was unobtainable. When he checked it with the operator, who put him through to the local exchange, he discovered that the number had been disconnected. When he rang directory enquiries and asked for the new number allocated to Wegelius he was informed that it was ex-directory. This, at least, told him that they were probably in residence. Four days later he received a card from Len suggesting that he should come down to Churt if he was serious about wanting a job.

Without telling his mother or Daniel what was afoot he drove down to Churt, timing his arrival to coincide with the end of Len's working day. Barbara gave him a warm welcome, bursting to pass on all the news about Mr and Mrs Wegelius and their generosity in not only keeping Len on as gardener but increasing his wages as well.

"And you should see the wife," Barbara enthused. "What a lovely girl she is. So nice and pleasant. Not like old Mrs Holt who was a right old tartar when she felt like it. When Len raised the question of having an assistant Mr Wegelius agreed without any argument, and Mr Holt had said no for ten years, the mean old devil. Mr Wegelius is so different, so open-handed . . ."

Eric sat and listened to Barbara rattling on. He had to hold back from interrogating her about Pauline in detail. While Barbara's flow of gossip swirled over him he watched her broad, smiling face, listening intently in case she let slip something important, which she failed to do. When Len came in he greeted Eric enthusiastically and continued his wife's paean of praise:

"Anything you need, he said. How's the lawn-mower? A bit past it? Get a new one. Do you need to replace any of your tools and implements? Do I? I said. Look at this lot! Labour-saving devices? I believe in them, he says. Can you handle a budget? he says. A budget? I've never had a budget, I used to have to ask Mr Holt for everything as it cropped up. From now on, he says, you have your own budget and you keep books. Books?" Len laughed and clapped Eric on the back. "I don't know one end of a book from the other, but I bet you do. You're educated, aren't you, son?"

Eric shrugged and smiled.

"I guessed you were. Anyway, I thought to myself, in for a penny in for a pound, so I asked him straight: can I have an assistant? I started to explain about the size of the garden, the orchard but he didn't let me finish. Find the right man, he said. And here you are."

"It's very good of you," Eric said humbly, "thanks a lot."

"Self-interest," Len retorted. "You'll have to earn your keep, and do the books!"

Barbara went off on one of her susurrating giggles.

"When can I start?" Eric asked.

"Tomorrow, if you like. I'll tell Mr Wegelius that you're here. He might want to check you over himself. Then, if everything is all right with him, we can go ahead."

Len invited Eric to stay that night. When Barbara took him up to his room she intimated to him that he could rent it, if he so wished. Len was saving up for his scooter and the money would come in useful. Eric accepted the offer.

After dinner he ferried them, one after the other, down to the pub on the scooter. Barbara clung to him, giggling, as they roared through the dusky woods.

They returned after closing-time and sat talking for an hour before going to bed. As Eric lay there listening to the night-birds active among the oak and beech, it pained him to admit that his enemy had made Len and Barbara so happy. He dispelled this thought as unworthy and a waste of his time; after all, he was now so close to his love who lay, he assumed, asleep in the same woods as himself.

*

The next morning he awoke early and discovered that he had been dreaming about what lay ahead. Decisions appeared to have already been taken in his mind. When he went to the bathroom and looked at himself in the mirror he encountered a new character. Since his first visit to Churt he had stopped shaving and now had a fortnight's stubble on his chin; his hair had been cut short recently; and, since the last time he had seen Pauline, his body had changed as a result of the intensive training he had undertaken. As he examined the person in the mirror he detected new overtones in the image. It was, above all, more sullen and dangerous, rougher, more compact and stripped down, more physical. He had moved down a class, he decided, tightening the muscles on his neck so the sinews showed like fan-vaulting. He was surprised to discover that he hoped she would walk straight past him, unaware of his identity. Rehearsing the encounter in his mind he went back to his room, dressed in a pair of old green corduroys (part of any genuine gardener's uniform, he had decided), a plaid shirt and a black sleeveless waistcoat very similar to the one worn by Len. On his feet he wore his old fell-walking boots which, he noticed, were still encrusted with mud from his walk by the estuary.

Len insisted that Eric should drive him on the scooter to the house even though it was a fine day and the half-mile walk through the woods would have been better in terms of giving him time to ease himself into his rôle. While riding up the track they were passed by a white Daimler going in the opposite direction. All Eric saw of the driver was a shape behind the wheel, any detail being made indistinct by the tinted glass of the windscreen.

Len waved as the car went past.

"That's him!" he shouted, twisting himself round on the pillion to watch the car disappear between the trees. "He's off to London."

Eric experienced relief at the thought that Wegelius would not be there on his first day. At the back of his mind he was not confident of his reception should Pauline recognise him. There was an element of burlesque and play-acting in what he was doing, deadly serious though he was, and she did not have much taste for that kind of thing. Her style would have been different if their predicaments had been reversed. As he accelerated through the orchard and the old house came into view in all its intricate, overlaid character, and he told himself 'She's in there!', he knew that Pauline would have been incapable of dreaming up this ploy.

As he drove through the courtyard he kept his head well down over the handlebars in case she should be watching through a window. When they reached the gardener's outbuildings he put the scooter on the hard standing and followed Len inside.

There was a table with a brand-new telephone on it and three chairs. Len sat in one and gestured to Eric that he should sit next to him.

"My HQ. He's even given me my own 'phone. I can ring the house and I can ring out, but I have to log all my outside calls, he says. No ringing my aunty in Australia." He leant back and pointed at a new electric kettle on top of a pile of well-thumbed gardening books stacked on a filing-cabinet.

"Make us a cup of tea, eh, Eric?" he said with a proprietorial air. "You'll find cups and saucers in the bottom drawer of the cabinet. Afterwards, I'd be obliged if you washed them in the sink provided in the shower-room. Isn't this great?"

After a chat about national insurance in which Eric had to confess that he had used Mullins as an alias (merely a student's psychological aid for his new life, he assured Len), they toured the gardens. Eric had bought a cloth cap and wore it pulled down over his eyes as they wandered along the paths. Len chattered as they strolled between shrubs and flowers, telling him the history of plants he had raised from seed, the ones which were thriving on the sandy soil, the ones which were only partially successful.

"Drainage is our main advantage here," he said. "So we do plants that don't like moisture retention, know what I mean? A lot of the soil here is pretty infertile but some plants like that. I grow a lot of broom, for instance. You look up on Frensham Common and you'll find tons of it, not the cultivated varieties, mind you, not like we have here, these pink ones. Another wild flower which does well in its cultivated varieties here is mallows, I like them, got them everywhere. . ."

Eric saw a set of french doors open on to the lawn. They were some distance away and there was a clump of tree-lupins partially blocking his view. Len caught the direction of his glance.

"Yes, she's up and about," he said. "Who'd want to waste a day like this?"

195

"What time do the indoor servants start work?" Eric asked.

"They don't have any," Len replied, supporting the dew-heavy heads of some early marigolds in his hands. "Mrs Wegelius doesn't like the idea."

"That's a bit of a waste, isn't it?" Eric said with a laugh. "All that money and no servants?"

"I admire her for it, actually," Len replied protectively. "She likes to do for herself. There is a char who comes in daily but Mrs Wegelius does her own washing and cooking. You don't find many young women of her class these days who can do that. They're all taught flower-arrangement and nothing else."

He conducted Eric to the fence by the meadow which led down to the stream. They were now out of sight of the open french doors. Stretching along the rusty metal fence was a plantation of grey-green shrubs not yet in flower.

"A rarity, Eric. In fact, a member of the potato family called fabiana," Len announced pompously. "One of Mr Holt's favourites. The flowers will be along in a week or so. Before they arrive I'd like you to cut away all the dead foliage from last year and trim them up. You could do a bit of weeding round them as well."

He produced a trowel and a pair of secateurs from his jacket pocket. Both implements were new.

"These are yours, Eric. Start a new job with new tools, I say. And I'd like to wish you the best of luck."

Eric took the trowel and secateurs and thanked him.

"Do this job well," Len advised, "because tomorrow I want to bring the governor over to have a look at it. I want to be able to say, this boy knows his business . . ." he paused, his eyes twinkling, "when I know you don't, do you, son?"

Eric hesitated, his fingers nervously working the handles of the secateurs. He finally shook his head.

"I knew that, but there's no need to worry. There's nothing mind-bending about gardening. Just use your commonsense and, if in doubt, ask. Why a lad like you wants to do this kind of work is your business, but I want it done properly. First tea-break at half-past ten, okay?"

He showed Eric how to cut away the dead foliage and how to

dig out the docks by their deep, straight root, then returned to his headquarters, leaving Eric to get on with the job.

It was a warm morning; the slight breeze reduced to a breath by the woods which surrounded the estate. The trimming of the fabiana was close, difficult work and after half-an-hour his back was aching, so he sat on the earth and did some weeding with his new trowel. This was work much more in keeping with his mood because the soil was light and the weeds came out easily. Soon he had a pile of dandelions, docks and groundsel heaped on the gravel path beside him.

"Hello, Mr *Mullins*."

His back was to her. Immediately recognising her voice he half-turned, keeping his head down so the peak of his cloth cap shielded his face. When he answered, saying "Mornin'" he heard himself using a parody of Len's accent.

"Oh, come on, you can't get away with that," she said laughing from far above him, her feet shifting on the gravel. They were clad in white canvas shoes and she was wearing a skirt. When he saw her ankles and the faint dark hair on the outside of her calves he felt his voice shrivelling up in his throat.

"It's all right, I know it's you, Eric," she said from far above him. "Stand up so I can look at you."

His face began to burn with blushing as he slowly got to his feet. When he was half-way up he felt her whisk the cap from his head. As the moment came for them to be face to face he could not look at her.

"You've got red in your beard," she said lightly. "I never knew that."

"How did you know it was me?" he muttered, his eyes on his cap as she dangled it from one hooked finger. "Did Leo tell you?"

"Good Lord, no. He'd let this go much further before tipping me off." She threw the cap back to him. "It's the scooter. Didn't it occur to you that I might recognise it? God, I've risked my life on the damn thing often enough and I even remembered the registration number."

Eric raised his head and looked at her, his heart hurting him with its violent beating. With a jolt he stared straight into the lenses of a pair of dark glasses.

"Will you take those off?" he said peremptorily.

"Steady on, Mr Mullins," she answered. "I'm supposed to be the boss around here."

"Take them off!"

She raised her chin and folded her arms, the black lenses giving him nothing but his own reflection. Then, with an odd smile, she took hold of one arm of the glasses and lifted them off her nose as if they were a theatre curtain, making a drum-roll with her lips.

"Ta-ra! Voila!" she exclaimed, sweeping the glasses away and shaking her hair, "It's me!"

Fearfully he entered her eyes. She was laughing but he saw how wary she was, keeping him at bay, her expression remote and disturbed. She had put on weight and her features had lost some pristine distinctness; now her face was moony, pale-golden and plump and she was wearing cosmetics, which he had never seen on her before. But beneath these changes and minor deformities she was more beautiful than ever; proofs of sadness, new knowledge and the haunting power of guilt having deepened the light of her expression.

"Why are you looking at me like that? I'm all right. Don't look so concerned." She touched his arm and frowned, then her brow cleared. "Isn't this a lovely place?" she said conversationally. "Have you explored it yet?"

"No, I haven't had time."

"You're staying at the gardener's house, *n'est-ce pas*? He told me all about you. Len thinks you're a bright prospect. Did he tell you that?" Her voice was edged with sarcasm.

"I took the job to be near you."

She put her hand in front of her face, furiously shaking it to silence him. The gesture repudiated anything he might say about his motives. When he attempted to by-pass the gesture and read from her eyes what she was feeling he encountered a splintery coldness.

"I've left university. . ." he continued doggedly, but she cut him short.

"That's your business."

"I know that," he replied, wounded by her attitude.

"Then why tell me about it?"

"Well, you jacked in university as well, didn't you?"

"Don't talk about it," she pleaded. "I have taken my decisions and you have taken yours. We are not responsible for each other."

"I'm not saying that you are responsible," Eric explained, "please don't think that."

"Don't worry, I won't."

She stared at him aggressively then her face softened.

"I think I'm going to like you with a beard," she said with abrupt caprice and coquettishness. "You'll look like a Viking. That's what the stockbroker-belt needs. Before long you'll be very popular around here."

He grinned back at her, fingering his stubble.

They talked for another five minutes then she returned to the house and left him to his snipping and weeding.

That night he went to bed and left his door open, listening for Len and Barbara coming upstairs. They stayed up late to listen to a radio programme and did not settle down to sleep until eleven. When Eric heard them stop talking he looked at his watch and decided to give them another twenty minutes. He tried to read a book to pass the time but could not concentrate. When the time was up he dressed in a dark track-suit and slipped out of the house.

There was a half-moon which gave enough light to walk up the track. Ahead of him he could see the gate-light shining through the trees. A bat fluttered across his vision, a piece of black silk blown by the nocturnal breeze. Born up by his elated mood he snatched at it like a child. He felt drunk.

Wegelius had flown to Turin that morning. Pauline had told Eric that the coast was clear until Saturday. Her approach had been startlingly matter-of-fact as if she had been partner in his scheme to re-assemble their relationship. As he had scouted around in their conversation in the garden, reconnoitring her attitude, she had gone straight to the point.

"Do you want to sleep with me?" she had said. "All I ask is that we keep quiet about it for Bruno's sake."

She had given him a key to a side-door which was seldom used as it gave its main access to an empty wing. The key lay in his palm in his pocket, warmed by constant contact with his hand.

"So much to talk about," she had said with an excitement he could see was sincere, "so many things to tell you about the places I've been."

As he approached the gate a shower began. He walked through the orchard, keeping off the drive and beneath the blossoming boughs, listening to the rain-drops on the leaves, whistling under his breath.

The courtyard lights were on so he skirted round the back of the house and approached the side-door through the kitchen garden, stealing down a corridor of bean-poles. Arriving at the door he used the key and entered.

As he did so he heard a dog begin to bark somewhere deep inside the house.

She had told him how to get to her bedroom. Due to the complicated plan of the old house it was not an easy matter to recall it and he dared not turn the lights on. The dog had stopped barking but Eric was very aware that it could be in any of the rooms he entered and he had estimated from the note of its bark that it was a large animal. Cautiously he edged through the dark passageways, hoping that he was going in the right direction, smelling the odours of the strange house, bumping into furniture, until he saw a light under a door.

As he knocked on it a frenzied barking began on the other side and he heard her commanding the dog to be quiet.

When she opened the door she stepped back, holding a long-haired Alsatian on a choke-lead. The animal lunged at him and Pauline yanked it back, bringing the dog up on its hind-legs.

"Come in," she said, "don't worry about the dog. He's my protector when Bruno is away."

He entered, watchful of the dog's snarling mouth.

"You might have warned me," he said with jealous reproof. "If I'd met him off the lead he'd have made a meal out of me."

"Oh no he wouldn't," she assured him sweetly as she closed the door behind him. "My Eric would never bite his namesake. Hold out your hand so he can sniff it then you'll be friends."

In a daze of insult and amusement he submitted his hand to the dog's eager examination.

"You called it after me?" he said wonderingly.

"Why not? He's attractive, his instincts are good, he's fierce when he needs to be and he can learn things if you have the patience to teach him," she answered, her smile fixed in a grimace of affection as she patted the Alsatian's black coat. "And I love him."

24

After a week at Churt he wrote to the university authorities, his mother and Daniel, telling them about his change of direction. These letters were difficult to write. He knew that the department would regret his decision because he had been doing well in the short time he had been there; his mother would be deeply upset and would need to think that he had given up one career in prospect for one that suited him better. What could he tell her? That he had decided to become a *gardener*? When he penned the letter he described his new occupation as trainee horticulturalist and told her that he was studying part-time at the Farnham College of Further Education with vocational attachments to the Royal Horticultural Society at Wisley. If that letter had been a torture to write, the one to Daniel was excruciatingly so: first he had to apologise for leaving him in the lurch about the flat they had rented together, then he had to provide reasons for abandoning university without giving Pauline as the cause. Daniel's opinion of love had been lowered of late; it was no longer a worthwhile experience. Against the ecstasy he set the humiliation and crucifixion and the irreparable ego-damage. If he now had an attitude it was historical and scientific, perceiving the influence of love as part of the necessary energy provided by Nature for survival. If Eric had told him that it had become the entire centre of his life Daniel would have treated him with the patronising delicacy people reserve for madmen; so he lied, blaming society for his decision, whose state of decadence was such, he claimed, that higher education and the professions were all part of a conspiracy to corrupt the innocent and exploit the ignorant, so he had opted out.

A week later he received a reply from Daniel; a piece of torn graph-paper in a re-used envelope. The message was scrawled in capital letters which had been deliberately blotched, some of the faded blue water spots ringed in red and marked 'tears'.

The message read: BOLLOCKS. YOU'RE BACK WITH HER. ENJOY YOUR MISERY.

Eric's reaction to having his carefully argued cover torn aside by his friend was mixed: on the one hand it made him apprehensive if his real motives for being at Churt were so transparent (he had not mentioned Pauline at all in his letter to Daniel), but, on the other hand, it meant that he could keep in touch with his friend with some degree of honesty and continue to share his problems with at least one peer other than Pauline who, he felt, had somehow grown distant because of the defeat she had accepted by marrying Wegelius. Making love to her was one-sided, passion against dalliance; for him it was only half-marvellous as she was only half-there.

It was not the same as it had been: she lacked any seriousness, thwarting any attempt he made to recover the erstwhile character of their relationship, deflecting his earnestness with nonchalant humour and teasing him when he became frustrated by it. Within the time made available by Wegelius's first absence Eric had hoped to re-establish everything on its previous best footing: the intimacy, trust and delight all making a return in full strength; but by the end of the period he knew that it was not going to be that way.

She had changed, but, what is more, she had made herself change. It had been an act of will on her part to suppress the past. The level of her success was remarkable, he thought. If she had loved him as completely as she had claimed to do up until the time of her mother's death, then what they were re-starting now at Churt should be a resurrection of that, its whole character cleansed and re-created, brought back to its former glory like a great temple excavated from mud. But that was not how it felt to him. She was not only holding back, she was denying the truth of what they had possessed before.

The only recourse which would salvage his pride and give the future some meaning was to woo her all over again. To do this he would need to re-interpret the present understanding on which their love-making was based, persuading her that it could not survive as the frolic of a mistress with a knowing slave, but had to be adjusted to the dignity of a secret truth beneath a sham.

The weekend came and went and Wegelius did not return. It was Sunday night before he rang up to give his excuses to Pauline, explaining that he had been forced to remain in Turin for longer than expected and now had to fly on to Washington. Eric had stayed away from Pauline from Friday night and found himself growing indignant over his enemy's cavalier treatment of time. He was appeased when Pauline told him that her period was due to start on Thursday, when Wegelius planned to return. As it happened, this was delayed again until the following Sunday and then Pauline received a call from a Berlin office to pass on a message that her husband could not give a firm date when he would be back.

From the time that call was received Pauline would not allow Eric to visit her at night. She was worried that Len and Barbara would become suspicious, even though Eric assured her that they never knew when he left the house at night and returned in the early hours. Pauline believed that the best solution was for Eric to find a room in the village and be independent. She followed this up with the suggestion that he should also find himself a girlfriend as a cover, a line of reasoning which enraged him. The argument it started dragged on until it filled the entire time in which Eric was stopped from making nocturnal visits to Fenlon Old Farm. He worked in the garden, avoiding any contact with her, while she affected to find his pique ridiculous and ignored his existence.

Eric worked Saturday mornings. As the row dragged on in its unspoken form, he was forced to find ways of passing the time. Up until the beginning of the disaccord he had spent the days anticipating the nights but now that pleasure had gone he became irritable with himself and began to lose faith. Reaching back into the immediate past he took up the javelin again, joined an athletics club in Alton, and took to practising in the meadow between the gardens and the stream. He had ordered a new javelin through the club and, while he waited for it to arrive, the secretary arranged for him to borrow one from their stock.

During his tea-break that Saturday morning he took the javelin down from the garage rafters where he had stored it and went down to the meadow. He had marked out a few lines there to give him an idea of his distances. When he made his first throw he was surprised at what he achieved. The second was even longer. As he had not been training hard he had not expected to throw so well. After he had finished the half-day he returned to the meadow to throw again, stirred by the thought that he had hit form without really working at it.

Half-an-hour later he knew that it had been a fluke which he could attribute to a following wind and perfect air conditions, both of which had eased off. Displeased with his lack of consistency, he took a final throw before going back for his mid-day meal and was surprised when he exceeded his first of the day.

"You know how to handle that thing," a voice said behind him. "Can you be accurate with it as a weapon?"

Eric turned to find a small, dark, bald man dressed in a blue T-shirt, khaki shorts and sandals grinning amiably at him, the Alsatian panting at his side. The man's face was round, graven by deep lines at the side of his wide mouth, and illuminated by lively brown eyes beaming with self-assurance. Eric recognised him as the birthday guest who had been at Joe Nash's party in Kew.

"I've often thought when watching athletes throw the javelin: how would they get on in a battle? Would they be able to hit anyone, or is it all just distance?" He continued affably, sticking out his hand. "I'm Bruno Wegelius and you're Mr Mullins. I won't call you by your Christian name because that will get the dog mixed up." He shook hands with a light, warm pressure. "I've talked to my wife and we've agreed that the dog will be called Rick from now on."

In his shock and confusion at meeting his enemy without being prepared, Eric murmured that he had no objection to sharing his name with a dog.

"No, no, that would be impractical," Wegelius said with a broad grin. "Every time I called for the dog you'd come running or vice versa. We'll call him Rick. I prefer it as a name for a dog. I told Pauline when she christened it: Eric's a name for a person, not an animal. Let's go and retrieve your weapon."

Eric walked over the meadow, the dog bounding at his side, leaving Wegelius to come along in his wake. His mind was in a turmoil of anxiety and doubt. How he would actually deal with Wegelius was something he had never worked out, being satisfied just to hate the man.

"The throwing-spear went out of fashion very early on because it was so inaccurate and it was so difficult to get enough power behind it to penetrate a shield. The Greek *hoplites* in phalanx were essentially a mobile anti-cavalry fence. Let's see if we can hit that tree."

Eric explained that the javelin was not his property and that he would rather not risk damaging it.

"Oh, come on, I'll replace it if we break it. I'll buy the buggers a dozen javelins if they like," Wegelius insisted cheerfully. "This is something that interests me. I've often thought about it. History is governed by the development of weapons. I'm not the first to say that, either. You go from bashing with a stone to throwing a stone; from bashing with a stick to throwing a stick, then you fire a stick from a launching-system — the bow — then you go back to the stone and you fire the stone from a gun, and everything changes. The day that the first stone was shot from a gun was the beginning of the modern age."

Seizing the javelin from Eric's grasp he hurled it at the tree and missed.

"See what I mean? Inaccurate. Now, if I was playing darts it would be different because I don't need to use so much energy. It's the application of energy to the weapon that's crucial. Now you have a go."

Wegelius trotted over to where the javelin had landed in the grass and picked it up, raising it over his shoulder and running back like a Zulu warrior, his bald head gleaming.

"Uh-huh-uh-huh!" he chanted. "The impis weren't bad at chucking spears but their real weapon was the stabbing-assegai. Shaka collected all the long throwing-spears together and made his *uFasimba* regiment cut them all short and got his smithies to re-forge the blades with blood-channels so they could withdraw them faster from the bodies of their enemies. They called these new weapons *Iklwa* which was the sucking sound they made when pulled out." He held the javelin out in both hands, amused mischief all over his simian features. "I'm a mine of useless information, Eric. Go on, imagine you're Achilles and that tree's Hector. Nail the bastard!"

Eric took the javelin, hesitating about the grip he should use. Finally he adjusted it to suit the short distance and Wegelius nodded his agreement.

"Much more of the pen-holder grip. Go on, chuck it, but you can't get much leverage on it, I bet," he said chuckling.

Eric did manage to strike the tree a glancing blow, making the hollow aluminium javelin ring. Wegelius winced then, without another word, wandered off towards the stream, the dog frolicking in his wake. Eric watched him go, affected by the man's directness and friendliness at the same time as he was affronted by such a carelessly overbearing character. Walking over to retrieve the javelin he worked at calming himself down, aware that he had learnt a useful lesson about his enemy. The man seemed to be of a piece, totally at ease. The fact that he was an arms-dealer could have emerged from his converstion at any moment and he would have owned up to it as an extension of his passion for weapons, just as anyone who talked lovingly about the law might reveal he was a judge. Wegelius appeared to be happy with himself, even blithe in spirit. Down by the stream he was throwing a stick for the Alsatian, trying to get it to jump into the water, his light voice raised like a boy's at play.

But how had she married such a mannikin? Such a small, sunburnt gnome with his chattering and showing-off? He knew Pauline's aversion to garrulous people; a left-over from the years she had spent being bombarded with words by her mother. Why had she chosen someone who would similarly afflict her?

He returned to Len's HQ where he found him cleaning the blades of the mower.

"See you've met the boss," he said with a grin. "I expect he wore your ear out."

"He can certainly talk when he wants to," Eric replied, glad that Len had given him the opportunity to be deprecatory.

"Nice bloke though," Len reminded him. "A lot of people in his position wouldn't be bothered to talk to the likes of us the way he does. At least he assumes we've got some brains, which is something to be grateful for when you're as thick as I am." He finished off his work, wiping the blades over with a rag. "Time for my lesson?"

Eric had given Len three driving-lessons on the scooter since starting work as his assistant. Each of these had been unsuccessful because Len could not keep the heavy machine in balance and some new scratches and dents on the bodywork showed how often he had come off. However, none of the accidents was serious and he had retained his determination to succeed, looking forward to the day when he had a scooter of his own.

"Don't worry," he said as he strapped the crash-helmet on and straddled the machine, bringing it down off its stand. "I'll pay for it to be restored to its original condition. Let's have the key."

Eric gave it to him, his face betraying his concern.

"Don't look so dismal," Len rebuked him with a grin. "You never know, I might get it right this time."

He started up the scooter, twisted the handgrip throttle as he put it into first gear, and pulled smoothly away, manoeuvring round the concrete yard.

"Better," Eric shouted. "You're improving."

Len grinned and drove up the gravel path towards the house, the flowers and shrubs whipping against his legs. Eric ran after him until they emerged in the courtyard, then trotted up through the orchard, out of the gates and down the track to Len's house.

When Len dismounted and put the scooter up on its stand beside the back door he was grinning proudly.

"Got the hang of it, I think," he said. "It's all a matter of confidence."

Wegelius stayed at home for a week before leaving on his travels again. During this time he encountered Eric on several days and always stopped for a chat, albeit a one-sided one. He displayed a knowledge of gardening which was far beyond Eric's (even with his recent reading to catch up and Len's tuition), as well as a nicely-calculated level of impudence and curiosity which was impossible to react against without bringing down an accusation of over-sensitivity. After their first encounter Eric deflected most of his questions with a shield of non-committal replies, but he had more difficulty with Wegelius's penchant for man-talk in the shape of queries about what the local girls were like and whether Eric was getting his fair share. Sometimes he suspected that Pauline was putting him up to it, recalling her suggestion that he should find a girlfriend. When Wegelius did depart on a trip to Japan and Eric resumed his nocturnal visits, he taxed Pauline on the subject but she laughed it off.

"Don't be ridiculous," she said, "he's only talking to you like that for fun."

"Well, I find it bloody insulting," Eric retorted, "especially when he's just got out of your bed."

"He doesn't sleep in my bed," she said acridly. "But you'd have never thought of asking whether he did or not, would you? You haven't got the sense."

"Where does he sleep, then?"

"In his own room."

He looked at her suspiciously.

"Show me," he said.

She got out of bed, put on her dressing-gown, then took him out of the room and down to the other end of the passageway. He followed her, naked, the dog nosing his buttocks from behind. Then she opened a door and ushered him into a large room which was bare and spartan, the only colour being provided by the golden tones of a parquet floor.

"I can't see you sleeping here I must say," he said, putting his arms round her from behind.

"Don't think of saying sorry."

"Sorry."

"No, I mean it," she replied, releasing herself. "You have to face up to the fact that I do occasionally have to let him."

Eric doubled up as if he had been smitten by a sudden pain in his gut and sat on the bed, his eyes closed.

"How often?" he asked when he knew that she was not going to retract.

"What does it matter?"

"HOW OFTEN!" he shouted, frightening the dog which sloped off into a corner. "I need to know."

She shrugged to show him that he had failed to frighten her then sat down beside him.

"Only now and again. You must have assumed he would, surely?"

"Oh, God," Eric groaned, rolling to one side. "You shouldn't have told me. I can't stand the thought of it."

Pauline pulled back the covers of the bed and levered him into it, her face as grave as a mother's with a sick child. He offered no resistance, lying on her as a dead weight. Dragging off her dressing-gown she pressed herself against him but he could not respond.

"Come on," she whispered. "Get your own back in his bed."

He moved, spurred by her brutality.

"What's happened to you?" he said, repugnance and astonishment mixing in his voice.

"I don't want to talk about it any more," she murmured into the hair at the base of his skull. "Why don't you just accept things as they are? At least we're together."

He lay with her clinging to his back for an hour, both of them refusing to move out of obstinacy and hope that the other would relent. Eventually she seduced him by the slightest movements of her finger-tips.

During his hour of paralysis he shredded the last of his illusions and abandoned any hold he had kept on their past. With this process of destruction went his last store of pride in anything other than his share of her. When, after a frenetic and unjoyful coupling, he did come into her, it was at the summit of a miserable haul out of himself: but the peace afterwards was serene in its way, restful as well as resigned, like the sleep of refugees who have escaped from old oppressions and have yet to wake up to the new.

25

In April Wegelius took Pauline to the Bahamas for a month in the sun while the English winter made its final retreat in wind and rain. Coming to hear of Eric's intention to find a place of his own, Wegelius asked him to house-sit at Fenlon Old Farm, offering to compensate Len for lost rent and mentioning to Eric that an arrangement was possible whereby a part of the house which had previously been made into a self-contained flat might be made available to him provided he would agree to house-sit whenever the need arose.

This offer sparked off a fierce dispute between Eric and Pauline as she saw no reason why he should not jump at the chance while he viewed it as just another humiliation; an attitude which had no logic for her at all. As far as she was concerned they had crossed the border into their own country months ago; the laws were their own, the way of life was peculiarly fitted to their own needs, and what they would undertake in terms of compromises must be governed by the one guiding principle; that their love was sacredly private, incapable of being judged by standards other than their own.

After a long, bitter battle, she won. Eric moved into the quarters which she, 'with her own hands' as Wegelius joked, had prepared for him. Linen, cutlery, crockery, a radio and television, a fully equipped kitchen, were waiting when he entered his new home after watching the Daimler drive out of the courtyard on its way to Heathrow Airport.

Her final act of loving treason had been to obtain Wegelius's consent to Eric having visitors to stay. When she informed him of this further act of generosity (the rent discussed in these negotiations already having been fixed at a peppercorn level, should he accept the offer), she made it clear that girlfriends were not excluded from the general licence to entertain guests. This had made him furious but she had argued, using sharp altruism, that as he had to endure her having another man there was no reason why he should not have another woman.

"Besides," she had added, "it will stop Bruno being so imaginative about your love-life if you're open about it. He just can't stand the thought of you being sex-starved."

Her coolness about these matters enraged him but the time for protest had passed. Day by day he had been drawn into the rhythm of being with her, having her, knowing she was near, and no matter how enormous her expectations, or how shameful her proposals, he acceded. Whatever arguments he could put up were always squashed by the strange, byzantine pragmatism which she had constructed as a basis for their life together; whatever pain it caused, the system worked. As he began to imagine what lay ahead, he knew that she had the flexible cunning to find a solution. She had become the leader because by marrying Wegelius she had pre-empted all his plans. When he conjectured as to whether she would have done the same to be with him if he had married someone else, he knew that she would not. Her pride was of a different grain to his, having grown out of a richer soil.

He wrote to Daniel and invited him down for Easter, having decided that it would be an unhappy choice to go and spend it with his mother and brother in Liverpool. He had received several letters from home after his initial one communicating the altered direction of his life. All of them had been plaintive, tinged with rebuke and regret for what he had done. The last had been accompanied by some notes from the family solicitor about his position with regard to the trust set up by his father's will. Under the provisions of the legacy both sons were bound to sell their shares to each other, or their mother, if they left the family business, and this option to sell came into force at twenty-one, but his father had hoped it would not be invoked. Taken in conjunction with a lump sum which he would also inherit on his twenty-first birthday — still two years hence — he stood to receive a sum between thirty-five and forty thousand pounds, provided the ironmongery business continued at its present level of profit. It was the solicitor's opinion, backed by his mother, that he would be mad to sell when the time came. Given this advice, she argued, would he not be better off becoming a working partner in the business rather than wasting his time at a job only a cut above that of a common labourer?

Surrounded by Wegelius's wealth as he was, he could not think about money. It was not a form of competition he could venture into because, although he was potentially well-off by middle-class standards, he could not compare himself with his rival. At root he knew that he was the man in Pauline's life and money had nothing to do with it so he aimed at reducing its importance. He was frugal, contemptuous of possessions, and never anticipated or made plans for the inheritance. It was so far away and, in his present style of looking at things, he could not imagine what those two years would bring.

He received some help in focusing on the future when Daniel accepted his invitation and came to spend a week with him at Fenlon Old Farm. After only a few months of interim political development Daniel had become an active radical socialist and it was into this fold he tried to shepherd his friend, woman-problems and all. Living actually inside the palace of a super-capitalist whose morality was so astoundingly and unrepentantly negative gave Daniel plenty of opportunities to make comparisons between Eric's situation and larger political issues. Also he made friends with Len and Barbara, and the dog, using them as figures in his long, perspicacious analyses.

"You've allowed yourself to become the victim of your own adolescence," he confided to Eric one night as they sat, at Daniel's insistence, eating haddock and chips at Wegelius's majestic William and Mary oak dining-table (one of many token gestures of defiance which Daniel had found necessary to practise while he stayed at Fenlon Old Farm), "and it basically comes down to your refusal to work out a system of values beyond this one woman. She's frozen your intellect. She's stopped you maturing. You've become en-tropic. You live here in this loathsome Shangri-la waiting for the scraps from this shit Wegelius's table, meanwhile your mind rots, your ambitions die. . ."

Eric objected to the idea that his mind was rotting and pointed out that he was learning as much as he could about gardening. He had already accumulated a library of his own on the subject and was becoming quite knowledgeable. In Len's opinion he was doing very well.

Daniel opened another bottle of the Margaux which he had persuaded Eric to filch fromWegelius's cellar.

"You're justifying every downward adjustment that you make," he lectured. "Don't imagine that doesn't satisfy her. She sees you in a woman's perspective, driven by a destructive urge to reduce your maleness to shreds."

"I didn't think you'd be able to talk more rubbish than you used to," Eric mused, crumpling the vinegar-soaked newspaper from his fish and chips into a ball and throwing it into the fire, "but you can."

"What's the future going to be like?" Daniel squawked indignantly, his ears edged with vermilion. "Your genes will travel backwards. Wouldn't you say that your family probably came from the servant class at some time? Your dad got you out of it through hard work and you're just undoing all he achieved. For what? Getting your leg over?"

Eric poured himself a full glass of wine and stared at the fire through it, pondering.

"Strange how conventional you've become," he said quietly.

"Me? Conventional?" Daniel replied, bridling.

"There's only one world for you, one interpretation of existence, one way of being, looking at things . . ."

"No, I deny that," Daniel came back at him. "You're the one imprisoned by a convention. You've become obsessed by the most poisonous and debilitating convention of modern times; love, the capitalist-Christian fallacy. I've escaped from it. With one heroic leap I sprang over the wall. So should you."

"Hennie has a lot to answer for."

"She was very like Pauline."

Eric was dumbfounded.

"Pauline? Like Hennie?" He shook his head violently. "Don't talk such a load of crap."

"She'll do anything to get her own way. It doesn't matter how much it hurts you, does it? She wants to be rich so she marries a multi-millionaire who just happens to be an arms-dealer. She wants to have a lover so she calls up her old boyfriend and moves him in."

"It's not like that!" Eric protested.

"Looks like it to me."

"I think you'd better go."

Daniel laughed and swilled his wine around in the glass.

"That's three times you've told me to do that," he scoffed. "And it's always when you're losing the argument."

"You don't change much, do you?" Eric snapped. "Same old tactics. Adopt the all-knowing pose, pour scorn on the opposition, then declare yourself the winner before the argument's over." He paused, his lips compressed as if contemplating a supreme risk. "Your trouble is this: you confuse sex with love."

"*I* do?" Daniel shrieked. "That's your blind spot. No one can love until they're forty. That's my view. From what I've seen, all the stuff before that is one variation of sex or another. What creates love is children and the experience of bringing them up."

"How do you know that? You haven't had a child."

"True, but I can work off real data, not fantasy. All you've done is use this woman as an excuse to reject reality. Your relationship with her is no more than a form of elaborated onanism. She induces the worst kind of romantic addiction in you. Know what that is? The narcotic pleasure of self-destruction. See what she's achieved? When I first knew you there wasn't another boy in the school with so much potential. You were mentioned in the same breath as candidates for Oxford and Cambridge, my dear fellow. Now, look at you. Up to your ears in manure, sharing your doxy with a rampant purveyor of pain and suffering, and a future staring you in the face which isn't far from desperate. When you're clapped out and completely ga-ga with the tension of it all she'll fire you for pruning the rose wrong and Wegelius will sell you as a human target to the Saudi Arabian camel corps, mate. That's my scenario." He put his glass down and ceremoniously got to his feet. "Now I suppose you'll throw me out so I'll just collect my hat and coat."

Eric attempted to hide his amusement but failed. When Daniel observed his success he sat down again with a sigh of satisfaction.

"All hope has not been abandoned," he murmured sanguinely.

"Let's talk about you for a change," Eric suggested with sardonic generosity. "We used to do that quite a lot, I remember."

Daniel dismissed the idea with a whinny of amusement.

"No point in that. My personality has been submerged in my political identity. There is no *me* to talk about. You see, unholy turd, the reason I understand you is that I have become as much a servant as you have, only my master is principle, not pussy."

"Who's running away from reality now?"

"Depends what you're running towards. We know where you're headed. Me?" He thumbed his chest. "I'm after a better society, not orgasm. You haven't got this woman in perspective. All you've done is absorb Hollywood into your bloodstream. Men and women aren't designed for great romance. They're intended to have relationships which are mildly but sporadically exciting in order to make the buggers breed, that's all. These liaisons don't bear thinking about beyond the supposition that they exist for the sake of mutual support and the preservation of social order." He paused for breath, pleased with himself. "And where does that leave you? You've taken this piece of ancient emotional folk-lore and made a fetish out of it.

"Is it so difficult to understand?" Eric pleaded. "Some people put their career first, others their family or their life's work or a vocation, with me it's a woman. Why not?"

"Know what they say in the Yorkshire coalfields?"

"They say a lot of things, if I remember rightly."

"The miners say that cunt will draw a man further than dynamite will blow him."

"Do they, really? How observant those lads are."

"And Aristotle said that some men are born to be slaves. They can't help it. It's just implicit in their natures. If you were a free man you would have told her to go to hell."

"I understand her need for a world outside me."

"That's just claptrap!" Daniel roared, flaring the wide nostrils of his heavy, high-mounted nose. "I just don't damn well believe you!"

"Neither did I until now," Eric admitted. "Talking to you has forced me to work it out. Strikes me you only do good when you least intend it, which is the result of being pissed on politics, I suppose."

In spite of the heat and insults generated by their nightly debates about whose life made most sense. Eric and Daniel enjoyed being together again. During the day Daniel helped out in the garden, winning Len's good opinion by his willingness to undertake drudgery for the sake of friendship; and his sense of humour which included calling Len Lenin because he was a natty dresser who favoured waistcoats and was bald.

On the third evening of Daniel's visit they went to a dance at the Working Men's Club with Len and Barbara. Before going they had dinner at Len's house and arrived at the dance in good spirits, already primed by several bottles of pale ale.

There were only a few unmarried girls at the dance, the majority of women being the wives of the members. Daniel paid a lot of attention to Barbara in fun once he discovered how easy it was to amuse her. Len drifted off to talk to other farm and estate workers he knew.

Daniel's jibes about slavery and dropping out had got through Eric's defences, stirring up his bile again about Pauline's unnerving proposal that he should find himself a second woman. He also felt, drunk as he was, that he needed to show Daniel that he was a free agent and not subservient to Pauline's whims. One of the girls was attractive; tall, thin, dark-complexioned with long, blonde hair tied up in a ponytail. She had spent most of the evening jiving with a girlfriend but he had noticed her snatching looks at him as she twirled around, showing her legs.

At the start of a new tune from the three-piece band on the rostrum at the end of the hall, Eric got up and went over to break up the jive that the two girls had embarked upon. As he approached them, the tall girl whirled around until her white skirt flapped against his legs. As soon as he held out his hand she accepted it with a grin, allowing him to take over the direction of the dance. As it was a fast number conversation was impossible. At the end of it he invited her to the bar in the next room for a drink. They sat at a folding table on a couple of chairs which he had to unstack from a pile. As he looked at her over the top of his pint she crinkled up her eyes and smiled.

"I haven't seen you here before," she said.

Eric gave her a minimal explanation of how he had come to be living in Churt, concentrating on his new career as a gardener rather than any aspect of his past. He discovered that her name was Stephanie and she was an apprentice hairdresser who lived and worked in Aldershot but Churt was her birthplace and her father and mother still lived there running a small market-garden on the southern outskirts. Her manner was chirpy and eager-to-please, her light chatter ornamented with gestures. What repelled Eric was her hair which was in the wrong style for the pointed shape of her face. It gave her a marginally mad appearance, forcing what good features she had into disequilibrium. When he had the opportunity to study her closer he saw that the ponytail was, in fact, a hair-piece.

"What are you looking at," she asked, catching the direction of his eyes, her hand flying up to the back of her head. "Is it coming off?"

Eric laughed and shook his head, his revulsion dispelled.

"Do you want me to take it off?" she said willingly. "I hate it. God knows why I allowed myself to be persuaded to wear such a thing. My friend Katrina made me do it, the fool." She paused, her hand still at the junction of the ponytail. "D'you mind if I do it here? It won't take a minute."

Eric assured her that he had no objection and watched as she unpinned the hair-piece. When she did so he was surprised at the difference that it made. Her own hair was cut neck-length and lay over her ears and forehead in a corona of bleached ends which was pretty and appealing.

She held up the ponytail.

"What shall I do with it now?" she said with a grin. "I've got nowhere to put it."

Eric took the hair-piece off her, folded it up and stuffed it into his pocket.

"I've got your scalp," he said.

"We'll see about that," she replied. "Come on, let's dance. I can read you better when we're on the dance-floor."

By the end of the evening he had kissed her a few times during the slow dances when the lights were lowered. She had responded but with reserve. When he asked if she would like to come back to Fenlon Old Farm for a cup of coffee, offering to run her home on his scooter afterwards, she declined the invitation because she had to return to Aldershot and she had a lift in a friend's car. Eric offered to run her back himself but she made a joke about it, having counted the number of pints of beer he had drunk that night. However, she did promise to see him two days later when she had the afternoon off from work.

When he got back to Fenlon Old Farm with Daniel after a large nightcap of cream sherry at Len's house, he sat in the kitchen waiting for Daniel's onslaught of questions and comments about the new girl. None came. Daniel appeared to be happy with yet another bottle of Wegelius's Margaux and a provocative diatribe about Britain's rôle in South African politics. It was only when he had spent himself on this subject and his eyelids were drooping that he spread himself across the table and patted his friend's arm.

"Tell me something," he said with a leer, feigning sleep.

Eric tensed, knowing the signs which heralded yet another foray into his psyche.

"What do you want to know?"

"It's of great anthropological interest to me, being, as I am, a stranger to the tribal rituals of Churt," Daniel hummed professorially. "Please give me details of the tabu which stipulates that she had to cut her hair off before turning you down."

He had arranged to meet Stephanie on the same day as Daniel was due to leave Churt to spend some of the Easter holidays with his family in Yorkshire. After saying goodbye to Len and Barbara, who made him promise to return soon, Daniel rode with Eric on the scooter to Farnham Station to catch a train to London and then on to Doncaster.

As they waited for the train Daniel raised the question of a trip to Greece that summer. It was something they had talked about in the past. When Eric said that he thought it was impossible, given his circumstances, Daniel was scathing.

"Don't be an idiot!" he fumed. "She'll want you to go away on your own holiday. Don't you understand the way her mind works?"

"I've got no holiday entitlement this year," Eric replied patiently. "I'll have only been here seven or eight months by August."

"Wegelius will give you time off. He'll give you anything you ask for because you're so useful to him. Gardener, dog-minder, house-sitter, wife-pacifier. See how it all works out?"

The train approached and Daniel slung his rucksack over his shoulder and gave Eric a strong embrace, digging the hinge of his spectacles into his cheek.

"You know where I am if you need me," he whispered, "but for any run-of-the-mill stuff I should go along to the nearest asylum if I were you. Give Pauline a bite on the nipple for me and tell her she's got it made. Adios, muggins."

He got into a carriage and pulled the window down, hanging out as far as he could go, his arms held wide.

"The Delphic Oracle! The theatre at Epidaurus! The pass at Thermopylae!" he shouted as the train drew away. "You need to visit these shrines of male supremacy if you're ever going to get your sanity back."

26

The house where Pauline and Bruno Wegelius were spending their holiday was situated on a low hill at the back of an inlet on the north-western coast of Andros Island, two hundred miles to the west of Nassau across the Northern Providence Channel. From the verandah of the comma-shaped stressed concrete mansion, lent to them by a business colleague of Bruno's, they had sweeping views over the Great Bahama Bank and the estate where young Neville Chamberlain, a future British Prime Minister, spent six formative years sweating to start a sisal plantation. As was the case with that product of his final years, the Munich Agreement of nineteen thirty-eight, premature euphoria led to humiliating disaster, his dreams withering in the blast of belligerent natural forces.

It was a perfect place to relax. There were six servants to run the house; the beach was three hundred yards away; the weather fair, warm and breezy. Most of the time there were other visitors coming and going, arriving by yacht and light aircraft from Nassau and staying for a few days of business discussions with Bruno. Sometimes they brought their wives or mistresses or hangers-on but Pauline preferred it when the men came unaccompanied. She had no wish to be convivial with women in her own predicament.

She spent most of each day reading. During the last six months she had worked her way through thirteen of the major texts set for her aborted degree course at King's College. From *Nostromo* she had gone to *Passage to India*; from thence to the *Dubliners* and *Portrait of the Artist as a Young Man*, then into Lawrence and Hemingway before reversing over four centuries to Sir Thomas Browne's *Religio Medici* and *Religio Laici* and Burton's *Anatomy of Melancholy*. The other books were mainly literary criticism, linguistics and linguistic philosophy and psychology. She had to admit that she enjoyed those less than the texts themselves as they seemed to provide no more than pretentiously-wrought insights into fabricated human mysteries written for purposes of escape.

After the first two months of her marriage to Wegelius she had begun to suffer from headaches which were being caused by straining her eyes with so much reading. She got some spectacles which helped but Wegelius complained. Now she only wore them when she was alone or in the safety of her room and she bathed her eyes regularly. An agreement had been reached that she would not read over meals or in company, except when circumstance permitted, such as a beach-party or when cruising. Also Wegelius had requested that she should stop larding what little conversation she offered with so much allusion to literature. It disturbed him and made his visitors feel that she was contemptuous of them. The result of these prohibitions was that Pauline developed a style of speedy, incongruous chatter which emanated from her like torchlight whenever she decided that it was needed. The effect of this was to make Wegelius's colleagues and their women believe Pauline to be eccentric; a diagnosis which she carefully encouraged as it made them leave her more to herself.

This defence was occasionally put under pressure when a man appeared on the scene who wanted to seduce her. This was not an infrequent problem because she was much more beautiful than the other women who accreted to Wegelius and his friends. Pauline's tactics were to accelerate volubility and incoherence and give signs which even a dunce could interpret as being evidence of a personality disorder. In this manner she protected herself from all but the most stupid of her admirers.

By the time she had arrived on Andros Island she had known that she was pregnant and there was no doubt in her mind that Eric was the father. She calculated that if Bruno had the wit to do it, he could catch her out. If the child was born when she estimated, Bruno could work out that she had conceived during the middle of one of his protracted absences. There was, however, little risk of his so doing; but if he did then she would simply tell him the lie that the birth was premature or late. Compared to the major untruth that she would have to tell him — that the baby was his — this deception would be of a minor order. What she would never admit to was that she had deliberately got pregnant during a time when he had been absent in order to be certain that Eric was the father. Only her lover would know that, and she had the entry in her diary to prove it to him should he doubt her word. She had rehearsed the scene in her mind when she would tell him: first he would be overjoyed, then would come suspicion, finally anger as the joy became discoloured with jealousy. The best approach she could make was to be direct and to show him how she had been able to anticipate his thinking. Once he had accepted that the child was his, she reckoned that Eric would never be uncertain of her priorities again.

She knew that Eric would hate the thought that Wegelius could believe himself to be the father. Although he tolerated the strange arrangement of their clandestine ménage, Eric saw his essential rôle as that of husband, a continuation of their earlier natural marriage being the underlying strength he counted on to sustain them through the tortuous complications she had led him into. This child would be proof to him that their original love had survived intact the estrangement which had followed upon Deidre's death. To Eric, Wegelius had no place in this; he was a deviation, a quirk of mad behaviour which Eric would never truly understand. But to Pauline it was Wegelius's surrogate fatherhood which made having the baby possible. Without it, Eric would take everything she had, destroy her success in fulfilling her mother's wishes in some part, drag her down into a domesticity she loathed, and reduce her horizons. His kind of love was darkly possessive, not enlightening; rich but not varied enough to suit her thoughts. Leo had given her a taste for the curious and artful in these matters which, although a curse, was now so ingrained and active in her psyche as to be ineradicable and, above all, she needed to feel that within whatever web was woven she could sit in the centre and be alone.

At the end of May the weather in the Caribbean deteriorated and there were warnings of hurricanes. As the winds closed in on Andros a group of American and Canadian guests were caught on the island, unable to leave by boat or 'plane. As their hostess, Pauline was forced to note her husband's request that she should put more effort into entertaining them as the customary pastimes of swimming and sunbathing were no longer available.

She surprised him by her ability to organise the party into playing cards, Scrabble, dice and all forms of indoor amusements, and by her easy-going manner. As the winds increased she became more and more affable towards people for whom she had previously nothing but contempt. As the days passed and the cooped-up guests turned to drinking as a relief from the oppression of the weather, one of the Canadians began to make surreptitious advances to her. He was a quiet, unassuming man of about forty whose only perceptible vanity was of his pure white hair which he wore shoulder-length. When he first spoke to Pauline about his feelings for her he was very drunk and it was past one o'clock in the morning. The wind was howling over the island and the surf was so high that it was visible through the trees, glowing with the animation of giant, phosphorescent dancers.

His name was Philip and he had a stutter which had got worse as he drank. When he cornered Pauline he could only manage to say that he ha-ha-had to ha-ha-ha-have her. As she moved away he followed her repeating this. It was so ludicrous that she could not stop laughing although she could sense that the man was in earnest. It was only when she saw Wegelius watching her that she was able to become stern enough to deal with Philip and send him away.

The next morning Philip did not appear at breakfast, lunch or dinner. The following day the storm abated and the guests were able to leave. Philip passed Pauline on his way to the car which was to take him to the airport. Although he turned his face away and held up the lapel of his coat she caught a glimpse of his injuries.

As he was driven away Wegelius appeared at her elbow and gave her a gentle nudge in the ribs, waving at the car.

"Ha-ha-ha-have a good trip, Phil!" he called out, putting his arm round her shulders and giving her a possessive squeeze. "Ho-ho-hope you ha-ha-haven't been b-b-bored."

That evening he came to her room. She was sitting on the balcony, reading. The sky was clear and the sea had calmed back into its usual blue repose.

"Well, I'm glad they've all gone," he said, bouncing on the end of the bed. "Thank you for all the hard work you did on them. We got something achieved."

Pauline testily flipped over a page, refusing to look at him. Getting down on all fours he crawled over and squinted up at the title of the book.

"What is it this time?" he asked boyishly.

"Milton," she replied. "D'you mind?"

"Sorry about Philip but I had to sort him out."

Pauline put the book down on her lap and looked into the starred darkness.

"Show me your hands," she said suddenly.

He held them out to her, palms upward. Taking hold, she turned them over and pointedly examined his knuckles.

"You couldn't even do it yourself," she remarked off-handedly, letting go of him. "Are you sure you didn't hire someone to get me pregnant?"

His face lost all its animal mobility. From his eyes, usually so vital, came a dull light.

"Come on, kid," he muttered. "What are you saying?"

She frowned and patted the book on her belly.

"It's true. I'm having a baby," she said, her head cocked on one side. "Aren't I good?"

He stopped absorbing the insult she had flung at him and began to deal with the announcement. Life came back into his eyes, he smiled, his mouth worked, his hands gripped her thighs, and, as a disguise for not knowing what to say, he allowed himself the luxury of noisy, demonstrative weeping.

Her husband's delight at the news that she was with child was harrowing. She had expected him to glide into the idea using the facility he employed on politics, war and business, subjugating all contemplation and conscience while coping with great issues to his profit; but her pregnancy shook him. He was frightened of the strength of his feelings and spent the remainder of their time on Andros in a daze. To her this was the worst reaction he could have had. It meant that Wegelius would hover over the event, seeing it as an extension of his power. For Eric to endure this transformation of his rival from part-time husband to full-time father, knowing the child was his, would be difficult. As Wegelius's enthusiasm and anticipation increased, so did her imagination of the strife which might be caused.

It was, at first, with shame then with bravura that she recognised the pleasure this prospect offered. She already accepted the notion of a two-fold father for her child, each part compensating for the other's inadequacies, as well as keeping herself out of the pit of maternal domesticity — a hell she feared far more than the danger of repercussions should the two men openly clash. For her it was a creative state, devoid of routine, and she was at the centre of it, and within that centre was the child, held in a secret orbit presided over by planetary ghosts.

Her last act upon leaving the Bahamas was to post three cards she had written, but been unable to mail, to Leo. Before putting them into the box at the airport post office she read them through, alarmed by the historical mustiness of what she had scribbled in the immediate past. She was changing so rapidly that it had become painful to encounter the person she had been barely a week ago. Every thought that woman had had was already obsolete: there was only the future and its transformations, the one beauty which she had come to respect.

Upon arriving home at Fenlon Old Farm she immediately went to look for Eric. It was three o'clock in the afternoon and he should have been at work. His damaged scooter was parked outside the gardener's buildings, the handlebars badly bent and one side of the machine severely scraped, but he was not in the office. Returning to the house she went to look for him in the flat and met a tall young woman who was bleaching her hair in the kitchen sink.

Pauline apologised for her intrusion and was about to leave when the woman finished rinsing her hair, bound it up in a towel and held out her hand.

"You must be Mrs Wegelius," she said. "I'm Stephanie, Eric's wife."

Pauline took the cold, damp hand and gave it a brief pressure, staring into the stranger's turbaned face. It was exotic, a beauty from a sultan's seraglio, the irises of her eyes brilliantly blue, her lips pale and lavishly-formed. Only the voice was wrong: high and strongly accented, and the longer she examined the stranger and listened to her voice, the more the beauty of the first impression diminished, until she was finally left facing someone quite ordinary.

"Eric's at the hospital with Len. He had an accident on the scooter this morning."

Pauline listened, watching runnels of water travel down the girl's pale cheeks. The kitchen was in a mess, half-eaten food was on the table, the stove was encrusted, used dishes were stacked high on the draining-board. The girl's feet were bare and dirty as she shuffled over to the electric kettle and filled it, still talking.

"Eric told him lots of times that he couldn't go on a public road until he'd got a provisional licence and learnt to control the bike better, but he wouldn't listen. The lorry driver was in a terrible state, he thought he'd killed him but, as it happened, he'd only broken his leg."

She plugged in the kettle and turned it on, smiling at Pauline in a soft, creepy way which made Pauline get ready to retreat.

"If you don't mind me saying so," she said timidly, "you're as pretty as my Eric says you are."

Pauline caught sight of herself in the kitchen mirror, a blur of tanned skin, her eyes mercifully hidden by sunglasses. There was nothing anyone could respond to except a received image culled from a magazine. Suddenly she felt wildly angry that he had seen fit to pick someone so credulous, so lame-brained.

"Would you like a coffee?" Stephanie offered, her accent adjusted upwards. "I'm just making some."

"No thank you," Pauline replied. "Do you know where Eric is?"

"He's gone to the hospital with Len. The accident only happened this morning."

"When he comes back please tell him that I'd like to see him."

"Is there anything wrong?" Stephanie said, her eyes wary. "You don't mind me being here?"

"Eric was given permission to have guests," Pauline said enigmatically, her self-control returning. "This is a new situation. We can talk about it."

"Oh, dear," Stephanie said, suddenly sitting down on a kitchen chair. "I told him we'd rushed things. Don't worry, though, Mrs Wegelius. We can sort it out. Eric and me will find somewhere local."

Pauline's attitude softened as she saw the distress in the woman's eyes. There was so much more in this situation that could hurt her if she knew why Eric had got married. But, now it was done, she could see from the victim how, by his hasty obedience, Eric had accomplished three things: he had satisfied her demand; he had ridiculed her thinking; he had got his own back.

"I didn't want to move in, Mrs Wegelius. I put myself in your place and I said to Eric, we have to wait and ask them when they get back from their holidays, but he wouldn't have it. No, he said, it will be all right, you'll see."

A taxi pulled into the courtyard and Eric got out. Pauline watched him through the kitchen window as Stephanie chattered on, her voice getting higher and higher as she saw the confrontation ahead. But Pauline was hardly aware of what she was saying. Eric had changed in the month that she had been away. He had put on weight. His beard was thicker and redder. He walked with a more powerful, defiant swing. She yearned to hear his voice and touch his skin.

"Oh, God, please don't have a shouting-match, Mrs Wegelius," Stephanie whined. "He's not in a good mood, I can see that by the look on his face. It's not surprising with his scooter smashed up, is it?"

Pauline heard him come through the side entrance and the sound of his boots along the corridor. She turned to face the kitchen door. He thrust it open. The air around him had its own smell, an aura of earth and indignation. As he spoke his reddened beard moved like an ox's head.

"That bloody old fool, Len!" he shouted with a laugh. "He'll never learn. He'll be three months off work, at least. Oh, hello, *madam*! How was your holiday."

"Eric!" Stephanie whispered. "Mrs Wegelius wants to talk to you about me being here."

He sat down at the kitchen table. She saw how his eyes were fiercer, set in his tanned brow, surrounded by luxuriant hair. Anger was everywhere, in every glitter, every detail, every contraction of his nostril.

"This is a business matter, Steph. I'll sort it out with my employer when he has a minute. Would you like to see all the work I've been doing in the garden, *madam*? I've re-designed much of it. I've got lots of plans for the future. I hope you'll approve. If you've got a moment I'd like to show you what I intend to do with the ground where I've pulled up those old blackcurrant bushes. Gypsophilia, I thought, and potentilla."

He left off, crossing his legs in the manner of a man secure. Stephanie had caught the note of insolence in his voice and was cringeing by the stove, her back turned.

"I hear that you're to be congratulated," Pauline said carefully. "May I add my good wishes?"

"Well, that depends if the first thing you're going to do for my wife is throw her out into the street," Eric replied, guffawing. "Only a joke, *madam*. Weather's been great while you've been away. I think you would have got just as sun-burned if you'd stayed here."

Pauline watched him as he stripped off his jacket, hung it up behind the door, then rolled his sleeves up. The skin of his hands and arms was scratched and roughened and his nails were broken and dirty. As he stood at the sink and washed his hands she noticed how forceful and urgent his movements were, using twice as much energy as the operation required.

"I'll look at the garden later," she said, moving towards the door. "But as you've given me some good news about your marriage I'll give you some good news of my own. I'm having a baby. See you later."

She saw his back stiffen as he rinsed his hands in the sink. Stephanie let out a little cry of delight and, flunkey-like, opened the door.

"Oh, that's wonderful!" she cooed, her eyes pleading for Pauline to approve of her. "You're so lucky."

27

It was a week before Wegelius went away. The weather broke and Eric could not work out-of-doors. During the hours he spent in the garden office or cleaning machinery and implements, Wegelius often came down to discuss the swimming-pool (a project which both Len and Eric were opposed to), but he was never accompanied by Pauline. Impatient to talk about the child, Eric noted with resentment that Pauline often dropped in to see Stephanie as soon as he left the house, and was deliberately befriending her, offering her rival help and advice while playing the rôle of the lady of the manor for all it was worth, and firmly establishing her superiority over his second-string woman into the bargain.

As a result of discussions with Pauline, Stephanie came up with the idea of setting herself up as a mobile hairdresser, going to people's homes in the Churt area on a bicycle. Pauline gave Stephanie the use of the telephone and helped to draft an advertisement for the local papers in Hindhead and Farnham. She offered to lend money to purchase equipment but Stephanie had acquired most of this during her employment in Aldershot and it was not necessary to avail herself of Pauline's generosity. When Eric was told about the new venture it was a virtual *fait accompli* and Stephanie had a timetable of twenty-five clients to visit. She had assumed that he would be delighted with her enterprise but he was not so until Wegelius had gone away and Stephanie had pedalled off on her first appointment. As soon as she had disappeared from the courtyard, her equipment strapped into a basket and two panniers, the telephone in the garden office rang and Pauline asked him to go up to the house. He had seen through her machinations by the time he reached the house and his admiration and amazement were battling with his conscience, the image of the willing girl on her loaded bicycle shadowing his pleasure with guilt.

She was already in bed, brown against the white sheets. Taking off his jacket he hung it over a chair.

"You smell of something," she said, wrinkling her nose.

"I've been mixing fertiliser," he explained, pulling off his boots. "D'you want me to have a shower?"

"No, it doesn't matter. It's quite a nice smell, actually."

He stood naked by the bed, his hands shielding his genitals.

"Is it my child?" he asked.

"Of course it is, you idiot!" she replied, opening her arms in the first natural, warm gesture she had given him since her mother's death. Suspicious at first, having been starved of such generosity for so long, he crept into her embrace with slow, cautious care, feeling his way forward like a blind man. But once he could believe her, and sense the truth of it in her, he exploded into ecstatic tears.

From that day he counted it as the time when he recovered all his lost ground. In his mind it was a complete marriage from that point onwards, a view he thought she shared. He told her of his happiness and she corroborated what he felt, offering no explanations or excuses for her treatment of him or submitting plans for the future.

"The main thing," she said as she comforted him, "is that we're together again. We'll just have to see what happens."

Len came out of hospital ten days later. After a month of convalescence he was told by the specialist that he should think of changing his job because the leg would never be the same as it was before the accident. When Len discussed the matter with Wegelius he found him to be not only sympathetic but peculiarly imaginative as to an alternative form of employment, suggesting that Len might like to become his chauffeur. As Len had been rendered *hors de combat* by failing to ride a scooter properly, the proposition that he should succeed in becoming a professional driver made him smart at first, assuming that Wegelius was mocking him. But in this he was incorrect. Once Len had recuperated, Wegelius had him taught by a driving school and within two months he had passed the test and was installed as the family chauffeur, driving Wegelius and Pauline around in the Daimler. He maintained an interest in the garden but was only allowed to do light work. As he had a form of compensation in his new post of chauffeur he gladly yielded up the post of *de facto* head gardener to Eric.

During this time excavations began for the swimming-pool which was to be located on the south side of the house. In order to provide space for the pool, the kitchen fruit and vegetable garden had to be destroyed and a new one made out of meadowland. Because so much work was being done in the garden which involved upset, Eric submitted designs for a whole new layout to Wegelius, the product of his studies. The previous owner, the parsimonious Mr Holt, had neglected the basic needs of the land, refusing to spend money on necessary enrichment of the sandy soil. Eric proposed a large investment in humus and fertiliser and some soil replacement. All in all, half of the garden would be dug out, improved and replanted. Wegelius approved the plan and Eric was given permission to hire temporary labour as he did not wish to bring in contractors who might dispute his design for, although his knowledge was new and often insecure, the important thing about it was that it was *his* and he must make it work.

Within all this upheaval Stephanie struggled to make her new life. The hastiness of her marriage to Eric had been based on equal parts of infatuation and pragmatism — she could not visualise a better opportunity presenting itself (even without being appraised of his potential wealth as he had kept this secret). She was a plucky, decent woman, determined to do her best and work hard, but she recognised that her honeymoon was over within a week of Pauline's return from Andros. Up until then she had had all of Eric's attention. Their sex-life had been a revelation to her of what pleasure and intimacy could do for the spirit. His temper had been cool but considerate, always friendly and only passionate when it mattered, but once Wegelius had returned he became bad-tempered, moody and difficult. With so much going on around her Stephanie assumed that this change was attributable to pressure of work in his new position as head gardener and the havoc taking place all around the house. When she taxed him with his peevish-ness and suggested these as the causes he would agree with her and apologise, and there would be a brief improvement. It was sad for him to watch her become so happy again so quickly and then, once he forgot his good intentions, become so confused and cowed as his ill-nature re-appeared, but he could not help it; her suffering was a form of compensation for his own frustration over Wegelius's power and he needed that counterbalancing pain.

Stephanie's business prospered, however. When the weather was too bad for her to go out on her bicycle she was able to afford taxis to take her to her clients and when Wegelius was away Pauline often allowed Len to run her around in the Daimler.

Before they had got married Eric had told Stephanie that he did not want any children for at least five years. She had obediently gone to the birth-control clinic and had a coil fitted but as she saw Pauline's pregnancy advance she began to yearn for a child of her own. All the arguments against it belonged to Eric in terms of their jobs and the need to remain at Fenlon Old Farm. They could not expect to be allowed to keep the flat if they had a baby, he reasoned. Stephanie accepted all he said but the yearning persisted and she went against Eric's wishes and asked Pauline if they would lose the flat if she had a child. Pauline's answer was a definite no. She saw no objection and many advantages to there being two young children in the house together. She also saw fit to undermine Eric's insistence on having a sound financial base before a child was born by hinting to Stephanie about his legacy, alleging that he had casually mentioned it one day. He was staggered at her strategy: it stretched far into the foreseeable future, inextricably mixing his fortunes with Stephanie's. Until then he had had a hope that one day there might be a return to their old privacy, just the two of them, freed from Wegelius and Stephanie; but now he knew that this was not one she shared. The complexity of his life would be a constant. In her way she had communicated to him that it was also a guarantee of her happiness and thus something which he should learn to accept.

But he maintained his refusal to have a child with Stephanie even after he had talked himself out of the recriminations which arose from his dishonesty in keeping his legacy secret, employing the argument that people must only have children when they feel ready for parenthood. She refuted it by pointing out that one cannot really prepare for children, only be sure that one wants them, which he could not deny doing in case he hurt her.

Upset by his procrastination she had the coil removed without telling him and fell pregnant immediately. It was August before she plucked up the courage to let him know. They were at the opening party for the new swimming-pool, an event Eric had been looking forward to as it meant he could get on with finishing the garden. He was in a good mood, able to cope with the presence of Wegelius and a crowd of his London friends, playing his rôle as servant-cum-guest while Pauline performed as bountiful hostess, deliberately paying him no attention at all because Joe Nash, her grandfather, had come down for the party; but behind the red beard and the thicker, coarser physique he could not recognise the youth who had troubled him only a year ago.

While Pauline ceremoniously took the first swim, Stephanie whispered into Eric's ear that he shouldn't think Mrs Wegelius the only one who was expecting a baby. When he turned to look at her she shrank from the cornered gleam in his eyes and the fierceness with which he gripped her shoulders.

"Are you telling me you're pregnant?" he hissed, shaking her.

"Yes, I am," she replied bravely, "and I'm glad."

It was a warm summer evening. Everyone at the party was wearing a swimming-costume of one sort or another. Some of the guests had hired Edwardian and Victorian versions, some were in conventional bikinis. Eric had chosen to wear trousers and a shirt and tie as he preferred to accentuate rather than disguise his separate status.

With a loud yell he dived into the pool and swam a length underwater. When he emerged at the other end he was side by side with Pauline who was holding on to the rails of the steps.

"I've just been given some good news, Mr Wegelius!" he shouted as the party laughed at him. "It's a big day for me. Not only have I got rid of those bloody swimming-pool contractors who've been messing up my garden for months but I've just been told that I'm going to be a father!"

Wegelius beamed with delight and thought it was all a wonderful joke and a good way to baptise his pool. As Eric climbed out in his dripping clothes he saw his two women: one standing at the edge of the blue water, her tall figure questioning him; the other climbing out above his head, her womb showering him; and, above them both, the drunken guests and the mouth of the pitted moon mocking him.

Negotiating for a curacy in the Churt area proved to be a tricky business for Leo. The local archdeacon was aware of his reputation and, even though he was no conservative in theological matters, he thought it his duty to warn the Bishop of Winchester about Leo's freethinking tendencies. Leo made two visits to the south in order to calm their fears. He claimed that he was a changed man who had fully returned to the faith of his fathers. When the archdeacon wrily pointed out that, to his knowledge, Leo's father had been a card-carrying Communist, Leo justified his use of the phrase by saying that he had been speaking metaphorically: what he had intended to convey was that he had rejoined the mainstream of Anglican thought on all questions of fundamental doctrine. His desire to move from the north was a reflection of this sea-change in his spiritual condition.

There was no reason for anyone in the Church to doubt the sincerity of his reasons. Many clergymen who had possessed wayward philosophies in their youth had, after years of enforced vegetation, returned to the straight and narrow in their mature years; some of them had even achieved eminence, contributing to the impression that early rebellion in religious matters often leads to a useful orthodox stringency in later years.

While he awaited the result of his application for transfer Leo did not inform Pauline of his hopes, nor did he attempt to contact her while he was in Winchester which was only twenty miles away. She had told him that her child was expected in the first week of November and he was anxious to have moved south by then but in August he was still waiting for the authorities to decide. He had not heard from Eric for six months but there had been no need as he had had a regular supply of information from Pauline about his activities.

In the middle of September he was advised that he was appointed to a curacy at Saint Luke's at Grayshott, a village only two miles south of Churt; and was expected to take up the position by October the tenth. Although it was impossible for him to keep the news a secret in Kirkby Lonsdale as he had to make arrangements to move, he did not tell Pauline, wanting to arrive on the lovers' doorstep and surprise them at about the time their child (and in that possessive adjective he included himself) was due to be born.

The lack of personal contact with Eric had not offended him; after all, it was not the first time he had been neglected this way. As he heard from Pauline about the job in the garden, the marriage to Stephanie, the children, he knew that it was Eric's immersion in these scenes attendant upon his love for Pauline which had shut him off from his old dependencies. Once Leo re-appeared and claimed his place he was sure all would be well. Pauline had warned him that Eric had altered but, from her description, it sounded as though it had been in the right direction, towards a more substantial, knowing, intricately-wrought character who was no longer anyone's fool.

What he did regret was Eric's loss of interest in the javelin. 'After his initial resumption of training and a few competitions in the club team he had lost interest,' Pauline wrote. 'Bruno tried to encourage him but it came to nothing. I did ask him why and, in his grumpy way, he told me that he had no energy to waste.'

By the end of September the new layout for the garden was finished. Wegelius, true to his word, had spent a very large sum on bringing Eric's design to fruition. The soil had been treated and enriched, old trees and shrubs torn out and replaced, new plant types brought in, the lawns re-laid. All that it required was a year's growth and settlement and all the signs of the recent upheaval would be gone. The one eyesore was the pool under its glass roof, supposedly hidden behind a bank of young conifers and connected to the house by a covered passageway. It was seldom used but was part of Eric's daily work-schedule as he had to maintain the heating and filtering equipment. With Wegelius's permission he planted wisteria, clematis and, for his own interest, an *Aristolochia macrophylla*, Dutchman's pipe, climber.

He was tending to the cuttings of the latter which he had planted in late August when Barbara came running over the lawn. It was an unusual sight, the woman's body bouncing and shaking as if it might fly apart at any moment. As she ran she tried to shout but her breath was broken and all he heard were squeaks and coughs.

He straightened up, feeling a chill in his heart. There was something in the abandon with which she ran that presaged a calamity. Forgetting that Barbara had come up that morning to have her hair done, he immediately assumed the worst. Before Barbara reached him he was running towards the house, Pauline's name on his lips.

When he got there he found that she was out. It took Barbara a while to find him in those rooms of the enormous old house which she knew were the province of Wegelius and his wife.

Unable to speak, she took his hand and dragged him along the corridors to his own part where Stephanie lay in the sitting-room, surrounded by her hairdressing tongs and lotions and the bloody mess of a miscarriage.

"I'm sorry, I'm sorry," she kept saying as he knelt down beside her, moved by an appalled pity. "We can start again."

28

Churt, the aloof colony of the rich hiding behind its trees and estate walls, re-asserted some of its neighbourly ways over Stephanie's loss. She was a local girl whom everyone had known since childhood and they had shared her modest aspirations and wished her well with her marriage to the outsider. His reticence and self-engrossment had made it difficult for them to strike up proper relationships, especially as he was part of the rarefied world of the super-rich which dominated the community. Their sympathy for Stephanie's loss was hard for Eric to accommodate at first as it conflicted with his own equivocal feelings but as he saw her strength emerge from the suffering she had endured, he began to let slip his controlled isolation and allow himself to be drawn more into her family and the life of the village. Sensitive to this change in him as she was, Stephanie proposed that they move from Fenlon Old Farm and find a place of their own before starting another baby, only to find both ideas rebuffed. In spite of the depressing memories which the flat now had for Stephanie, and her natural desire to be an independent woman in her own home, Eric refused to contemplate moving, claiming that the present arrangement suited him in terms of being close to his work and convenient for hers. When she told him that she blamed her constant cycle-rides with heavy loads up and down the steep lanes for her miscarriage and said that she would like to give up her hairdressing business for a while, she found him angrily opposed to the notion. In view of the fact that she now knew he did not really need the money she earned, Stephanie could not stop herself becoming more and more resentful of his attitude. During the weeks after the miscarriage they often fell into dispute on these issues and he was torn between his increasing affection and respect for her and his necessary interest in keeping things as they were at least until Pauline was delivered of his child.

On two occasions Stephanie walked out of the flat during an argument and went to Barbara's for the night. Eric refused to follow her, going about his business the following morning and making no comment when he found her waiting for him back at the flat when he came home for lunch. When she went to her parents' house after a major row and stayed there for three days he was forced to discuss the matter with her father. She returned with Eric that afternoon but not without Eric having been forced to agree that by the end of the year he would have made alternative arrangements, 'to keep the peace', as Stephanie's father had said morosely, hinting that Eric's tight grip on what looked like a very temporary set-up at Fenlon Old Farm would have to be released for the sake of his daughter's well-being.

From then on Stephanie lapsed into a quiet watchfulness, waiting for him to evince proof of his intention to keep his promise. She did not resume her mobile hairdressing business but applied herself to being the perfect housewife, taking pains to dress well, cook with flair, keep the flat spotless and talk when he was inclined to listen, inching herself into the full status of wife and partner in a conformable marriage which she had intuitively felt he had, until then, denied her.

It had been Wegelius's plan to be at home for two weeks on either side of the date of the child's anticipated birth and he had made strenuous attempts to prevent himself having to travel outside the country during this period but in the middle of October he was forced to go to Israel on urgent business with the military. As it was trouble and not gain which drew him there he was doubly displeased but Pauline serenely assured him that there was no need to worry; there had been no problems with her pregnancy to date and she had Stephanie, Barbara, Len and Eric close by should she need help, "And besides," she added with a smile which was beyond his powers of interpretation, "God will be with me."

Wegelius took this unusual expression of faith as something she had culled from recent reading: of late her conversation had become increasingly prolix, larded with quotations and the doings of characters from fiction as she continued to plough through her university reading list. This artificiality in their relationship did not torment him unduly, nor did it make him feel culturally inferior, but it did make him believe that his wife was lonely, turning to books as a surrogate for friends. When he had taken her from her student days to be his wife this danger had crossed his mind but he had forgotten about it. Now, when he heard her mention God as a friend, he, as a oncetime Roman Catholic, hastened to echo her piety, reminded her of his Polish ancestry and bought her a gold cross to wear round her neck. When she laughed at him for this he assumed that it was purely in pleasure at his readiness to re-awaken a childhood myth in order to be close to her.

Since being told that she was pregnant he had not been allowed in her bed. He had accepted this with good grace but not without suspicion that she was using her condition as an excuse. With the difference in their ages and the inviolable authority of her beauty he had not expected passion from her and had certainly received none. For passion he paid, as he had always done, going to women with superlative skills in love-making. In his mind they were hardly of the same sex as his wife: her chasteness forbade any comparison. What she lacked in artistry he attributed to innocence, glad to believe this to be the cause of her coldness.

When he arrived in Jerusalem he spent an hour in the Via Dolorosa buying postcards and souvenirs to take home to her, tears in his eyes as he wandered from shop to shop. Adjacent to the site of what had once been the palace of Pontius Pilate he purchased a large pictorial guide book, in colour, of all the holy places. That night, as he lay in bed at his hotel, he leafed through it and found himself weeping again. This was unaccountable behaviour, he decided, being a person who was confident that he knew himself well. As, on the morrow, he was scheduled to meet many hard men, veteran negotiators who were not prone to sentiment, he carefully wrapped the book in one of his spare shirts and put it at the bottom of his bag.

The gardens of Fenlon Old Farm were patched with late flowers, and the turves of the new lawns had nearly knitted together, the joins sporadically visible. The expenditure on the soil was showing its first signs of value, the last burst of growth coming through with vigour.

As he worked, Eric did not see the landscape he had created in its present phase; for him it already had a second existence which was the ghost of the next growing season. While the asters, kaffir lilies and Michaelmas daisies flowered around him and the roses blossomed on he saw only the movement through winter into spring, these colourful tokens being attached to a year that was essentially dead.

He did not ask himself if he was happy, nor did he offer the question to Pauline on her account or his own. As the days passed they saw each other fleetingly, sensing the inexorable stream which had carried them along as it began to pour through their lives in flood. With Wegelius away Pauline had many opportunities to see Eric in private but she made little use of them, keeping to her part of the house. Since the miscarriage she had avoided Stephanie; this apparently cruel behaviour was correctly interpreted as being more a matter of delicacy and the avoidance of bad luck. Len took her out in the car; she read; she did exercises; she waited.

Having become accustomed to this temporary expulsion from her daily life — something he believed to be natural when a woman was close to giving birth to a man's child — and finding that it was, in fact, congenial to his own mood, Eric kept away from the part of the garden nearest to her living-quarters where she might see him. If there was necessary work in that area he got up very early in the morning and did it before she arose.

It was on a damp, misty morning when he was stealthily rooting out a diseased grandiflorus from beneath her bedroom window that he looked up and saw her watching him. She was wearing a white nightgown and held a cup and saucer cradled in her palms. Raising her eyebrows she turned side-on so he could see the full extent of her belly, then crooked her finger at him and opened the french doors.

He went over and stood on the step, his spade still in his hands.

"Won't be long now," she said, "I can feel it kicking."

"I love you," he told her, holding up his hands for her to see how dirty they were, "but I can't give you a kiss."

Stepping out into the garden she pecked his cheek and put her arm through his.

"When it's born I want you to be there," she murmured. "I don't care how impossible it is, I want you there. Promise me?"

He nodded dumbly, holding down powerful surges which shook him as soon as she touched him. Glancing at her vast, white womb he told himself that his lust was wrong. Sensing his struggle she let go of his arm.

"While you're here I'm all right," she assured him. "As long as I know you're around, I don't mind Bruno being away but I'll need your support."

He drove the spade into the earth and crouched down on his haunches, covering his inner turmoil by fussing with a clump of dead nettle which had strayed on to the path.

"I don't think I can stand it any longer," he muttered gloomily. "Let's get out of here, go away somewhere and start all over again."

"With me like this?"

"Women can have babies anywhere. If you were in Africa you'd have it under a bush and think nothing of it."

"And what about Stephanie? She'd be heart-broken."

"She'd be better off without me."

Pauline shook her head and poked her finger into a blown rose, making it shower spent petals.

"Too late for all that," she said sententiously.

"Why?"

"Because I'm used to it. The whole situation suits me fine. I don't want it changed, ever."

Eric rose from his haunches, angry disbelief inflaming his eyes.

"Well, it doesn't suit me much!" he protested.

"Oh, it does, it does," she replied with a gay smile. "You'd be bored if it were any different, darling. Lend me your clippers, will you?"

She held out her hand. Taking his secateurs out of his pocket he unfastened the safety-catch and gave them to her. Holding a rose-stem delicately between finger and thumb she cut it off and held the flower up, cradled in her big hands.

"Heap not on this mound
Roses that she loved so well;
Why bewilder her with roses
That she cannot see or smell?"

242

she chanted, studying his eyes for a response. "Edna Saint Vincent Millay? Ever heard of her? Some say she was a proto-feminist but I have my doubts. At heart I think she was just momma from mid-West America."

Yanking his spade out of the ground he swung it and struck her across the head with the edge of the blade, felling her instantly. Without looking at her, he ran to the garage, took down his javelin from the rafters and impaled himself through the heart.

29

Before moving down to Grayshott, Leo took a week's holiday in Rome, staying with the friends he had missed seeing the previous year when he had cancelled his visit because of Deidre Nash's death. They were both friends he had made at theological college who had abandoned their Anglican faith for Roman Catholicism and had become lecturers at seminary colleges in the city. Like Leo, their careers had ground to a halt and they took the opportunity of his visit to discuss whether they would be wise to return to England.

As they sat and talked it seemed to Leo that a quarter of a century had rolled back. All the thoughts they had had, the opinions and ideas, the ceremonies and sermons, were little more than molecular exchanges in a test-tube, mere adjustments to show for their labours, apart from the excitement of their apostasy which still sustained them. There was no underlying strength; no original, unique achievement. When he left them to return to England he felt wrung-out and arid from contemplating their futures. From then on the world would ignore them. They had concentrated their lives on love so pored over, so explored and squeezed of meaning, so battered, that nothing fresh would ever emerge. Without admitting it his friends were locked in despair, having pursued the irrelevant proofs of scholasticism at the expense of the truths of the natural God.

In contrast, his strength had grown. With the knowledge that his one small experiment in the management of souls had been a success and was shortly to perpetuate itself, he would build a new future within the Church, working for total revision of its values. So much that was archaic and hidebound would have to be swept away: the ancient emphases on family and the paternal power of God would have to be revised. The true authority behind the existence of the Supreme Being was a love which sprang from recognition in innocence, not experience. The love of God came from the creation, generated by the same forces which enabled all matter to find its mate, particle to particle. It had never been proposed that it should be subject to human bargaining and horse-trading.

When he got back to Kirkby Lonsdale he found a long letter from Pauline waiting for him. It was oddly disjointed, written at different times and in different styles of printing and handwriting. Although he smiled as he read it, recognising the books she quoted from, enjoying her thumb-nail sketches of Eric in the garden, it made him feel uneasy. There was no consistency to what she wrote. She progressed by means of a stream of *non sequiturs* which disguised a lack of content.

He moved south three days later. Saying good-bye to Kirkby Lonsdale was not difficult for him. It had been the scene of many disappointments and hardships of the spirit and he remained unmoved by the farewells and gifts which his parishioners showered upon him, convinced that they were merely a demonstration of their gladness that he was going.

Grayshott was the start of a new life and he approached it as if he were a young priest at the beginning of his pastorship; with energy, good-nature and commitment. The husk of village life was as unlovely to him as it had been in the north but he had the sense of the gleaming, pure kernel inside to sustain him.

Once he had settled into his house and got to know his way around the village and its institutions he began to make plans for his arrival at Churt. Pauline had told him in her letter that Wegelius had gone to Israel but hoped to be back for the birth of the child. As he wanted everyone to be present when he made his entrance, Leo decided to ring the house to check that Wegelius was back.

Pauline had given the number but he had lost it in the move. As it was ex-directory he had no way of obtaining it so he was forced to write to Pauline to ask her to ring him. Three days later the letter was returned. It had been opened, re-sealed with sellotape, and was marked 'deceased'.

Within an hour of receiving the letter he was at Fenlon Old Farm. The only person there was Len. He told Leo the story and showed him the spot where Pauline had died then limped over to the garage and showed him where Eric had killed himself. Because Leo was a churchman Len felt that he could talk to him about the anguish he felt and how much he had liked Eric.

"He was always straight with me. I didn't ask him too many questions because he seemed so solid, if you know what I mean, someone who knew what he wanted." He held on to the big, green lawn-mower for a moment, then continued, "We never suspected . . . well my wife started to . . . poor kids." He faltered, his face paling. "Best you go off and pray for them both, vicar. I do every time I think about it. Only nineteen, the pair of them, God help us."

Len left Leo in the garden and returned to the house. Half-an-hour later he looked out of the window and saw the clergyman back at the place where Pauline had died. When he came back to the courtyard to get in his car and leave, Len saw that he was wearing a grey and green white-flaked leaf.

Limping out he opened the car door for the visitor.

"Quite an achievement of Eric's, getting that to thrive here," he said. "That dead nettle doesn't favour our light soil."

Leo reached into the back seat of the car and handed Len a flat parcel.

"What's this?" Len asked. "There's no one here any more."

Leo began to speak but could not put the words together. Such was his obvious distress that Len, accustomed though he had become to living with the tragedy, started to be re-shaken by its strangeness. He kept his questions to himself, letting Leo drive off leaving him with the parcel in his hand, then dutifully took it into the house and laid it on the dining-table, unopened.

Having no desire to be involved in any further ramifications of the great misfortune which had befallen the house, he avoided reading what was written on the parcel, which would have confused him even more than he was already. It read:

For E & P. Nos cedamus amori. L.

Fenlon Old Farm was cleared by a firm of auctioneers three months later upon the instructions of Wegelius who had never returned to the house after the day of Pauline's funeral. All the furniture and effects in the building were sold at the auction-rooms in Farnham, including an item listed under *Antiques, Bric-à-brac and Pictures*, which was described as: *Oil on canvas, 20" x 12", titled and signed: Girl in a wheelbarrow with ruins, Mansergh. Oswald Nash, 1945.*

Len and Barbara attended the sale. When Len saw the tall clergyman who was determinedly bidding for the picture he thought that he recognised him from somewhere, but, in his mind, he could make no connection with the parcel and its delivery to the house because he had never opened it. When the auctioneer knocked the lot down to Leo for a sum which reflected the escalating value put on the work of Oswald Nash, Len noticed what he took to be bemusement in the clergyman's expression and guessed that it must be caused by the great price which the man was having to pay to get what he wanted. But in this Len interpreted wrongly. Leo was neither disconcerted nor resentful at having to go so high to be successful in his bid. To him it was satisfyingly just and redemptive that he should be chastised in having to buy back at such cost what had so recently belonged to him; a gift made to lovers which, by death, they had returned.

With the picture under his arm, Leo threaded his way through the crowd and items for sale and went briskly out into the town.

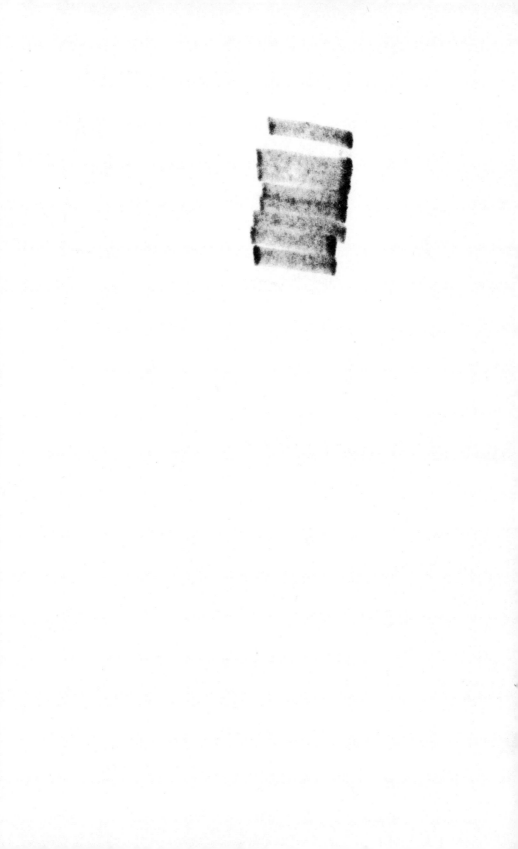